RUNAWAYS™

THE GOOD DIE YOUNG

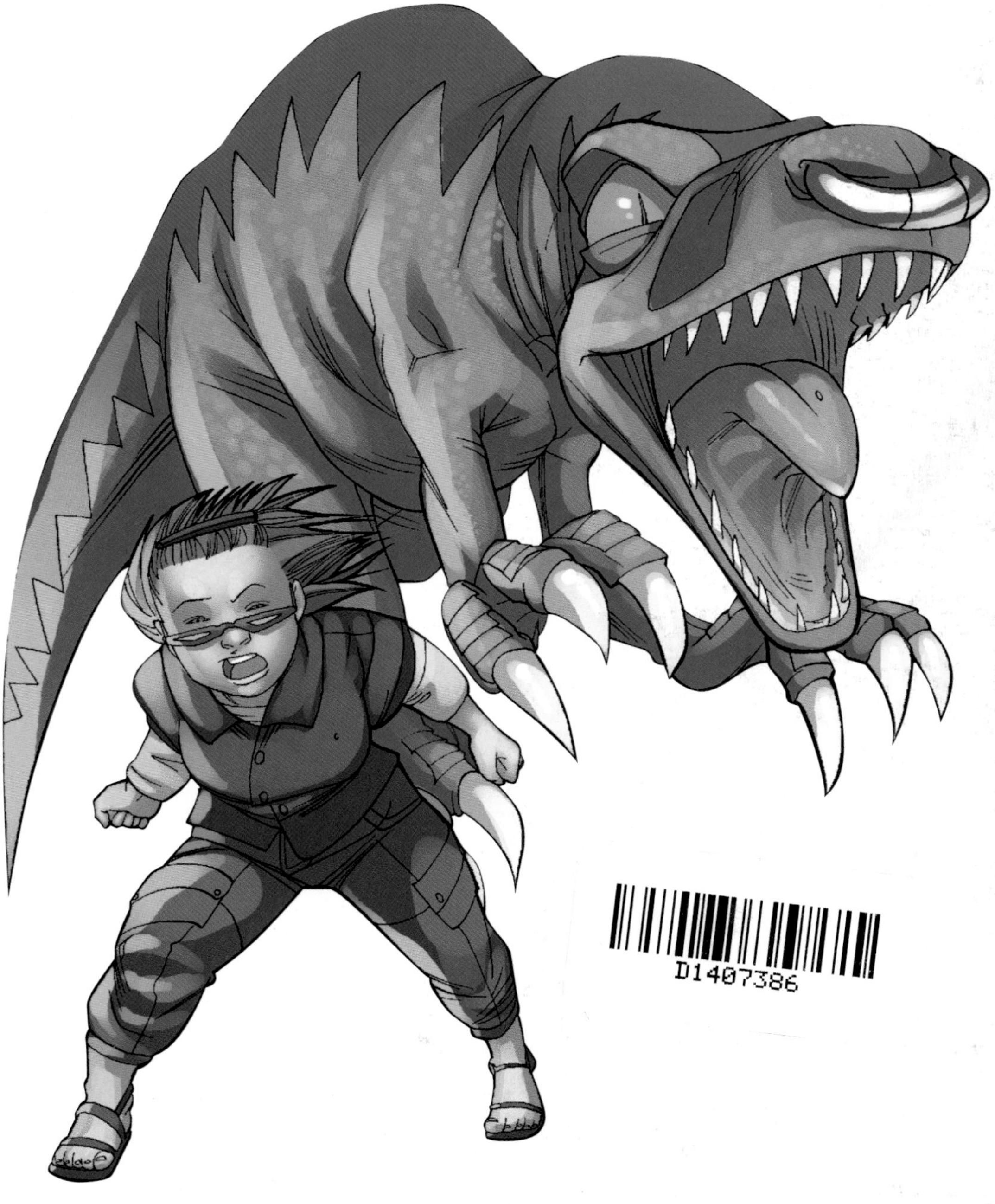

RUNAWAYS™

THE GOOD DIE YOUNG

PREVIOUSLY...

Teenager Alex Wilder and five other children always thought that their parents were boring Los Angeles socialites, until the kids witness the adults murder a young girl in some kind of dark sacrificial ritual. The teens soon learn that their parents are part of a secret organisation called The Pride, a collection of crime bosses, time-travelling despots, alien overlords, mad scientists, evil mutants and dark wizards.

After stealing weapons and resources from these villainous adults (including a mystical staff, futuristic gauntlets and a genetically engineered velociraptor named Old Lace), the kids run away from home and vow to bring their parents to justice. But when the members of The Pride frame their children for the murder they committed, the fugitive Runaways are forced to retreat to a subterranean hideout nicknamed the Hostel. Using the diverse powers and skills they inherited, the Runaways now hope to atone for their parents' crimes by helping those in need. But the Pride has other plans for their children...

WRITER: BRIAN K VAUGHAN
PENCILS: ADRIAN ALPHONA
INKS: CRAIG YEUNG

COLOURS: UDON'S CHRISTINA STRAIN
LETTERS: VIRTUAL CALLIGRAPHY'S RANDY GENTILE
COVER ART: JO CHEN
ASSISTANT EDITOR: MACKENZIE CADENHEAD
EDITOR: C. B. CEBULSKI

EDITOR IN CHIEF: JOE QUESADA
PUBLISHER: DAN BUCKLEY

MARVEL presents: **RUNAWAYS: THE GOOD DIE YOUNG**

RUNAWAYS VOLUME 3: THE GOOD DIE YOUNG. Contains material originally published in magazine form as RUNAWAYS VOLUME 1 #13-18. Published by Panini Publishing, a division of Panini UK Limited. Mike Riddell, Managing Director. Alan O'Keefe, Managing Editor. Mark Irvine, Production Manager. Marco M. Lupoi, Publishing Director Europe. Brady Webb, Reprint Editor. Luigi Mutti, Assistant Editor. Will Lucas, Designer. Office of publication: Panini House, Coach & Horses Passage, The Pantiles, Tunbridge Wells, Kent TN2 5UJ. Tel: 01892 500 100.
 ISBN: 978-1-905239-78-8

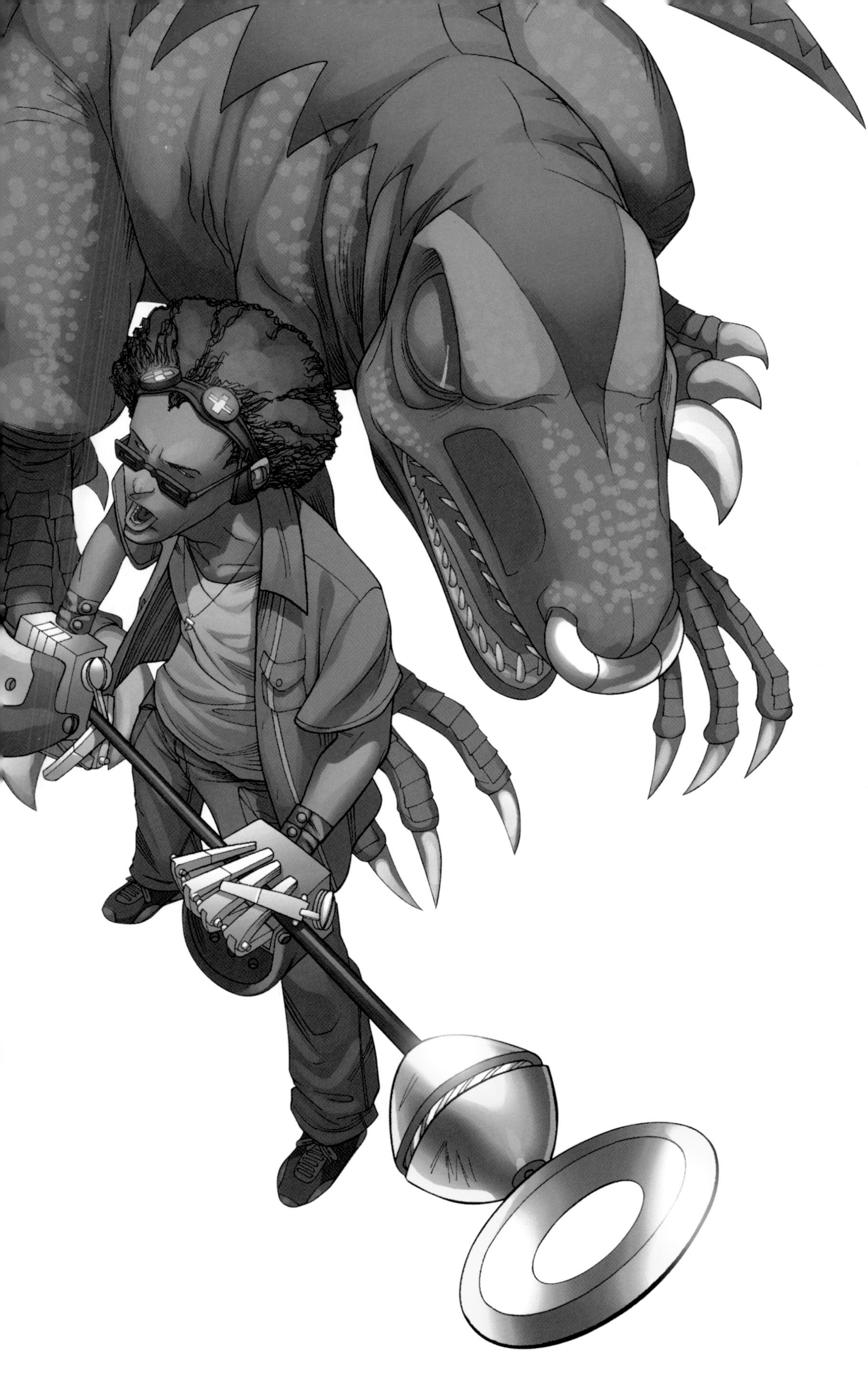

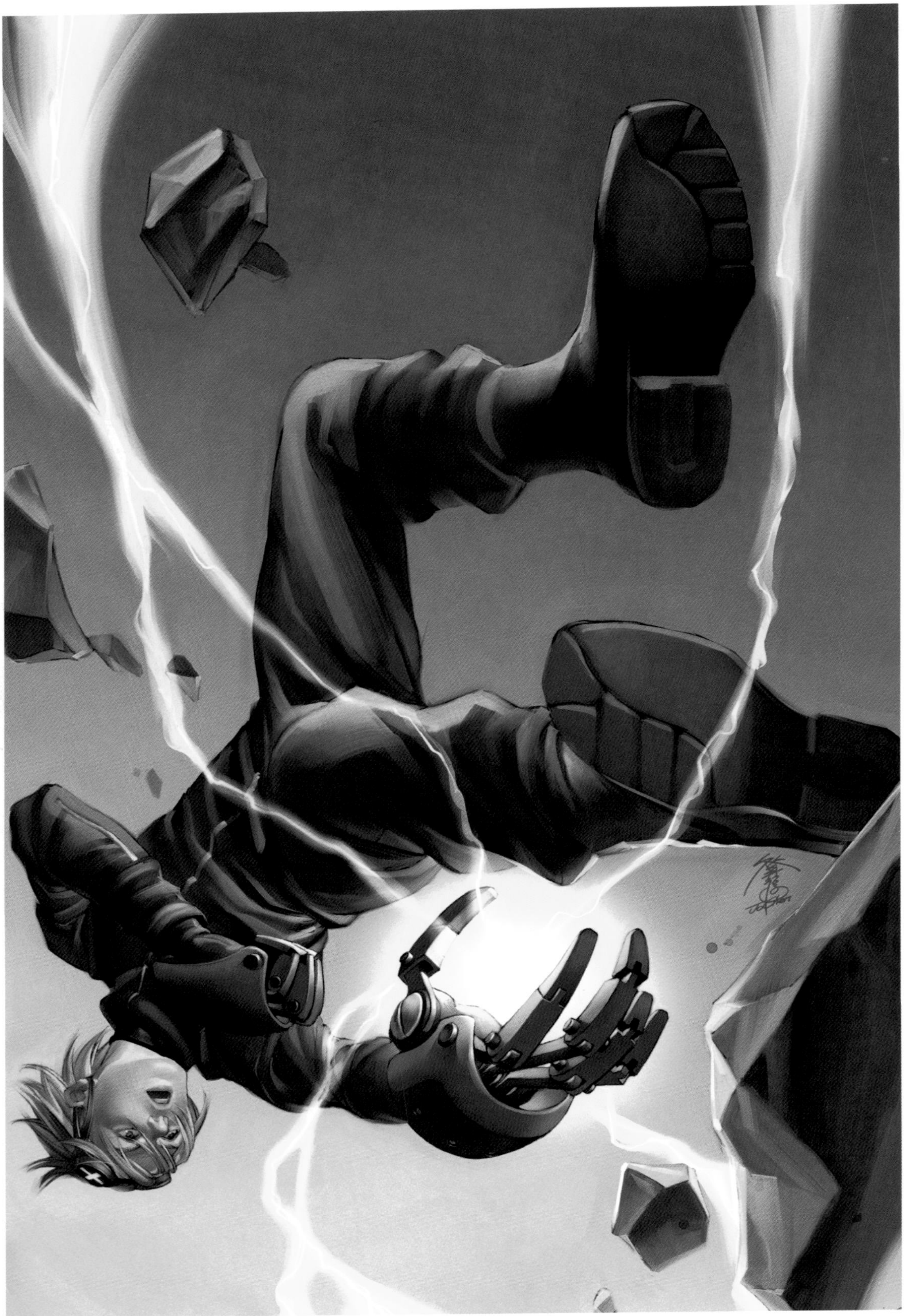

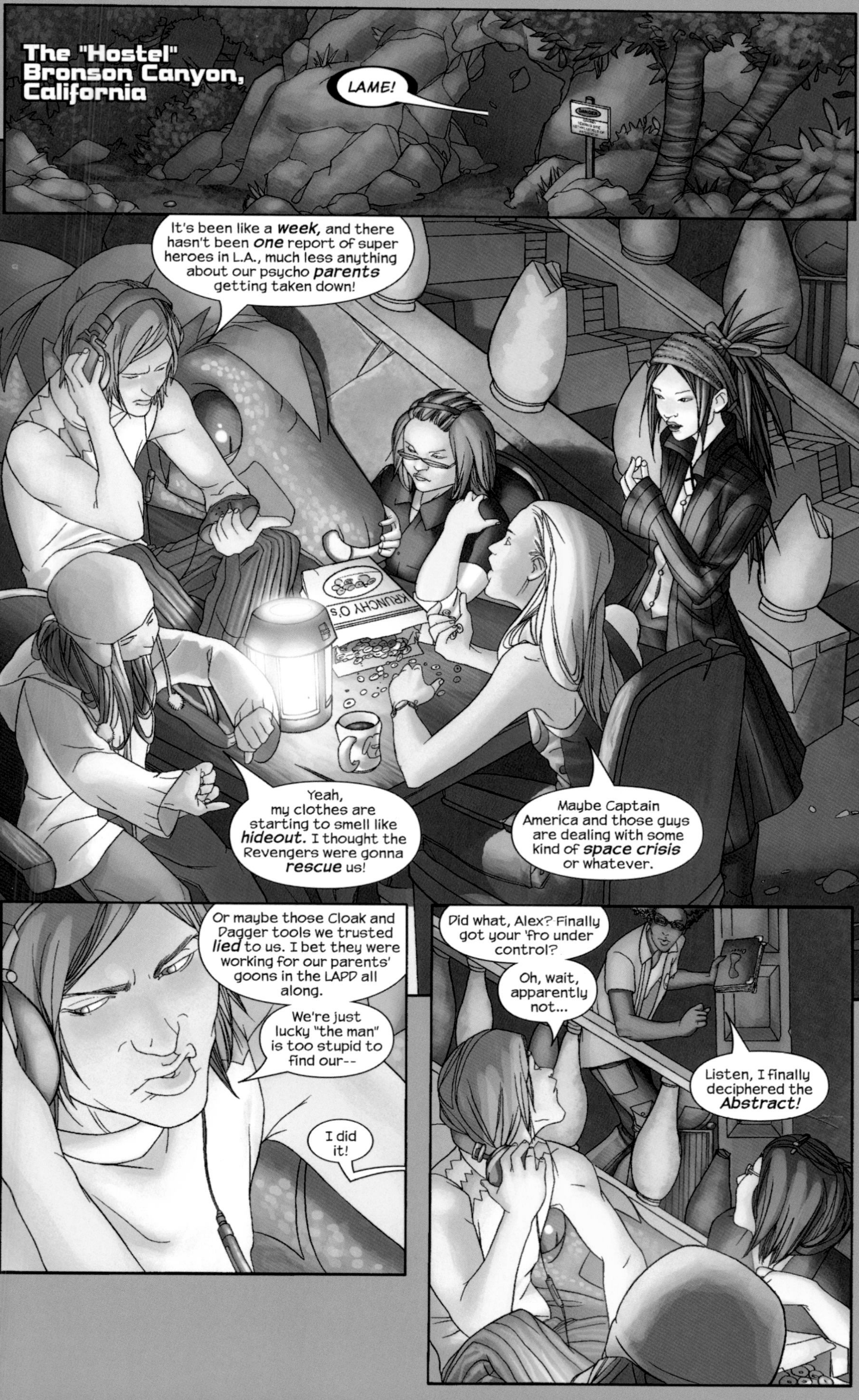
The "Hostel"
Bronson Canyon,
California
LAME!
It's been like a week, and there hasn't been one report of super heroes in L.A., much less anything about our psycho parents getting taken down!
Yeah, my clothes are starting to smell like hideout. I thought the Revengers were gonna rescue us!
Maybe Captain America and those guys are dealing with some kind of space crisis or whatever.
KRUNCHY O's
Or maybe those Cloak and Dagger tools we trusted lied to us. I bet they were working for our parents' goons in the LAPD all along.
We're just lucky "the man" is too stupid to find our--
I did it!
Did what, Alex? Finally got your 'fro under control?
Oh, wait, apparently not...
Listen, I finally deciphered the Abstract!

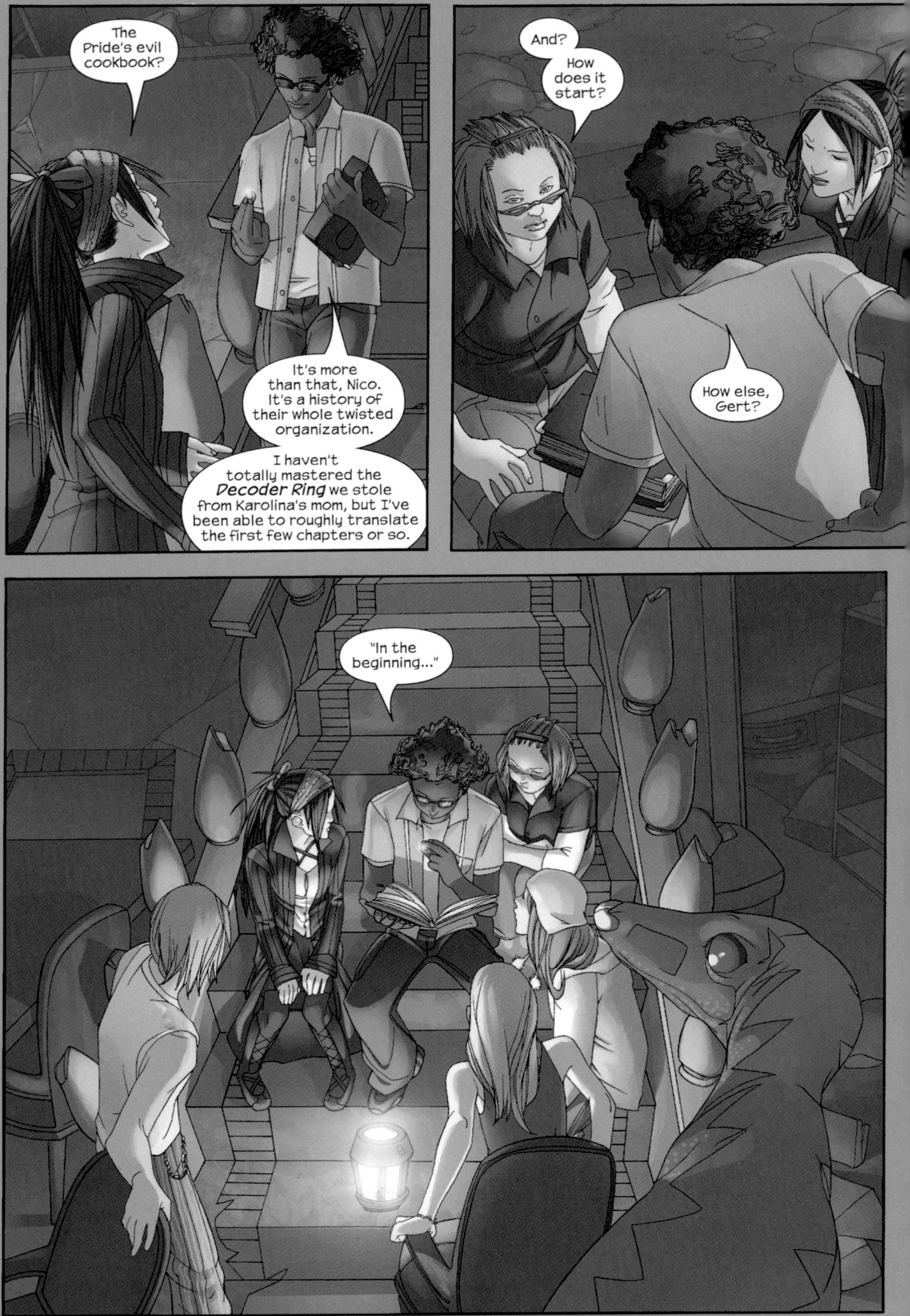

The Pride's evil cookbook?
It's more than that, Nico. It's a history of their whole twisted organization.
I haven't totally mastered the *Decoder Ring* we stole from Karolina's mom, but I've been able to roughly translate the first few chapters or so.
And?
How does it start?
How else, Gert?
"In the beginning..."

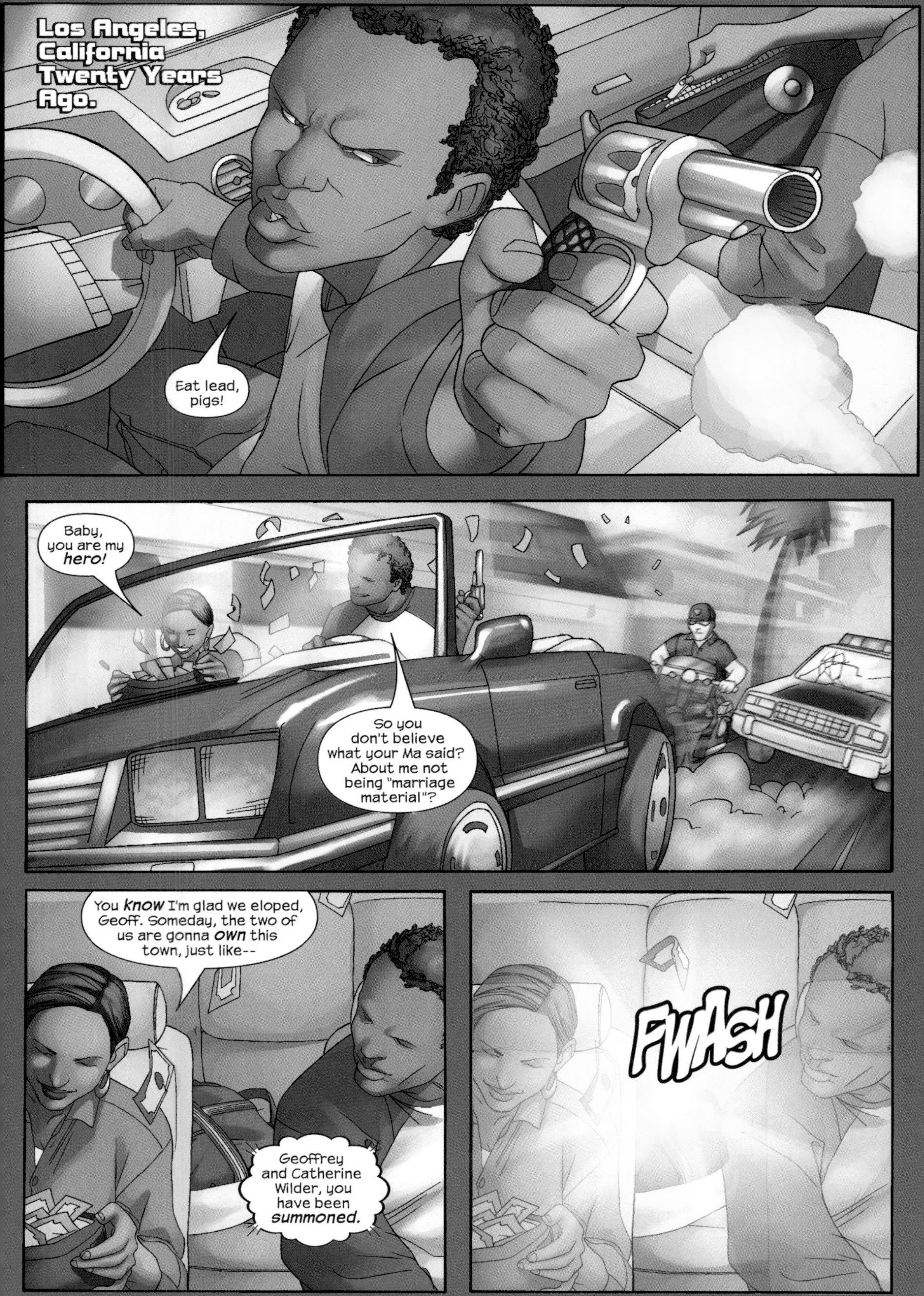
Los Angeles, California Twenty Years Ago.
Eat lead, pigs!
Baby, you are my *hero!*
So you don't believe what your Ma said? About me not being "marriage material"?
You *KNOW* I'm glad we eloped, Geoff. Someday, the two of us are gonna *OWN* this town, just like--
Geoffrey and Catherine Wilder, you have been *summoned.*
FWASH

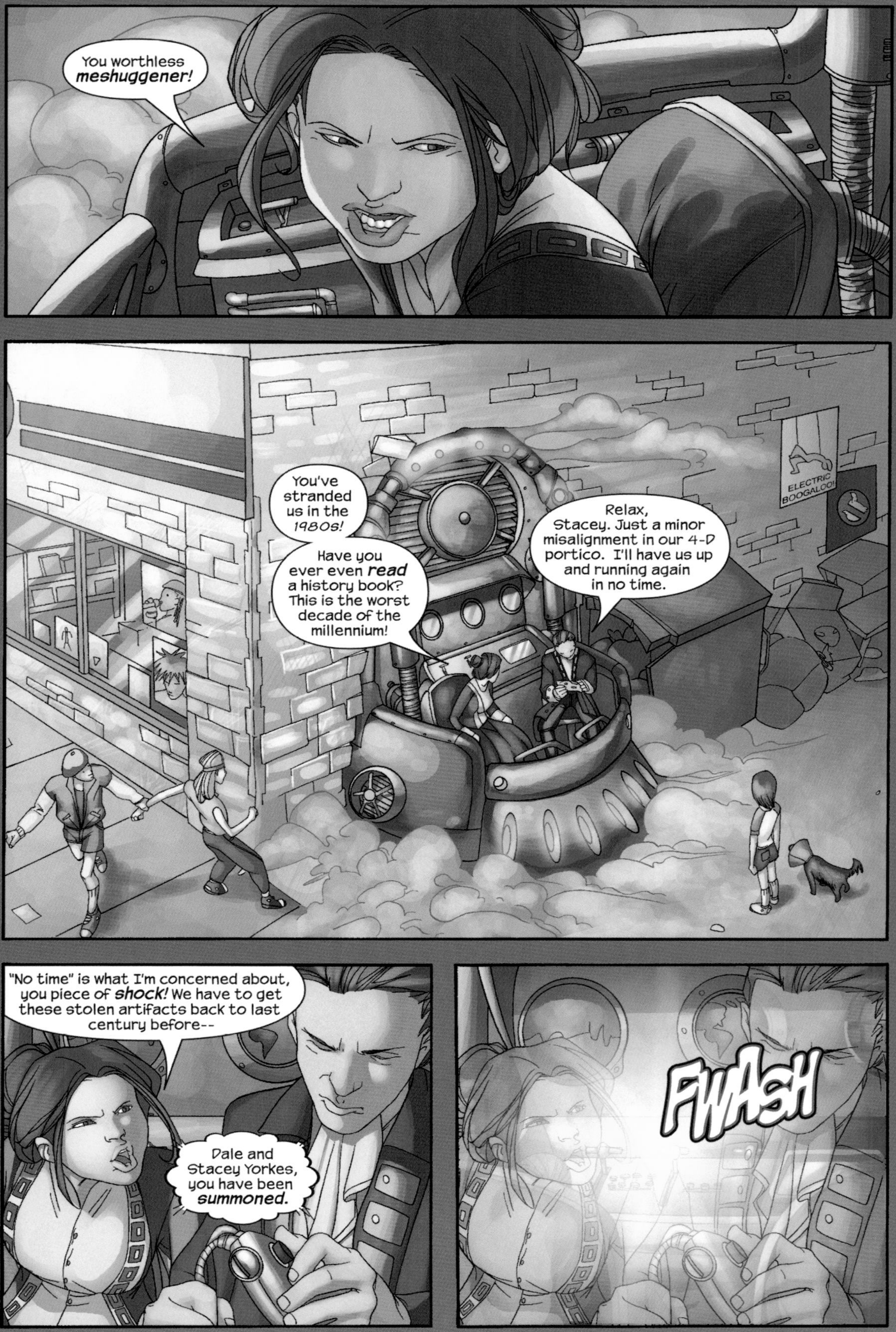
You worthless *meshuggener!*
ELECTRIC BOOGALOO!
You've stranded us in the *1980s!*
Have you ever even ***read*** a history book? This is the worst decade of the millennium!
Relax, Stacey. Just a minor misalignment in our 4-D portico. I'll have us up and running again in no time.
"No time" is what I'm concerned about, you piece of ***shock!*** We have to get these stolen artifacts back to last century before--
Dale and Stacey Yorkes, you have been ***summoned.***
FWASH

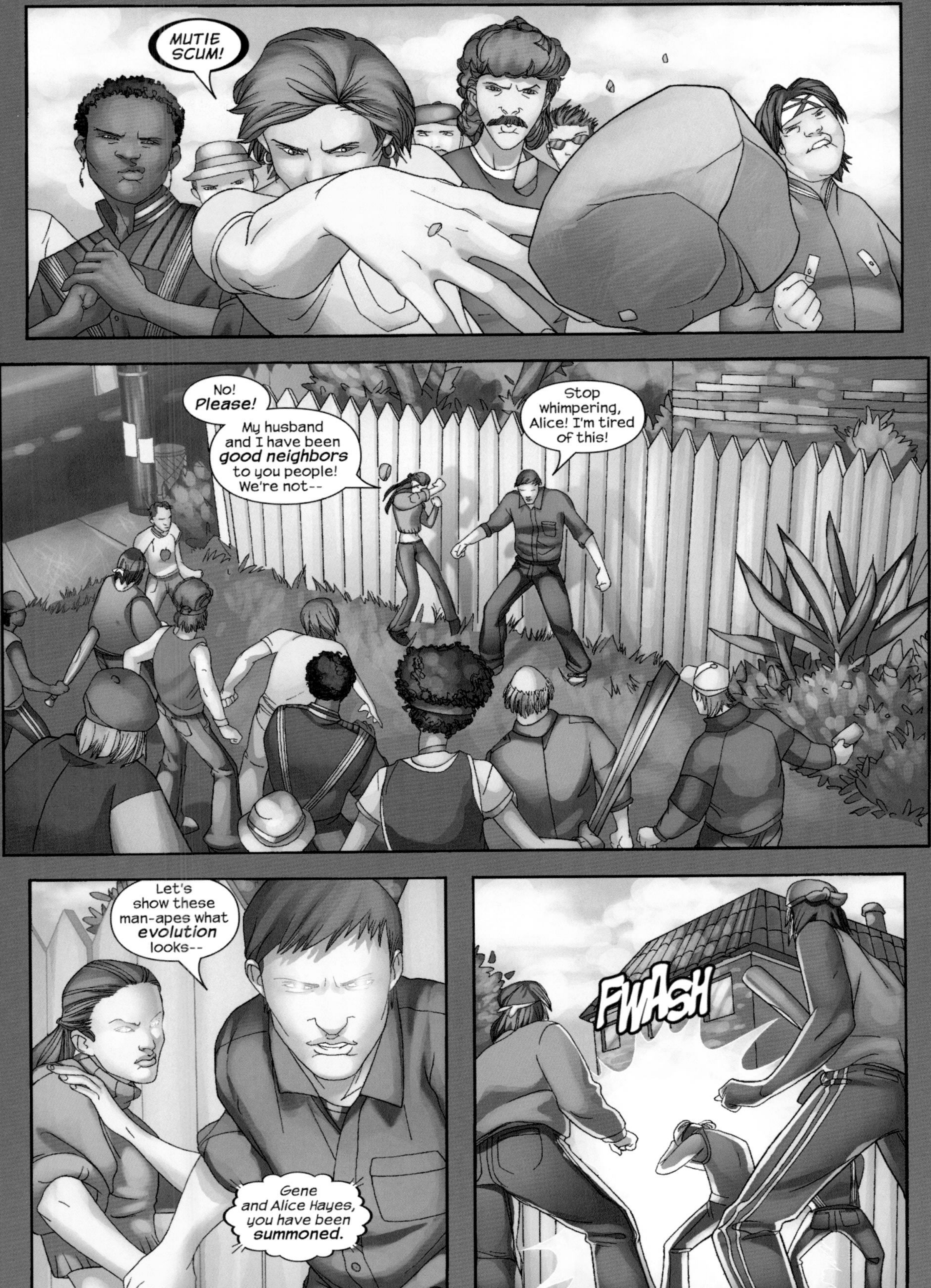
MUTIE SCUM!
No! Please!
My husband and I have been good neighbors to you people! We're not--
Stop whimpering, Alice! I'm tired of this!
Let's show these man-apes what evolution looks--
Gene and Alice Hayes, you have been summoned.
FWASH

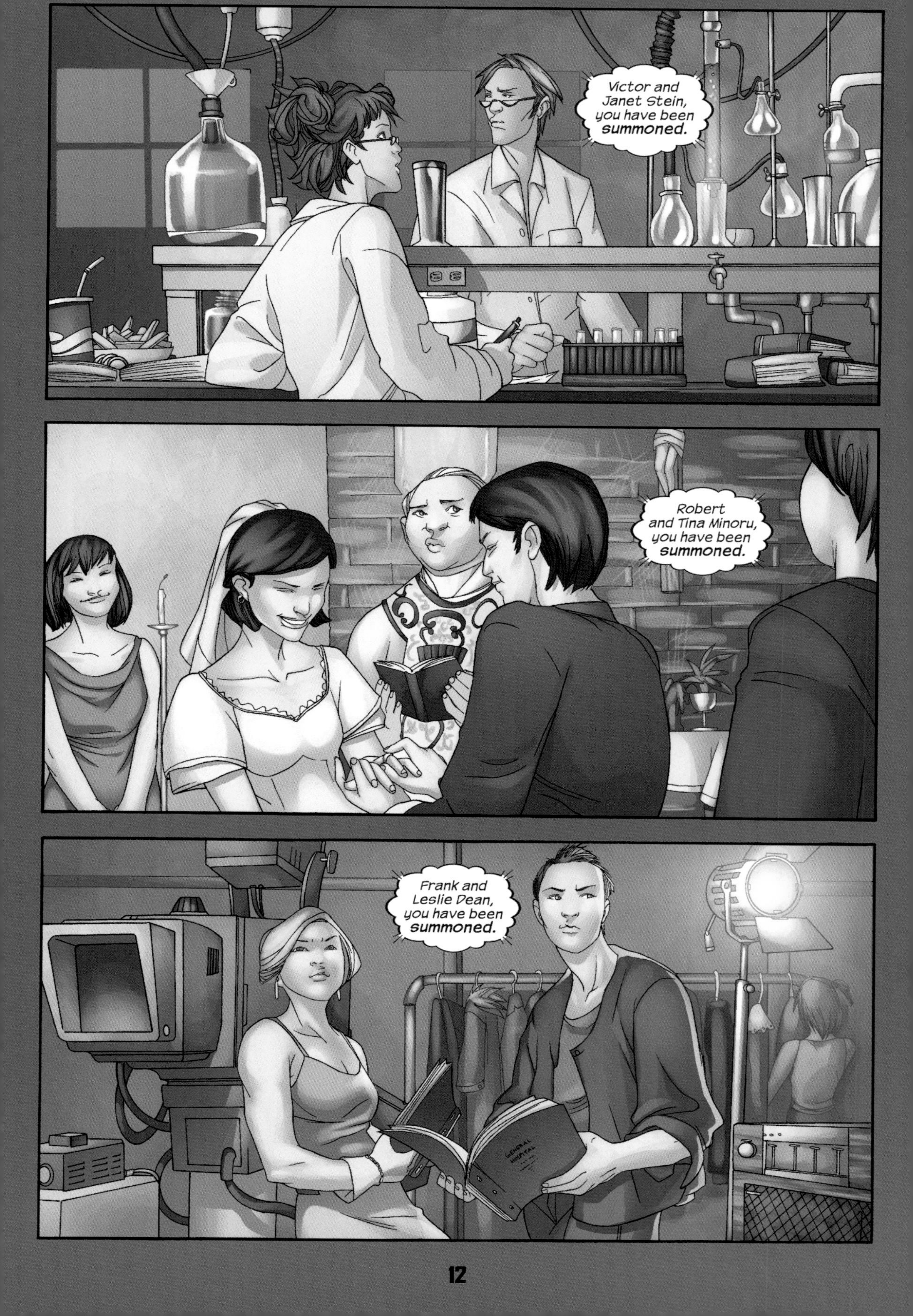
Victor and Janet Stein, you have been summoned.
Robert and Tina Minoru, you have been summoned.
Frank and Leslie Dean, you have been summoned.
GENERAL HOSPITAL

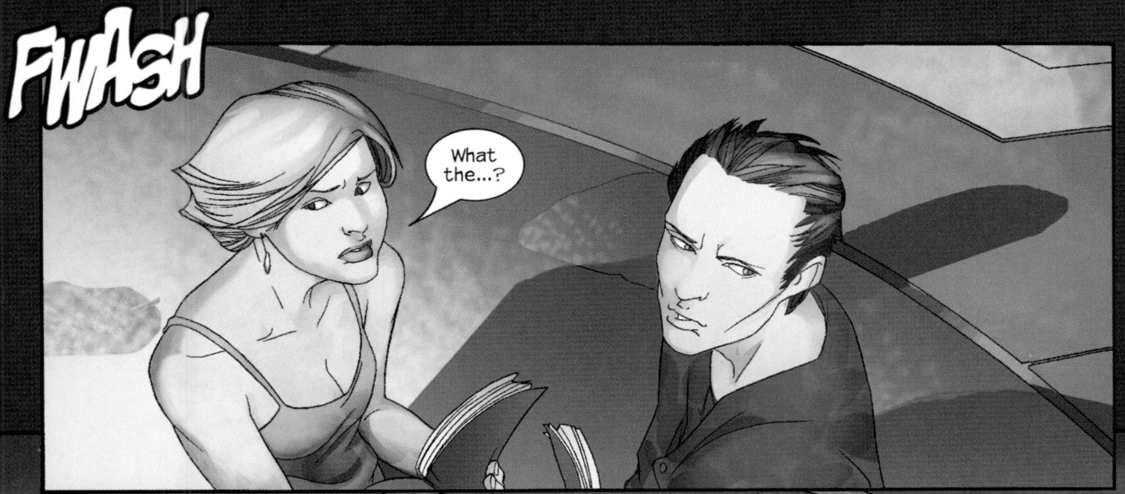
FWASH
What the...?

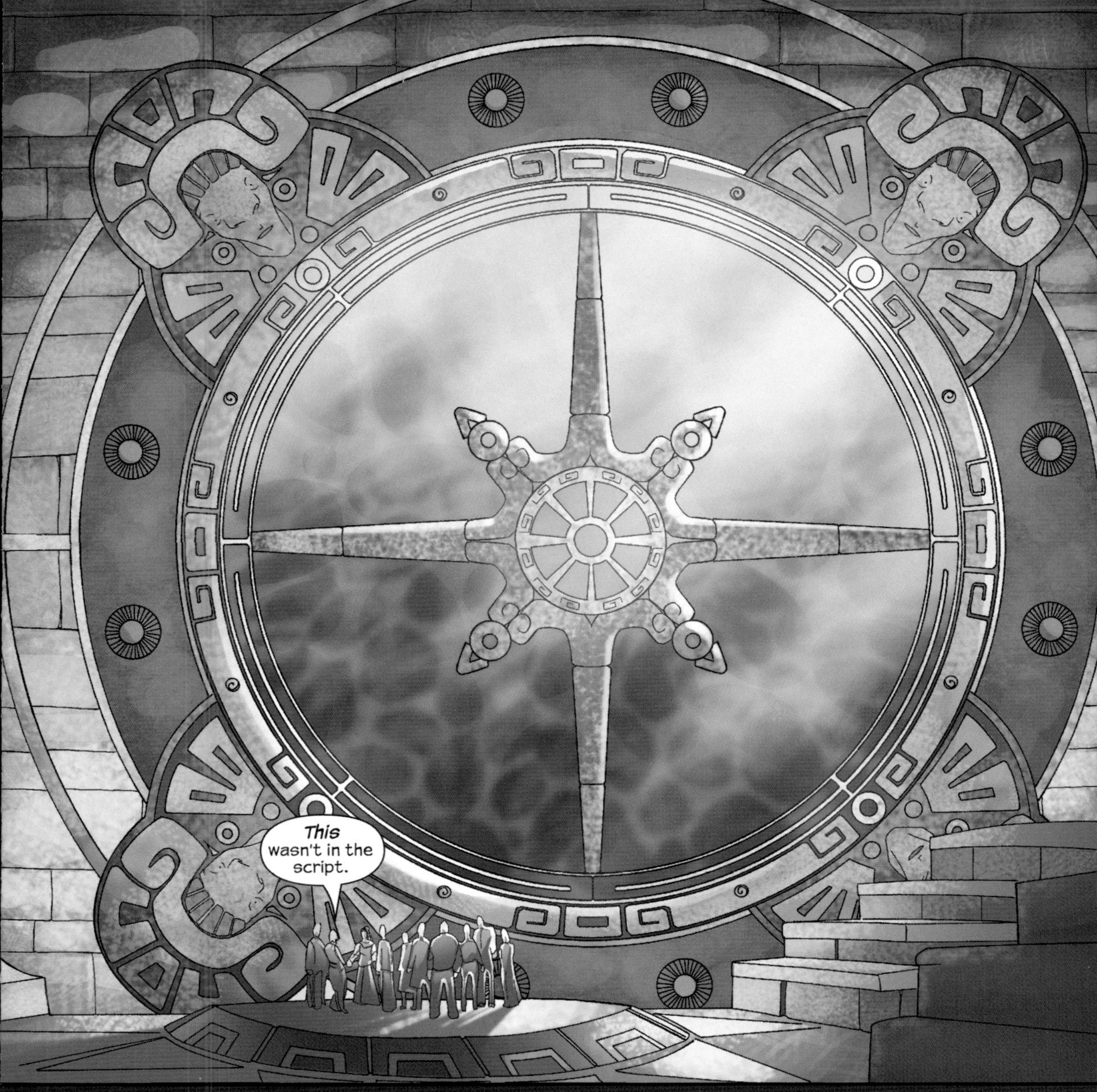
This wasn't in the script.

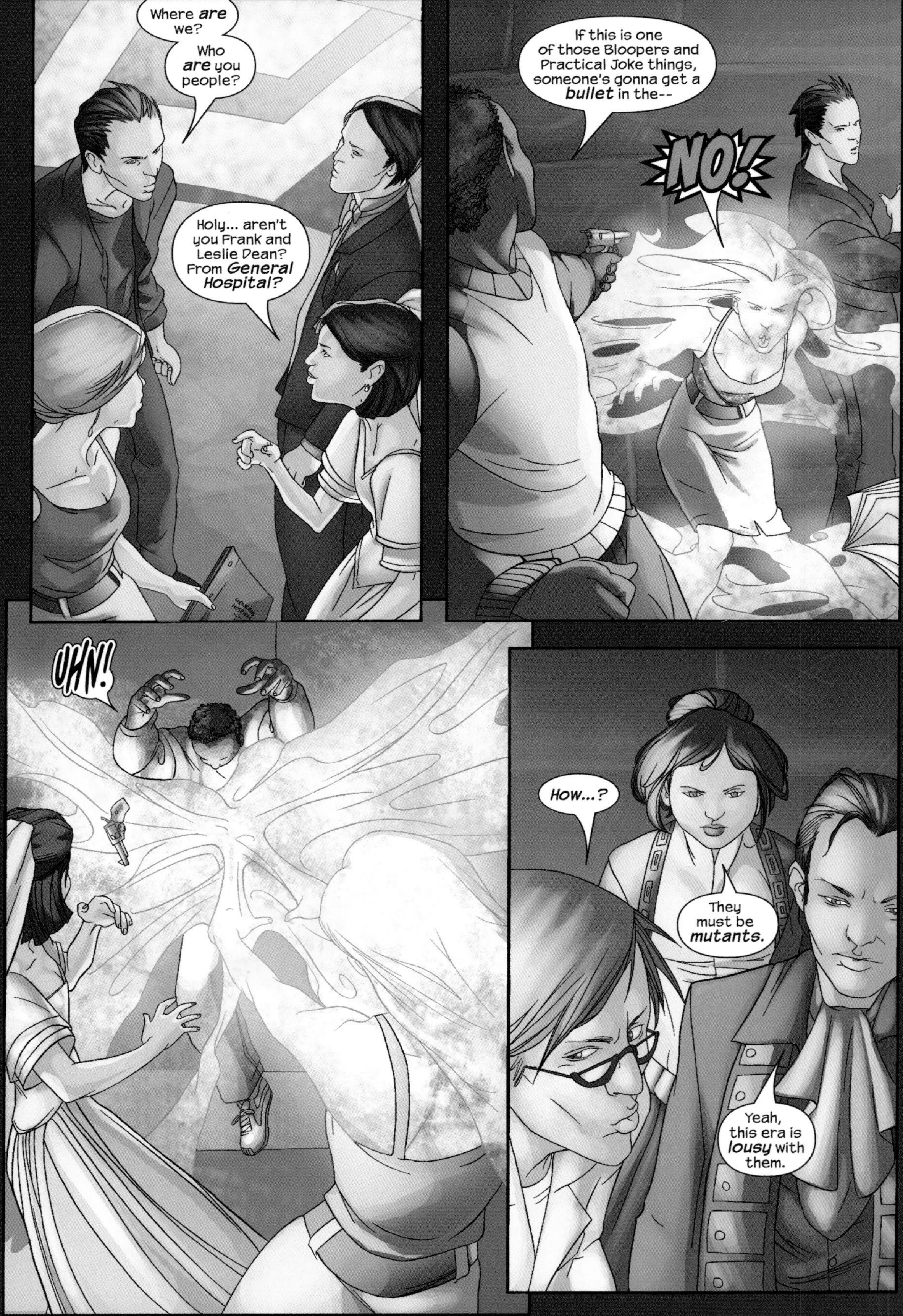
Where are we?
Who are you people?
Holy... aren't you Frank and Leslie Dean? From General Hospital?
If this is one of those Bloopers and Practical Joke things, someone's gonna get a bullet in the--
NO!
UHN!
How...?
They must be mutants.
Yeah, this era is lousy with them.

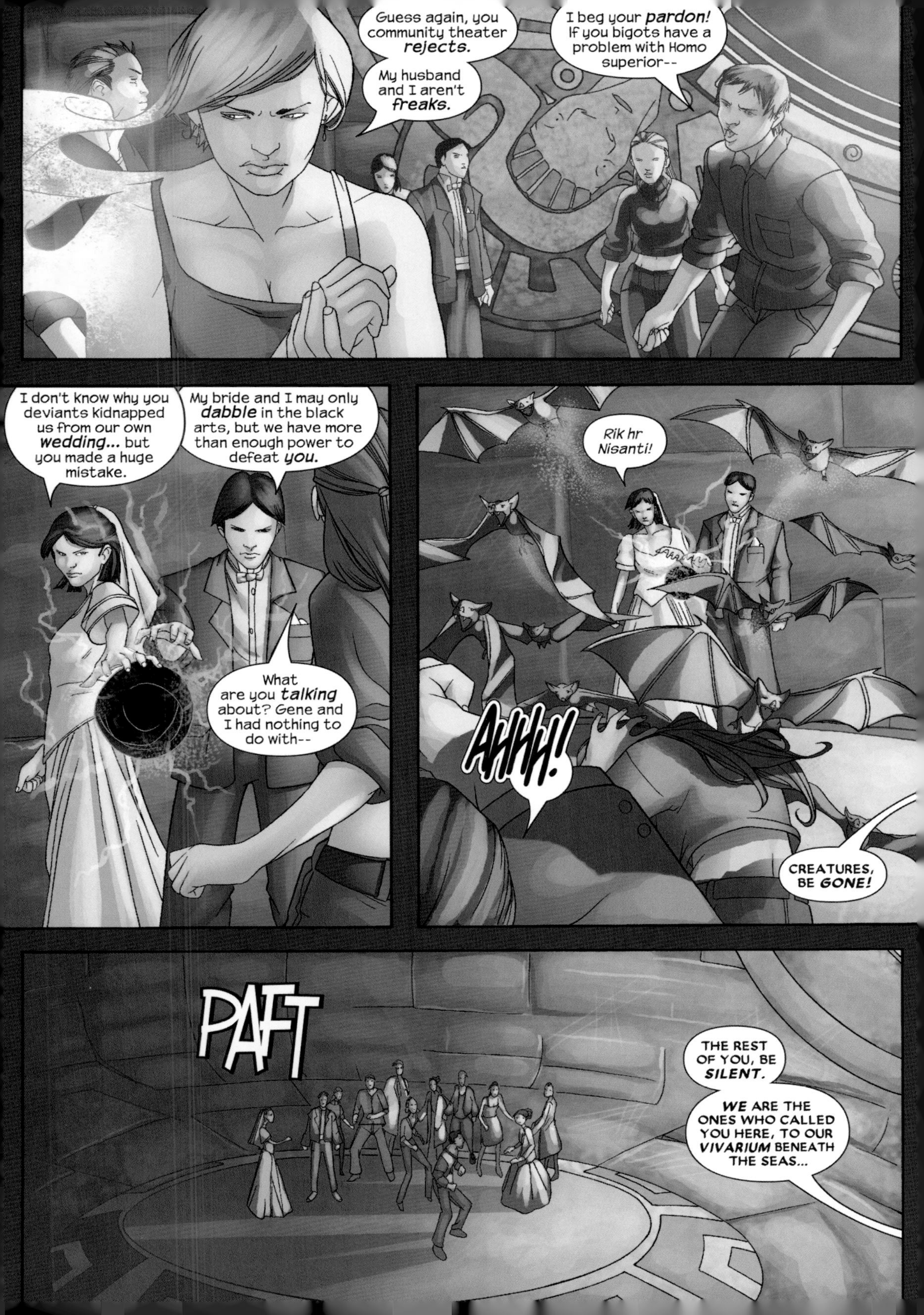
Guess again, you community theater rejects.
My husband and I aren't freaks.
I beg your pardon! If you bigots have a problem with Homo superior--
I don't know why you deviants kidnapped us from our own wedding... but you made a huge mistake.
My bride and I may only dabble in the black arts, but we have more than enough power to defeat you.
What are you talking about? Gene and I had nothing to do with--
Rik hr Nisanti!
AHHH!
CREATURES, BE GONE!
PAFT
THE REST OF YOU, BE SILENT.
WE ARE THE ONES WHO CALLED YOU HERE, TO OUR VIVARIUM BENEATH THE SEAS...

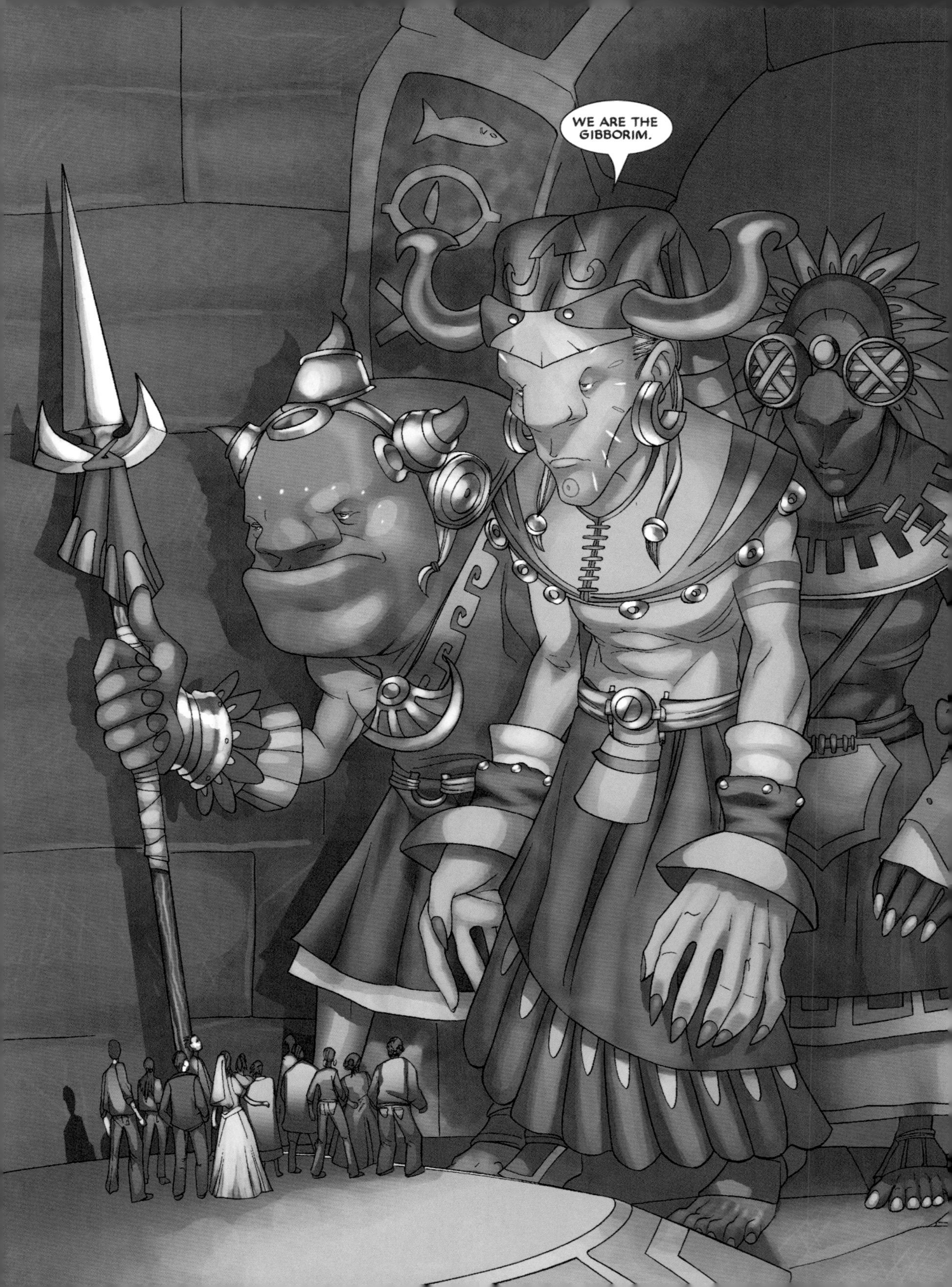
WE ARE THE GIBBORIM.

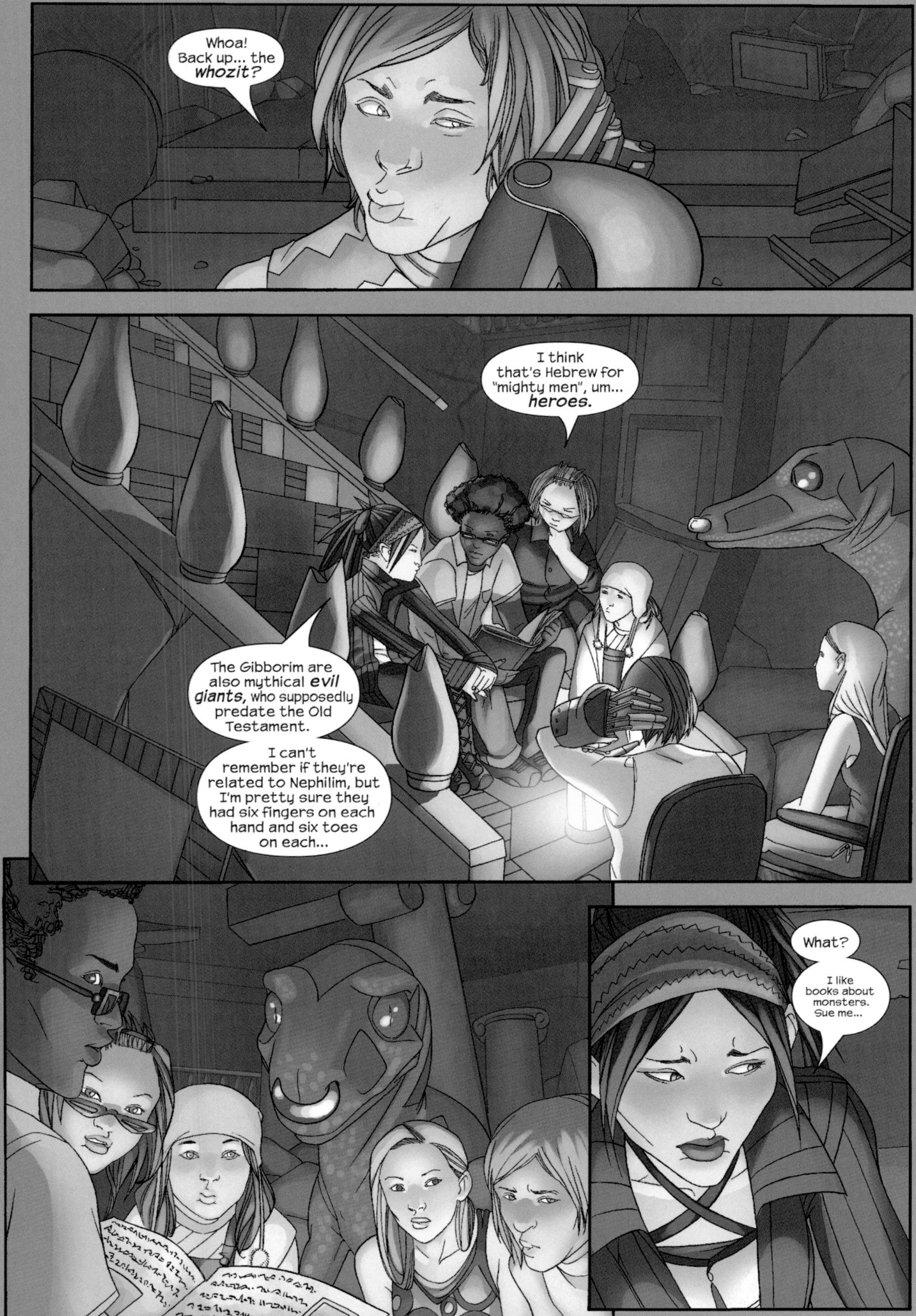

Whoa! Back up... the *whozit?*
I think that's Hebrew for "mighty men", um... **heroes.**
The Gibborim are also mythical ***evil giants,*** who supposedly predate the Old Testament.
I can't remember if they're related to Nephilim, but I'm pretty sure they had six fingers on each hand and six toes on each...
What?
I like books about monsters. Sue me...

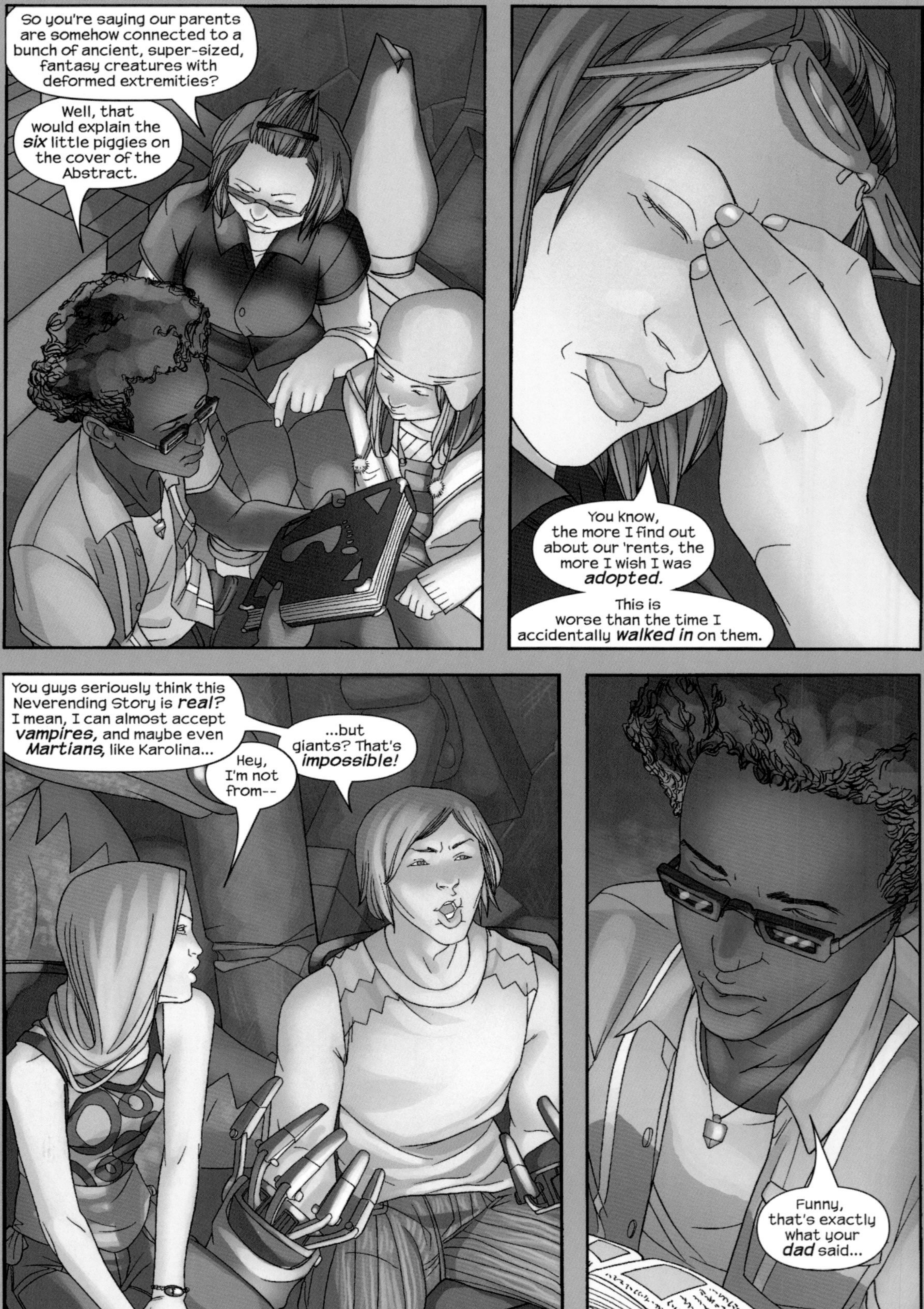
So you're saying our parents are somehow connected to a bunch of ancient, super-sized, fantasy creatures with deformed extremities?
Well, that would explain the *six* little piggies on the cover of the Abstract.
You know, the more I find out about our 'rents, the more I wish I was *adopted.*
This is worse than the time I accidentally *walked in* on them.
You guys seriously think this Neverending Story is *real?* I mean, I can almost accept *vampires,* and maybe even *Martians,* like Karolina...
Hey, I'm not from--
...but giants? That's *impossible!*
Funny, that's exactly what your *dad* said...

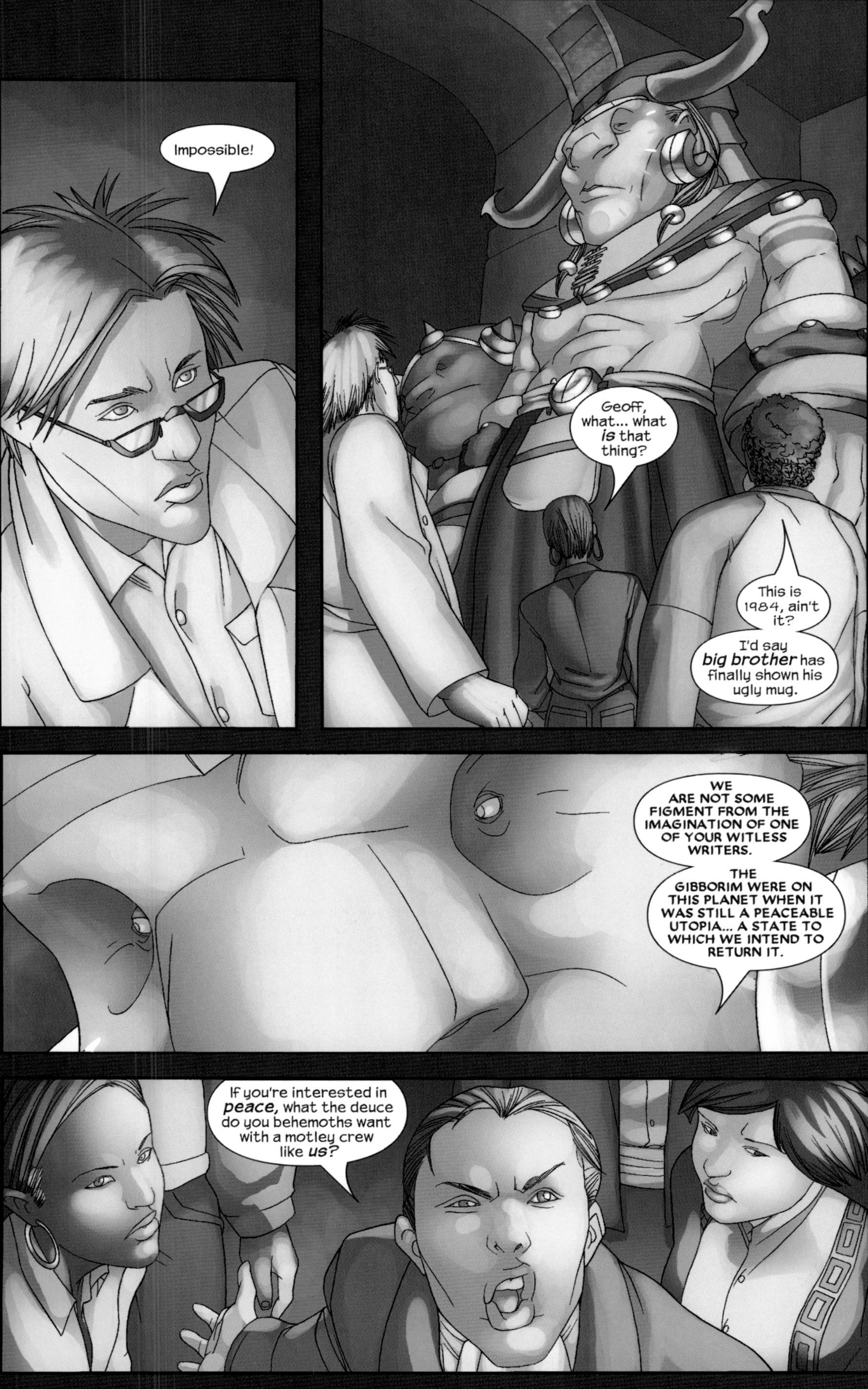

Impossible!
Geoff, what... what *is* that thing?
This is 1984, ain't it?
I'd say **big brother** has finally shown his ugly mug.
WE ARE NOT SOME FIGMENT FROM THE IMAGINATION OF ONE OF YOUR WITLESS WRITERS.
THE GIBBORIM WERE ON THIS PLANET WHEN IT WAS STILL A PEACEABLE UTOPIA... A STATE TO WHICH WE INTEND TO RETURN IT.
If you're interested in ***peace,*** what the deuce do you behemoths want with a motley crew like ***us?***

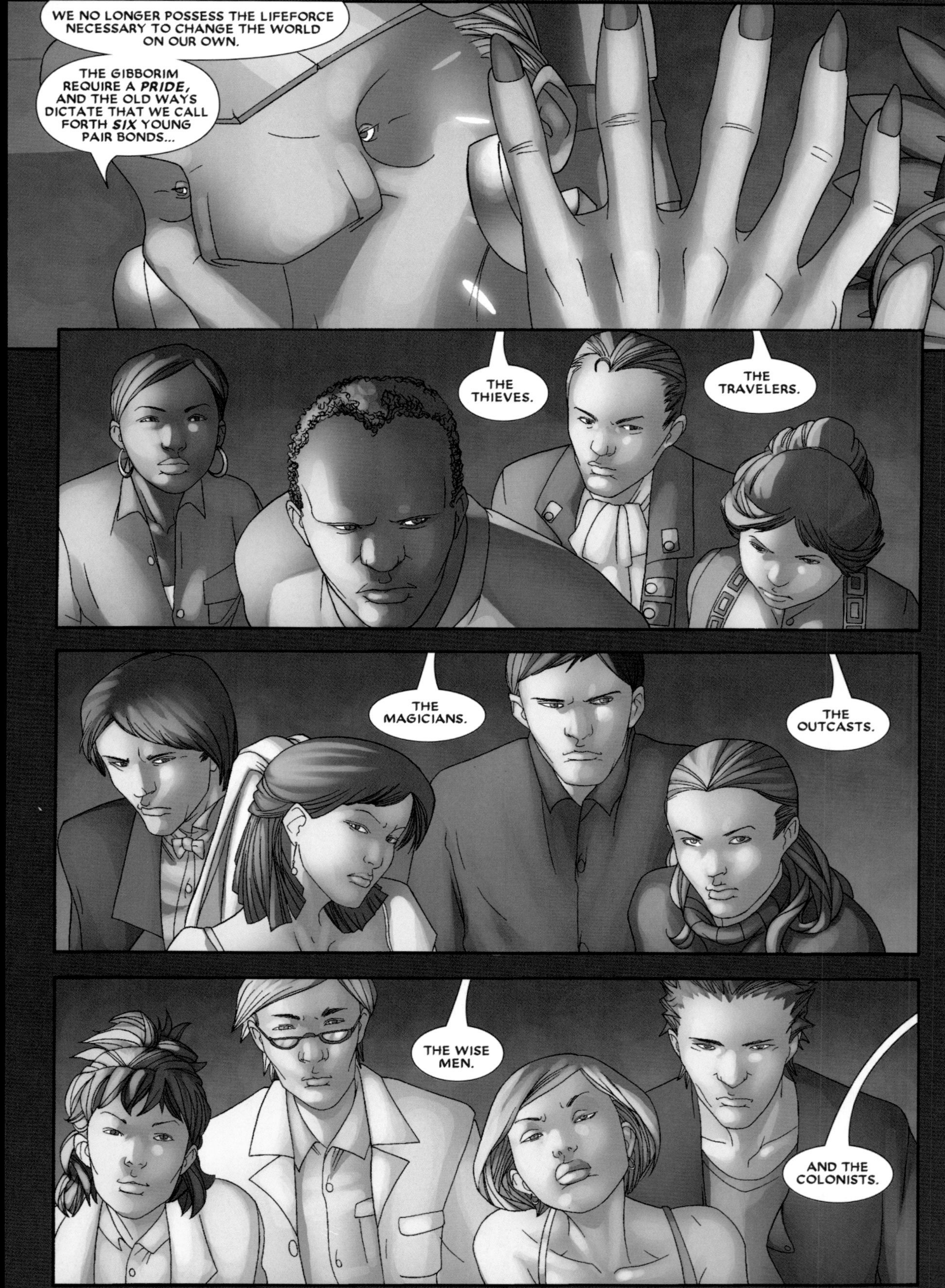
WE NO LONGER POSSESS THE LIFEFORCE NECESSARY TO CHANGE THE WORLD ON OUR OWN.
THE GIBBORIM REQUIRE A *PRIDE*, AND THE OLD WAYS DICTATE THAT WE CALL FORTH *SIX* YOUNG PAIR BONDS...
THE THIEVES.
THE TRAVELERS.
THE MAGICIANS.
THE OUTCASTS.
THE WISE MEN.
AND THE COLONISTS.

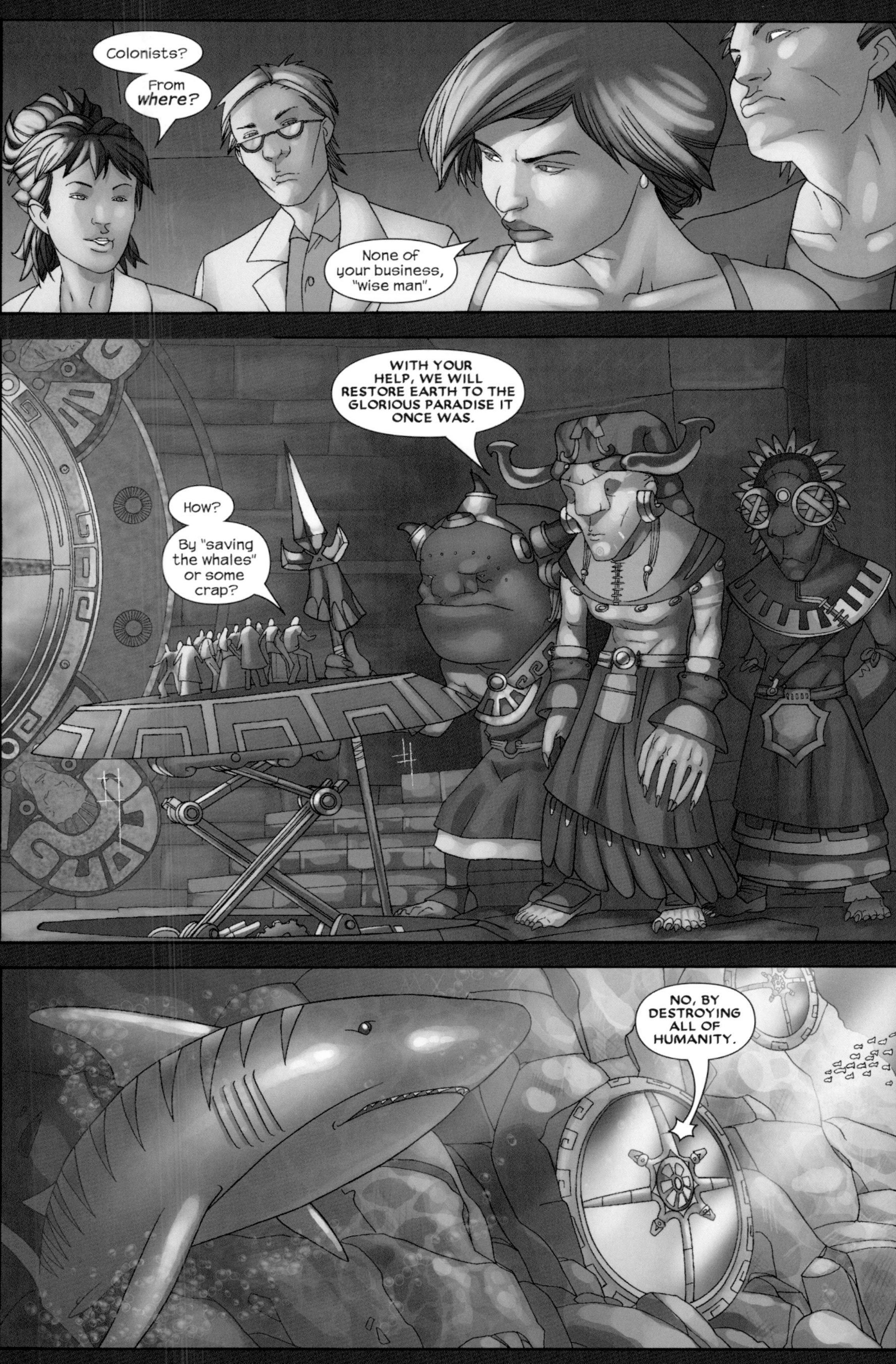
Colonists?
From where?
None of your business, "wise man".
WITH YOUR HELP, WE WILL RESTORE EARTH TO THE GLORIOUS PARADISE IT ONCE WAS.
How?
By "saving the whales" or some crap?
NO, BY DESTROYING ALL OF HUMANITY.

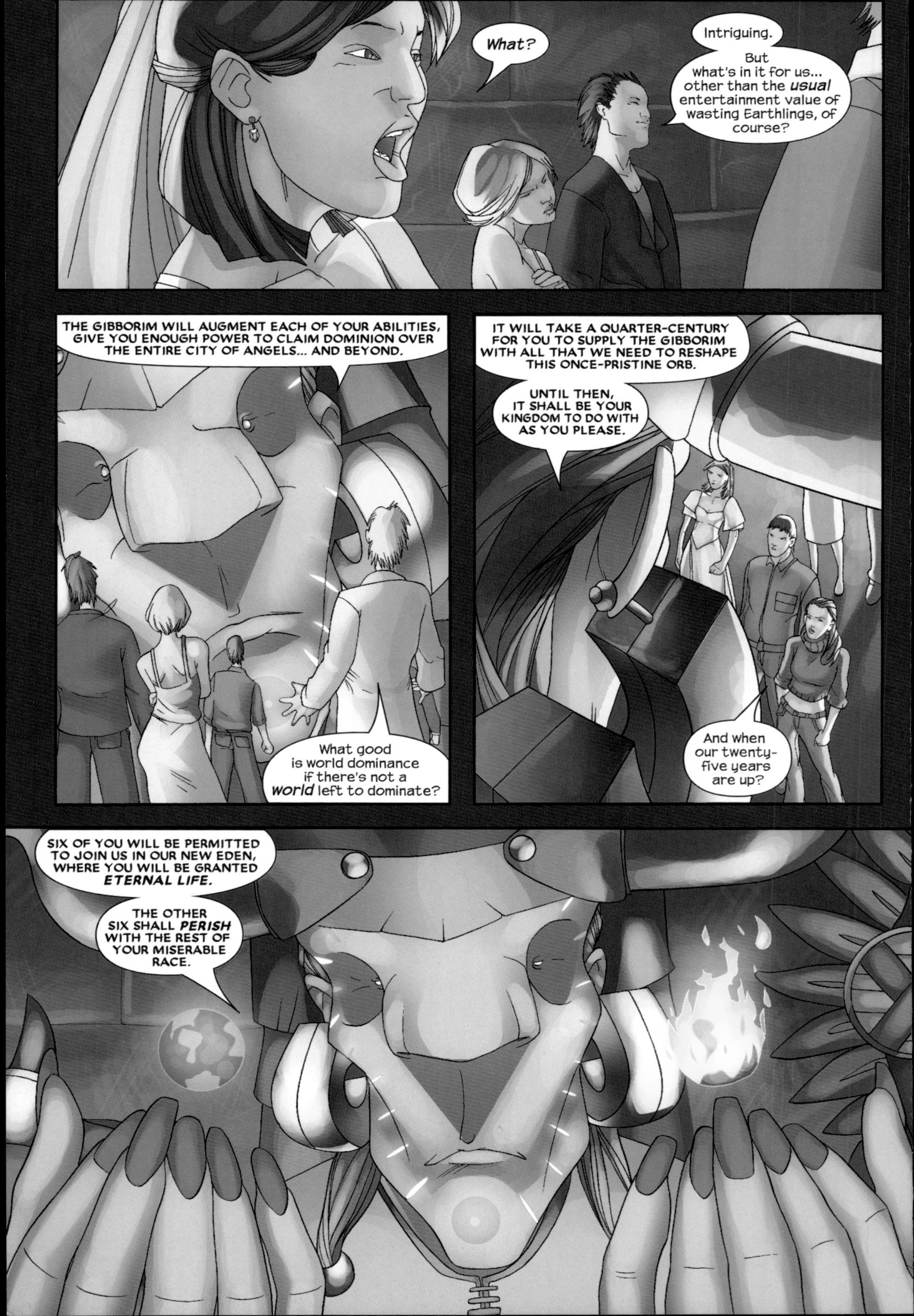
What?
Intriguing.
But what's in it for us... other than the *usual* entertainment value of wasting Earthlings, of course?
THE GIBBORIM WILL AUGMENT EACH OF YOUR ABILITIES, GIVE YOU ENOUGH POWER TO CLAIM DOMINION OVER THE ENTIRE CITY OF ANGELS... AND BEYOND.
What good is world dominance if there's not a *world* left to dominate?
IT WILL TAKE A QUARTER-CENTURY FOR YOU TO SUPPLY THE GIBBORIM WITH ALL THAT WE NEED TO RESHAPE THIS ONCE-PRISTINE ORB.
UNTIL THEN, IT SHALL BE YOUR KINGDOM TO DO WITH AS YOU PLEASE.
And when our twenty-five years are up?
SIX OF YOU WILL BE PERMITTED TO JOIN US IN OUR NEW EDEN, WHERE YOU WILL BE GRANTED *ETERNAL LIFE.*
THE OTHER SIX SHALL *PERISH* WITH THE REST OF YOUR MISERABLE RACE.

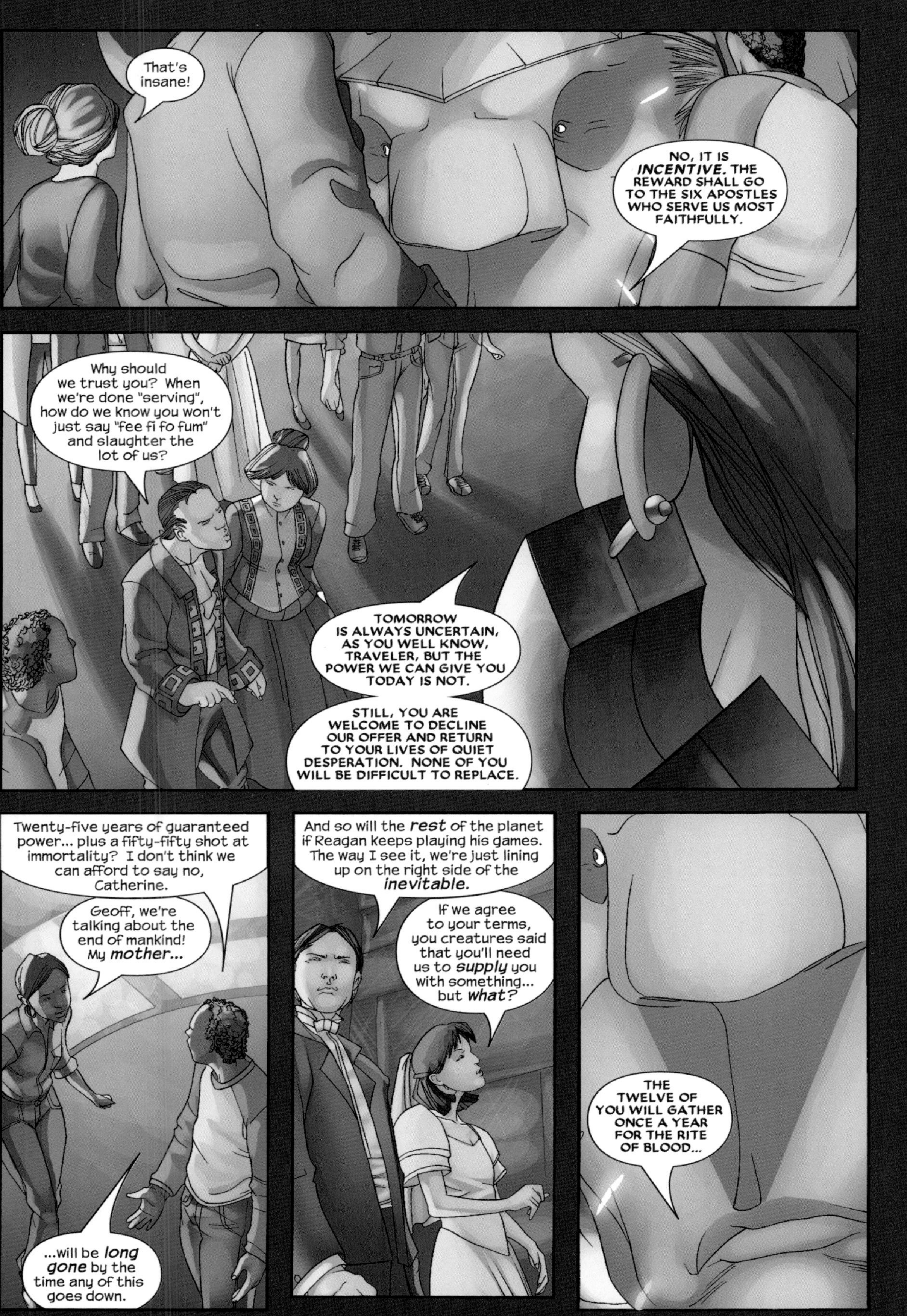

That's insane!
NO, IT IS INCENTIVE. THE REWARD SHALL GO TO THE SIX APOSTLES WHO SERVE US MOST FAITHFULLY.
Why should we trust you? When we're done "serving", how do we know you won't just say "fee fi fo fum" and slaughter the lot of us?
TOMORROW IS ALWAYS UNCERTAIN, AS YOU WELL KNOW, TRAVELER, BUT THE POWER WE CAN GIVE YOU TODAY IS NOT.
STILL, YOU ARE WELCOME TO DECLINE OUR OFFER AND RETURN TO YOUR LIVES OF QUIET DESPERATION. NONE OF YOU WILL BE DIFFICULT TO REPLACE.
Twenty-five years of guaranteed power... plus a fifty-fifty shot at immortality? I don't think we can afford to say no, Catherine.
Geoff, we're talking about the end of mankind! My mother...
...will be long gone by the time any of this goes down.
And so will the rest of the planet if Reagan keeps playing his games. The way I see it, we're just lining up on the right side of the inevitable.
If we agree to your terms, you creatures said that you'll need us to supply you with something... but what?
THE TWELVE OF YOU WILL GATHER ONCE A YEAR FOR THE RITE OF BLOOD...

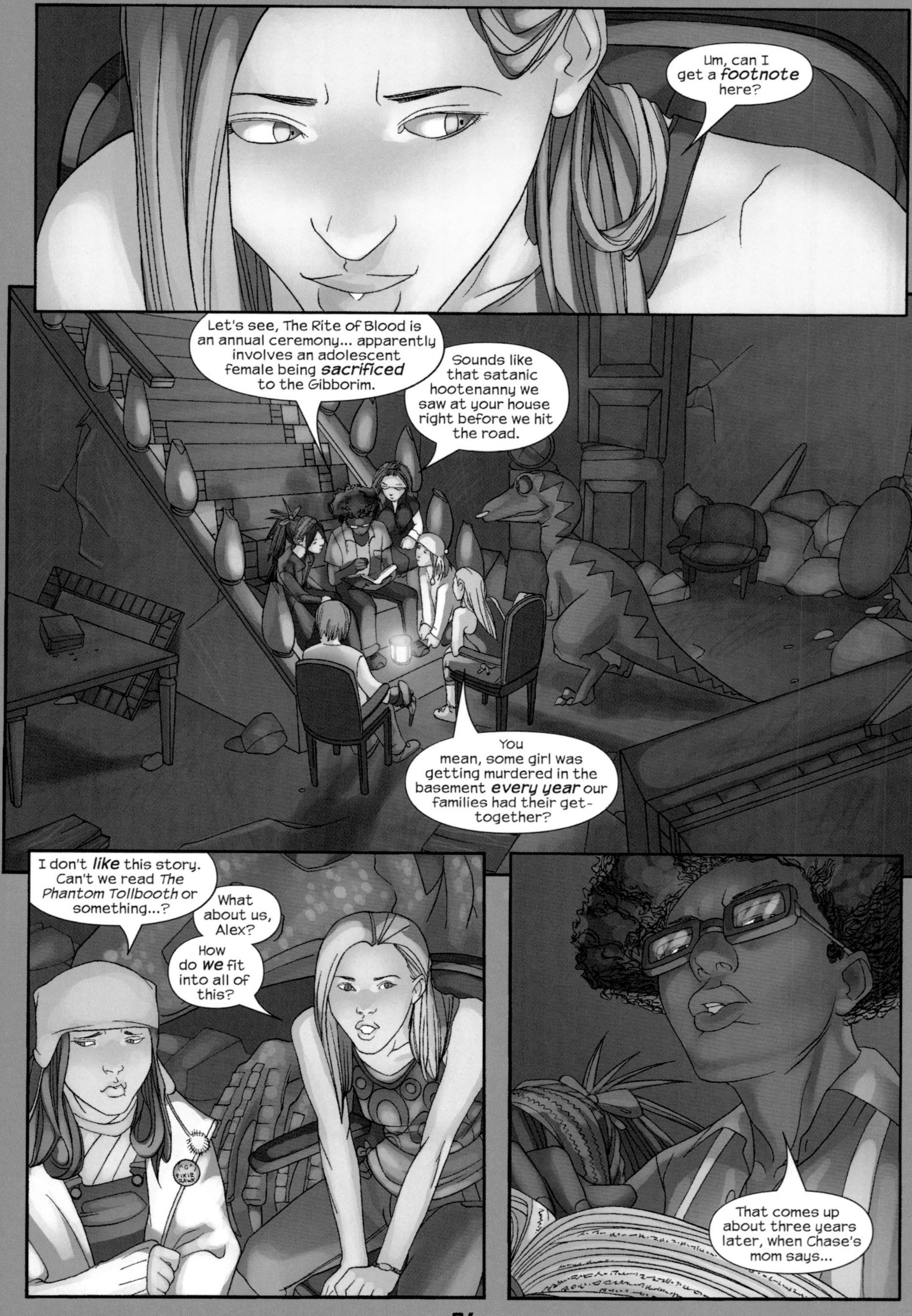

Um, can I get a *footnote* here?
Let's see, The Rite of Blood is an annual ceremony... apparently involves an adolescent female being *sacrificed* to the Gibborim.
Sounds like that satanic hootenanny we saw at your house right before we hit the road.
You mean, some girl was getting murdered in the basement *every year* our families had their get-together?
I don't *like* this story. Can't we read *The Phantom Tollbooth* or something...?
What about us, Alex?
How do *we* fit into all of this?
That comes up about three years later, when Chase's mom says...

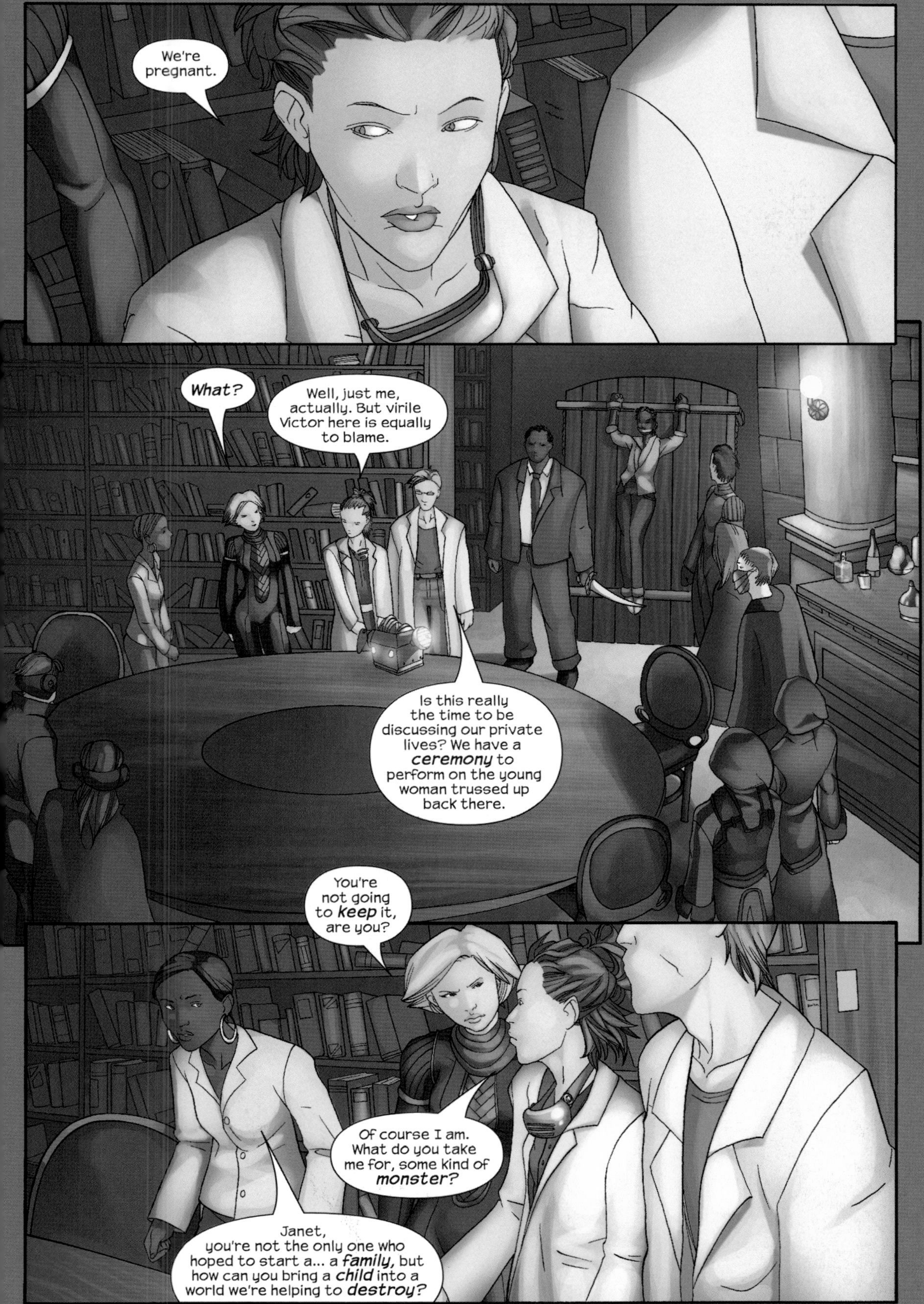

We're pregnant.
What?
Well, just me, actually. But virile Victor here is equally to blame.
Is this really the time to be discussing our private lives? We have a *ceremony* to perform on the young woman trussed up back there.
You're not going to *keep* it, are you?
Of course I am. What do you take me for, some kind of *monster?*
Janet, you're not the only one who hoped to start a... a *family,* but how can you bring a *child* into a world we're helping to *destroy?*

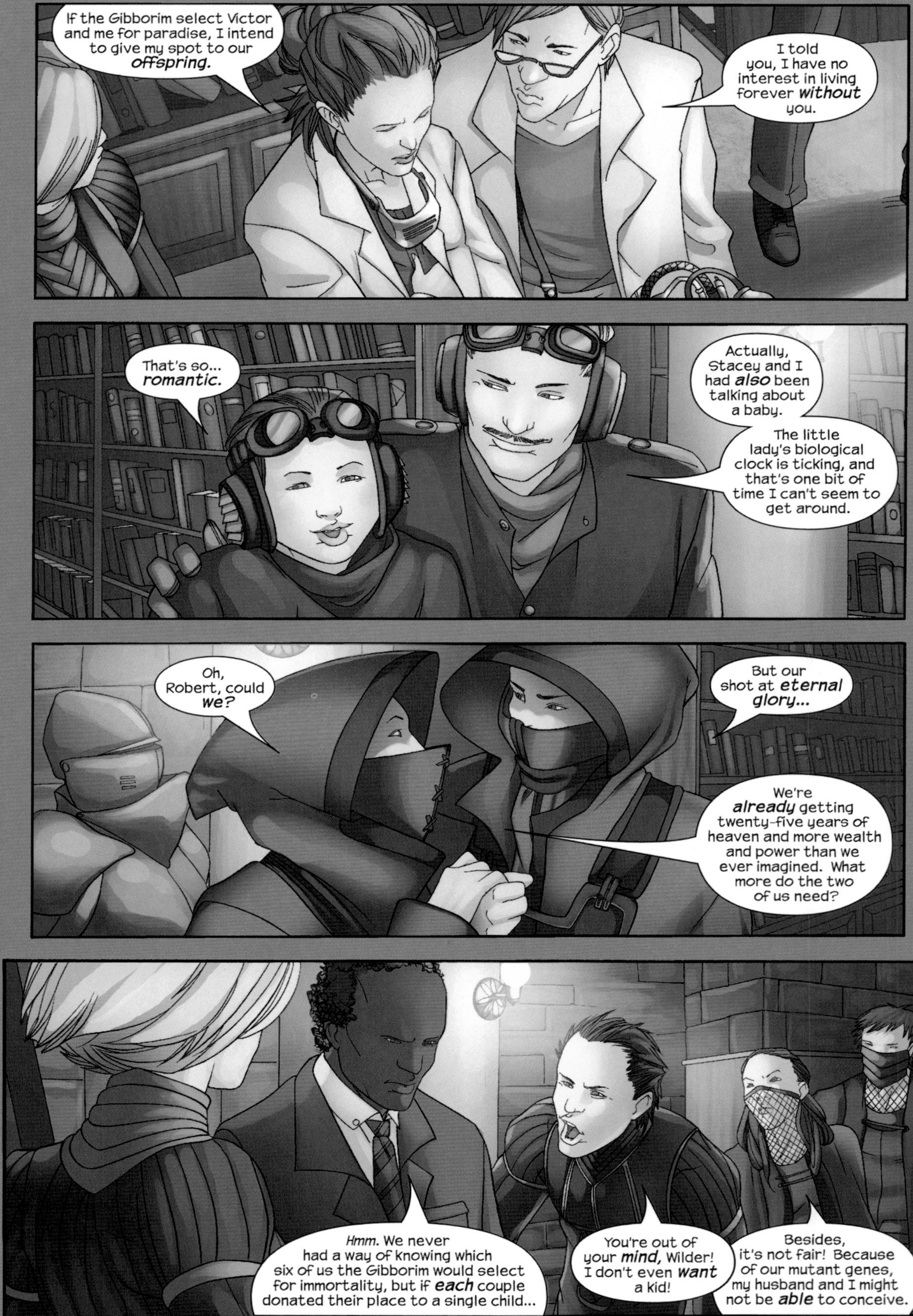
If the Gibborim select Victor and me for paradise, I intend to give my spot to our *offspring.*
I told you, I have no interest in living forever *without* you.
That's so... *romantic.*
Actually, Stacey and I had *also* been talking about a baby.
The little lady's biological clock is ticking, and that's one bit of time I can't seem to get around.
Oh, Robert, could *we?*
But our shot at *eternal glory...*
We're *already* getting twenty-five years of heaven and more wealth and power than we ever imagined. What more do the two of us need?
Hmm. We never had a way of knowing which six of us the Gibborim would select for immortality, but if *each* couple donated their place to a single child...
You're out of your *mind,* Wilder! I don't even *want* a kid!
Besides, it's not fair! Because of our mutant genes, my husband and I might not be *able* to conceive.

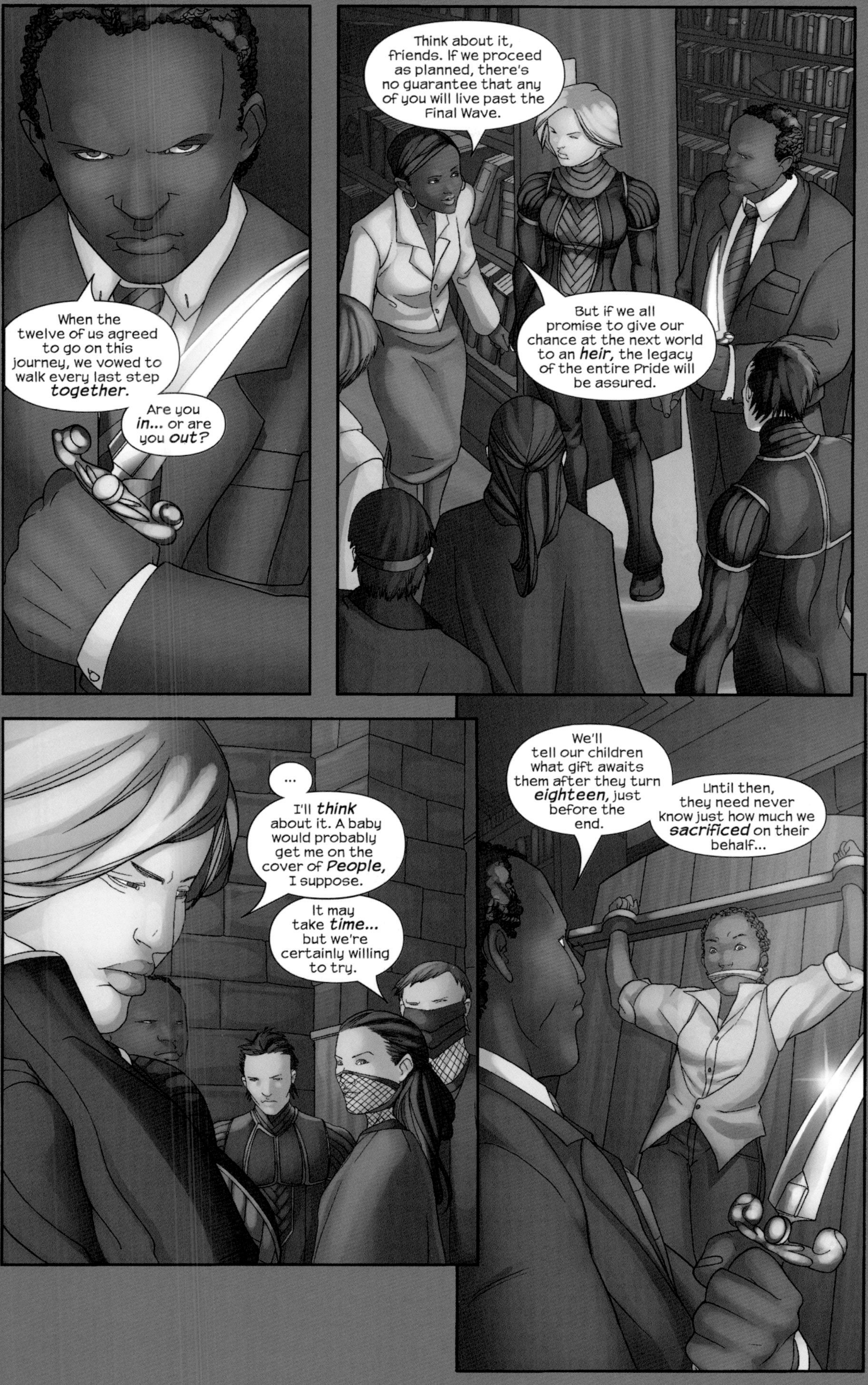
When the twelve of us agreed to go on this journey, we vowed to walk every last step *together.*
Are you *in...* or are you *out?*
Think about it, friends. If we proceed as planned, there's no guarantee that any of you will live past the Final Wave.
But if we all promise to give our chance at the next world to an *heir,* the legacy of the entire Pride will be assured.
...
I'll *think* about it. A baby would probably get me on the cover of *People,* I suppose.
It may take *time...* but we're certainly willing to try.
We'll tell our children what gift awaits them after they turn *eighteen,* just before the end.
Until then, they need never know just how much we *sacrificed* on their behalf...

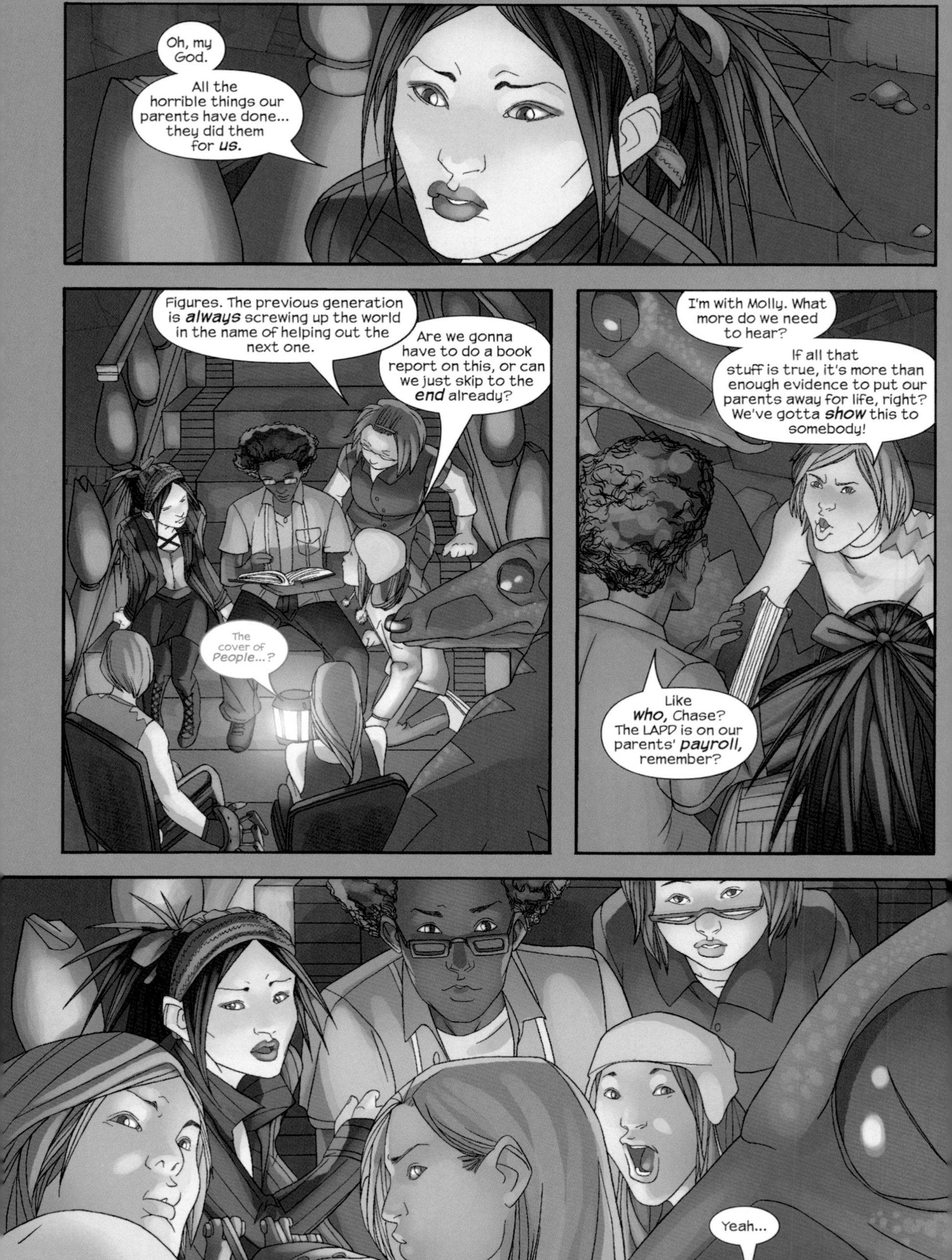

Oh, my God.
All the horrible things our parents have done... they did them for *us.*
Figures. The previous generation is *always* screwing up the world in the name of helping out the next one.
Are we gonna have to do a book report on this, or can we just skip to the *end* already?
The cover of *People*...?
I'm with Molly. What more do we need to hear?
If all that stuff is true, it's more than enough evidence to put our parents away for life, right? We've gotta *show* this to somebody!
Like *who,* Chase? The LAPD is on our parents' *payroll,* remember?
Yeah...

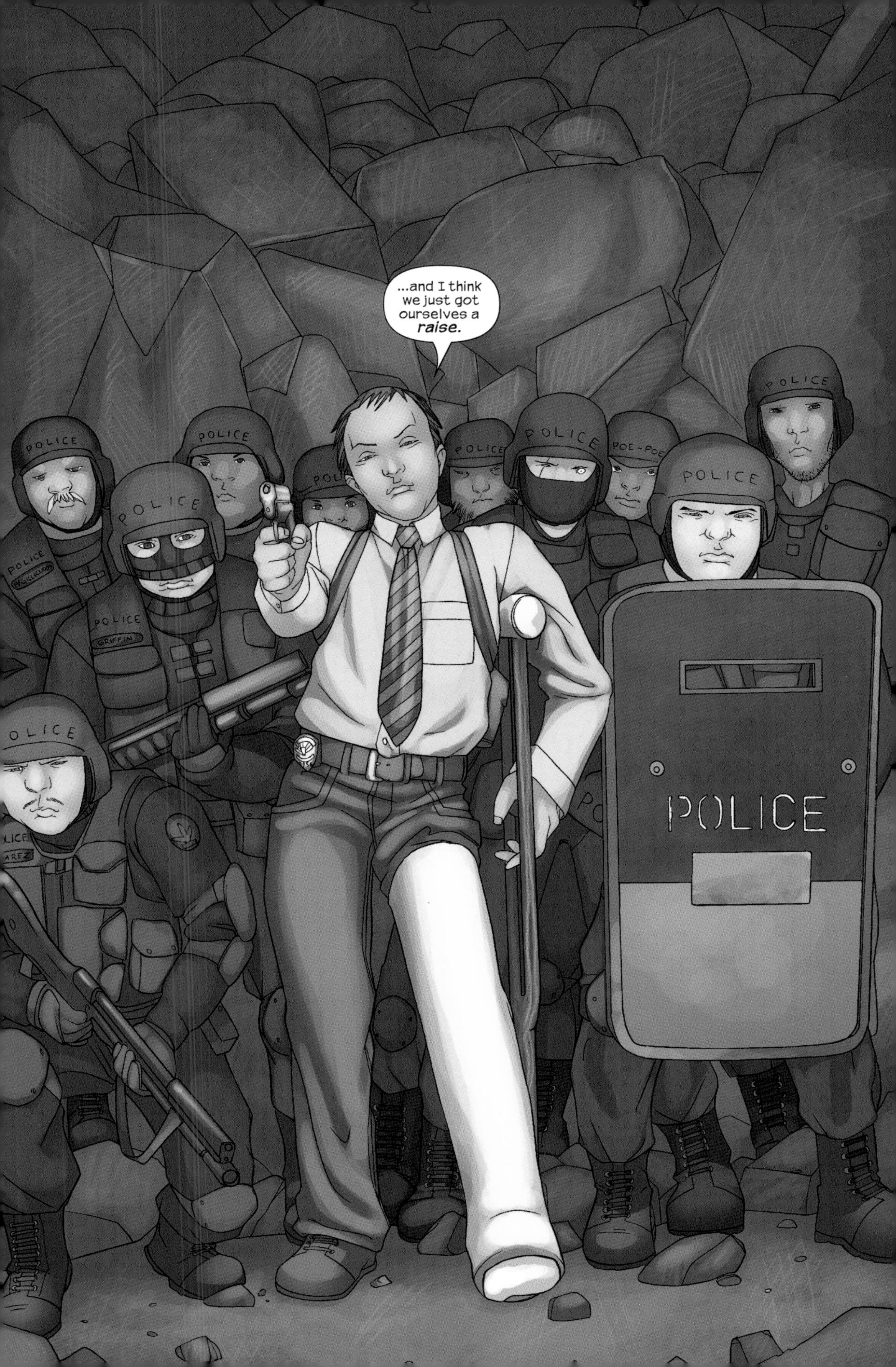
...and I think we just got ourselves a *raise.*
POLICE

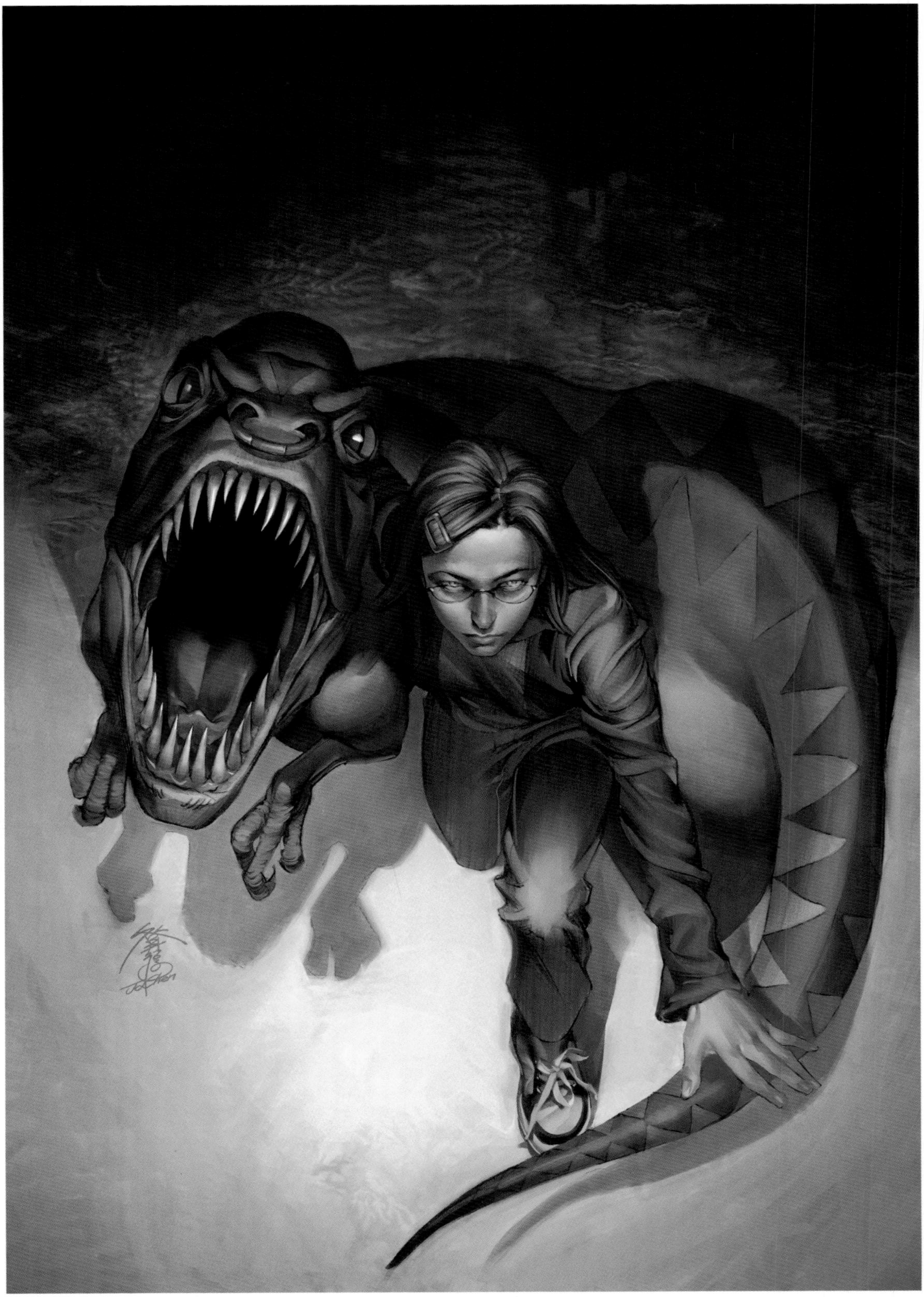

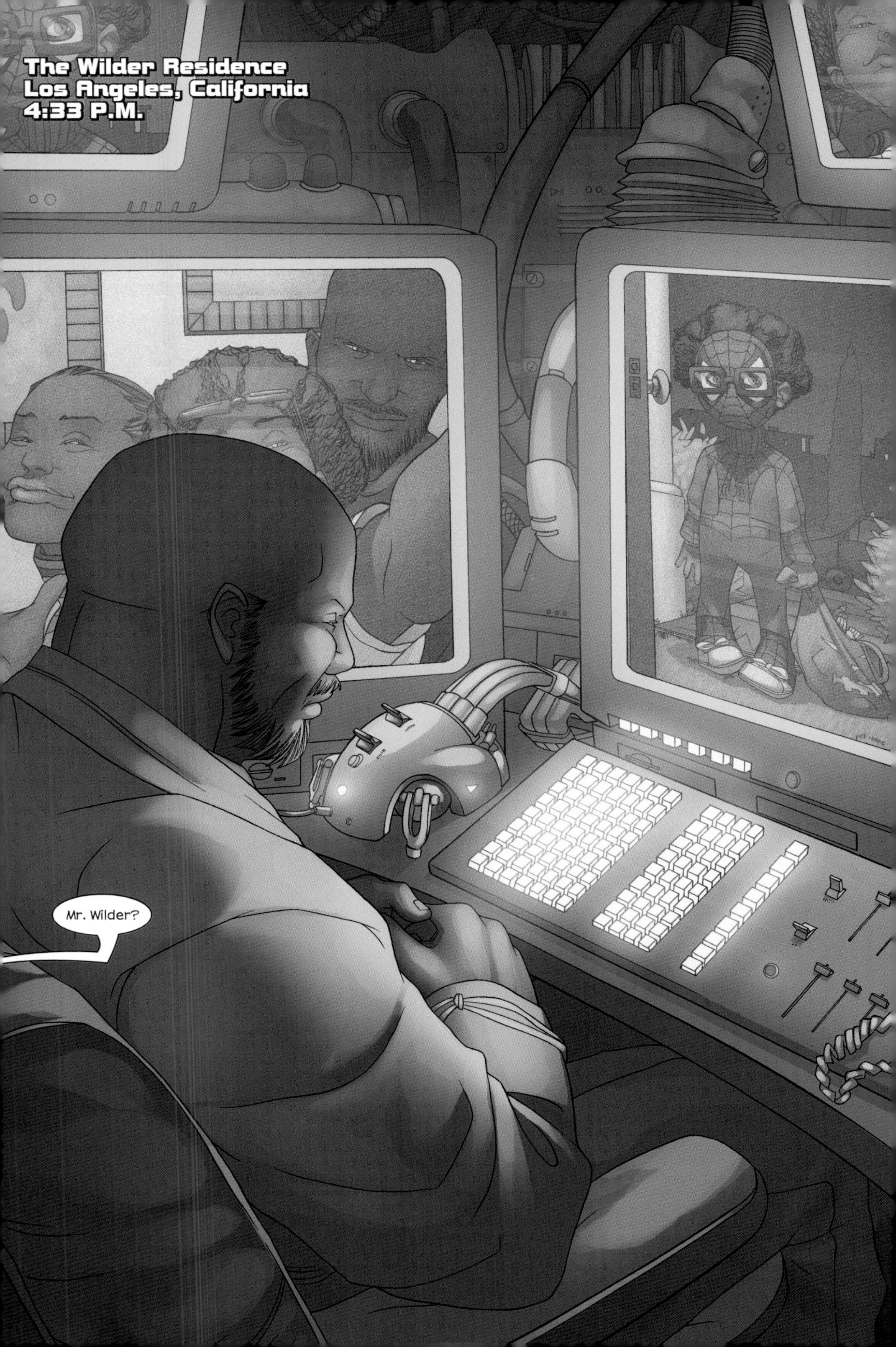
The Wilder Residence
Los Angeles, California
4:33 P.M.
Mr. Wilder?

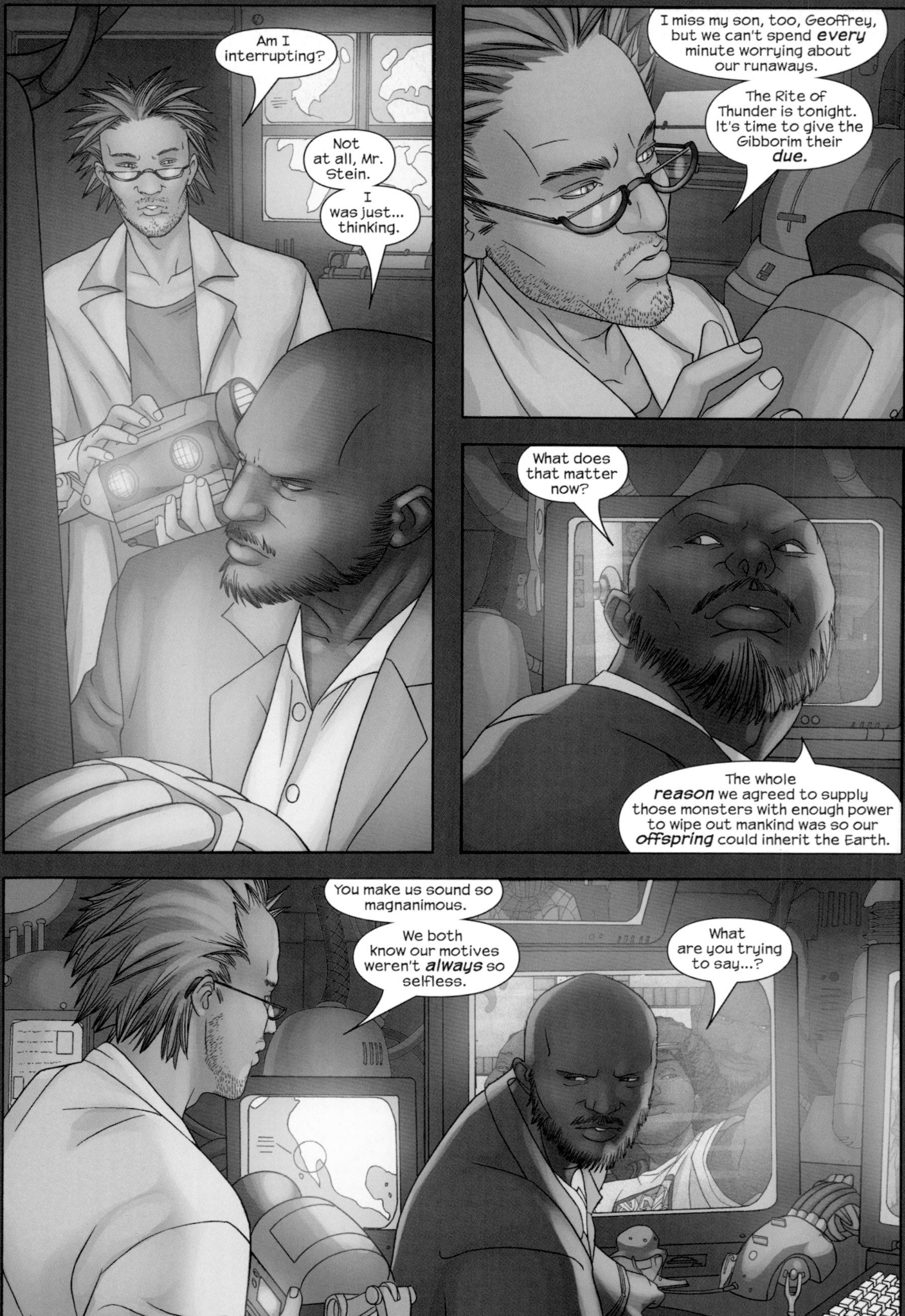

Am I interrupting?
Not at all, Mr. Stein.
I was just... thinking.
I miss my son, too, Geoffrey, but we can't spend *every* minute worrying about our runaways.
The Rite of Thunder is tonight. It's time to give the Gibborim their *due.*
What does that matter now?
The whole *reason* we agreed to supply those monsters with enough power to wipe out mankind was so our *offspring* could inherit the Earth.
You make us sound so magnanimous.
We both know our motives weren't *always* so selfless.
What are you trying to say...?

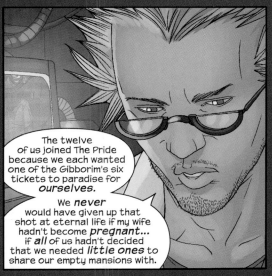

The twelve of us joined The Pride because we each wanted one of the Gibborim's six tickets to paradise for *ourselves.*

We *never* would have given up that shot at eternal life if my wife hadn't become *pregnant*... if *all* of us hadn't decided that we needed *little ones* to share our empty mansions with.

But it was *years* ago that we agreed to donate our chance at immortality to those six kids. Back then, none of us imagined that we would ever *want* to live forever.

Surviving to an age like *forty* sounded like an eternity already, more than enough time to enjoy all the Gibborim had granted us.

But now we're *old men,* rapidly approaching the Final Wave, and the ungrateful brats we sacrificed everything for have *abandoned* us.

Admit it, some nights, you think about *letting* your son perish with the rest of this wretched populace... and taking his spot in the Next World for *yourself.*

NEVER!

‹hkk‹

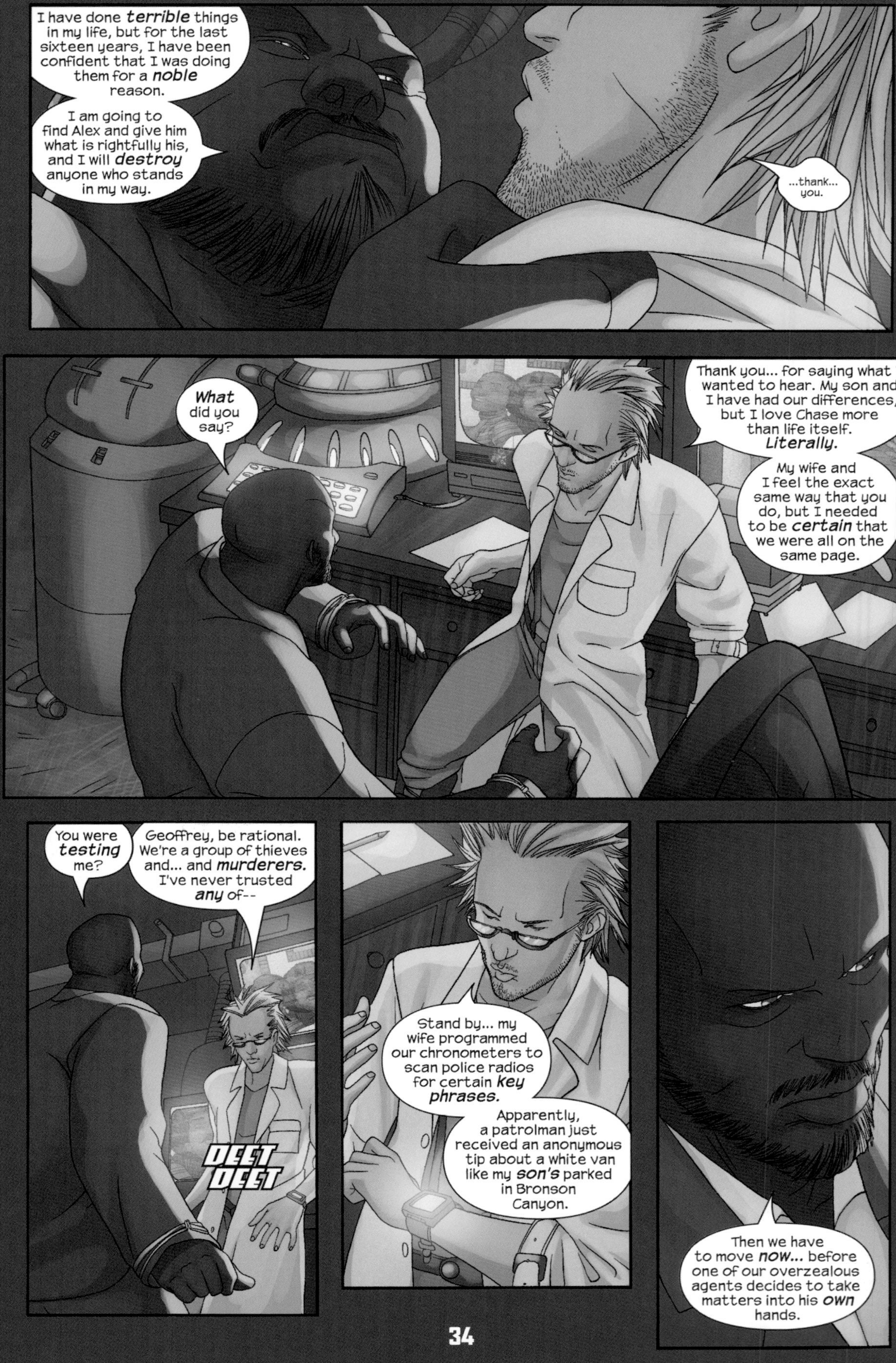

I have done *terrible* things in my life, but for the last sixteen years, I have been confident that I was doing them for a *noble* reason.
I am going to find Alex and give him what is rightfully his, and I will *destroy* anyone who stands in my way.
...thank... you.
What did you say?
Thank you... for saying what I wanted to hear. My son and I have had our differences, but I love Chase more than life itself. *Literally.*
My wife and I feel the exact same way that you do, but I needed to be *certain* that we were all on the same page.
You were *testing* me?
Geoffrey, be rational. We're a group of thieves and... and *murderers.* I've never trusted *any* of--
DEET DEET
Stand by... my wife programmed our chronometers to scan police radios for certain *key phrases.*
Apparently, a patrolman just received an anonymous tip about a white van like my *son's* parked in Bronson Canyon.
Then we have to move *now...* before one of our overzealous agents decides to take matters into his *own* hands.

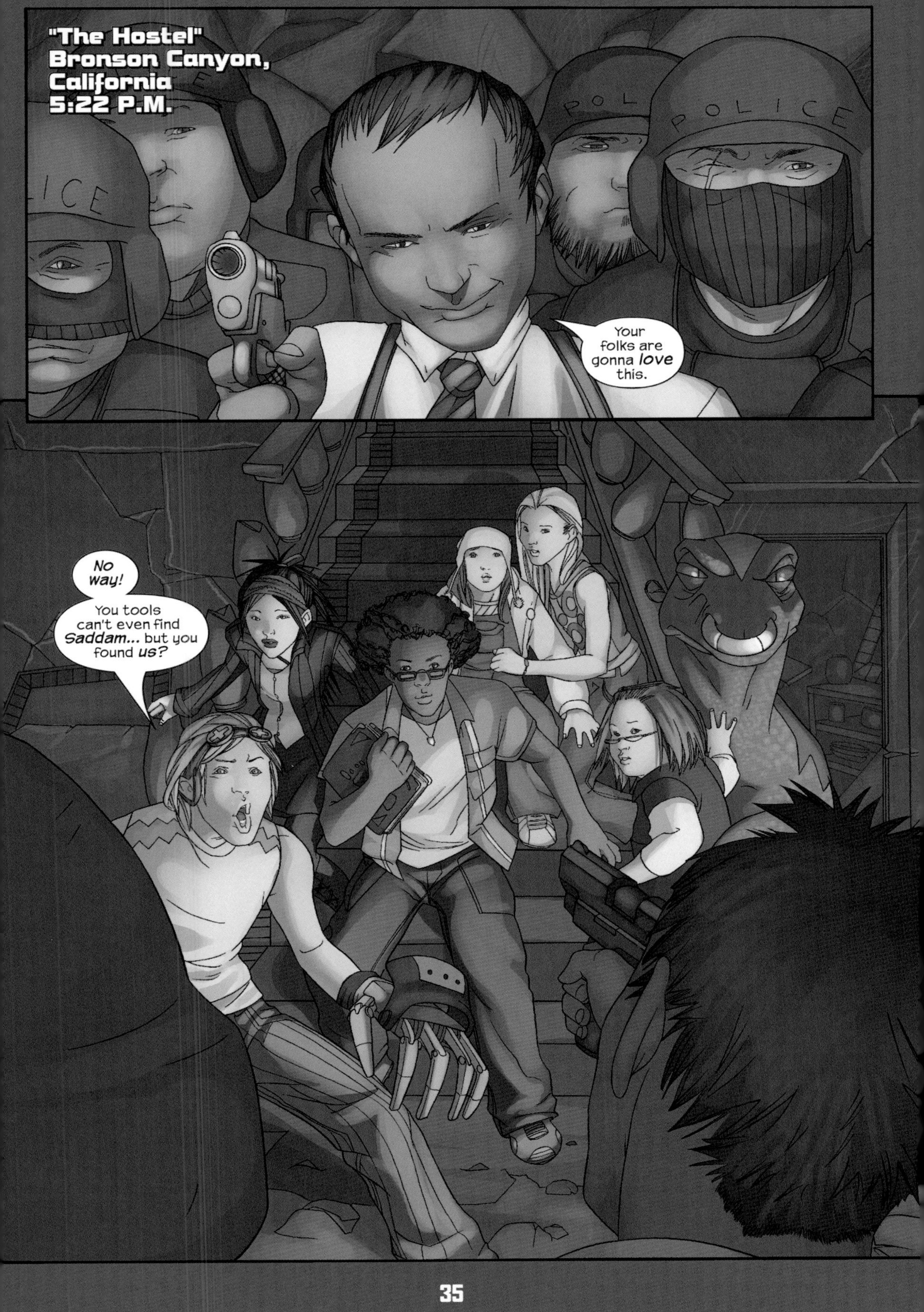
"The Hostel"
Bronson Canyon,
California
5:22 P.M.
Your folks are gonna *love* this.
No way!
You tools can't even find *Saddam...* but you found *us?*

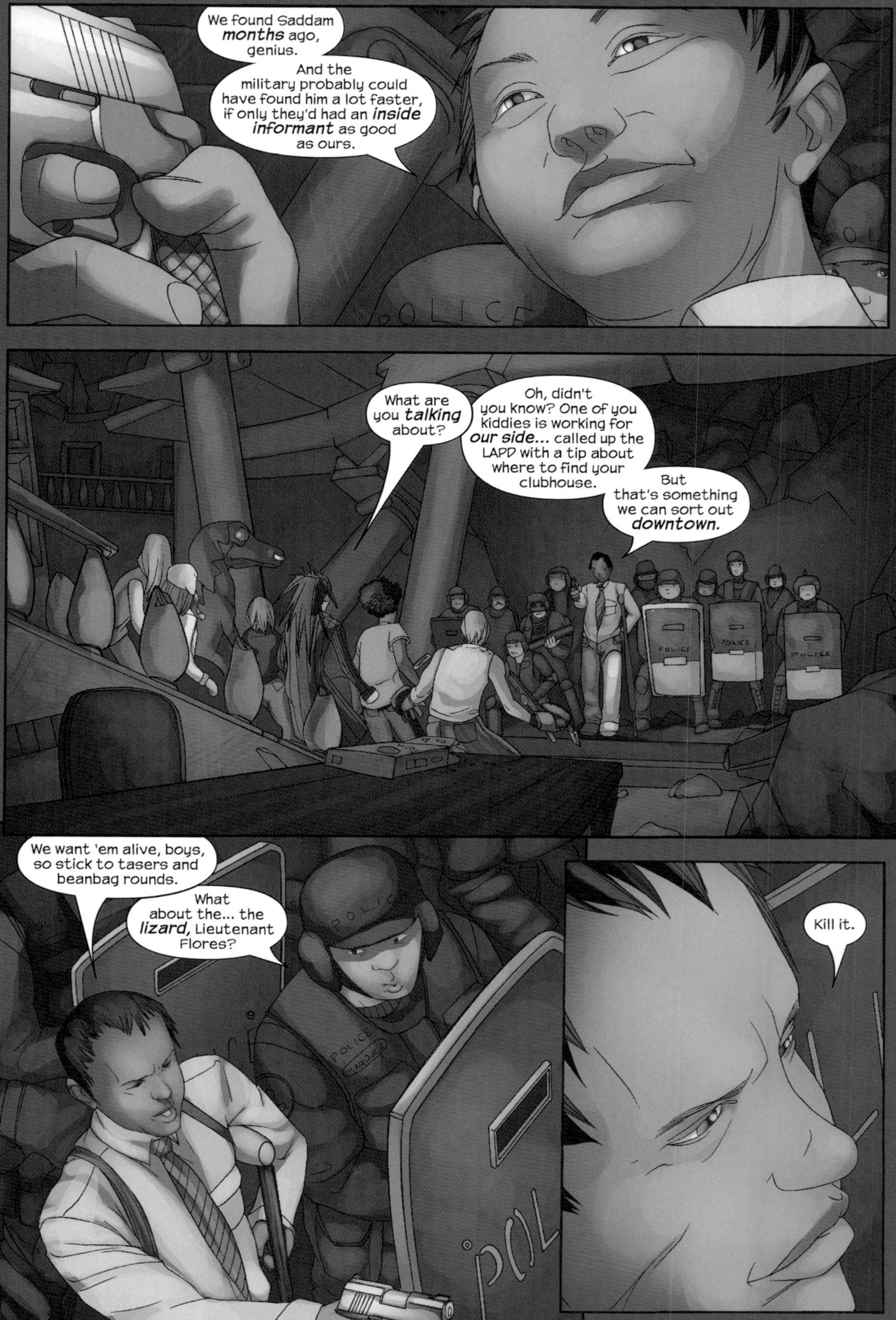
We found Saddam *months* ago, genius.
And the military probably could have found him a lot faster, if only they'd had an *inside informant* as good as ours.
POLICE
What are you *talking* about?
Oh, didn't you know? One of you kiddies is working for *our side...* called up the LAPD with a tip about where to find your clubhouse.
But that's something we can sort out *downtown.*
POLICE
POLICE
POLICE
We want 'em alive, boys, so stick to tasers and beanbag rounds.
What about the... the *lizard,* Lieutenant Flores?
Kill it.

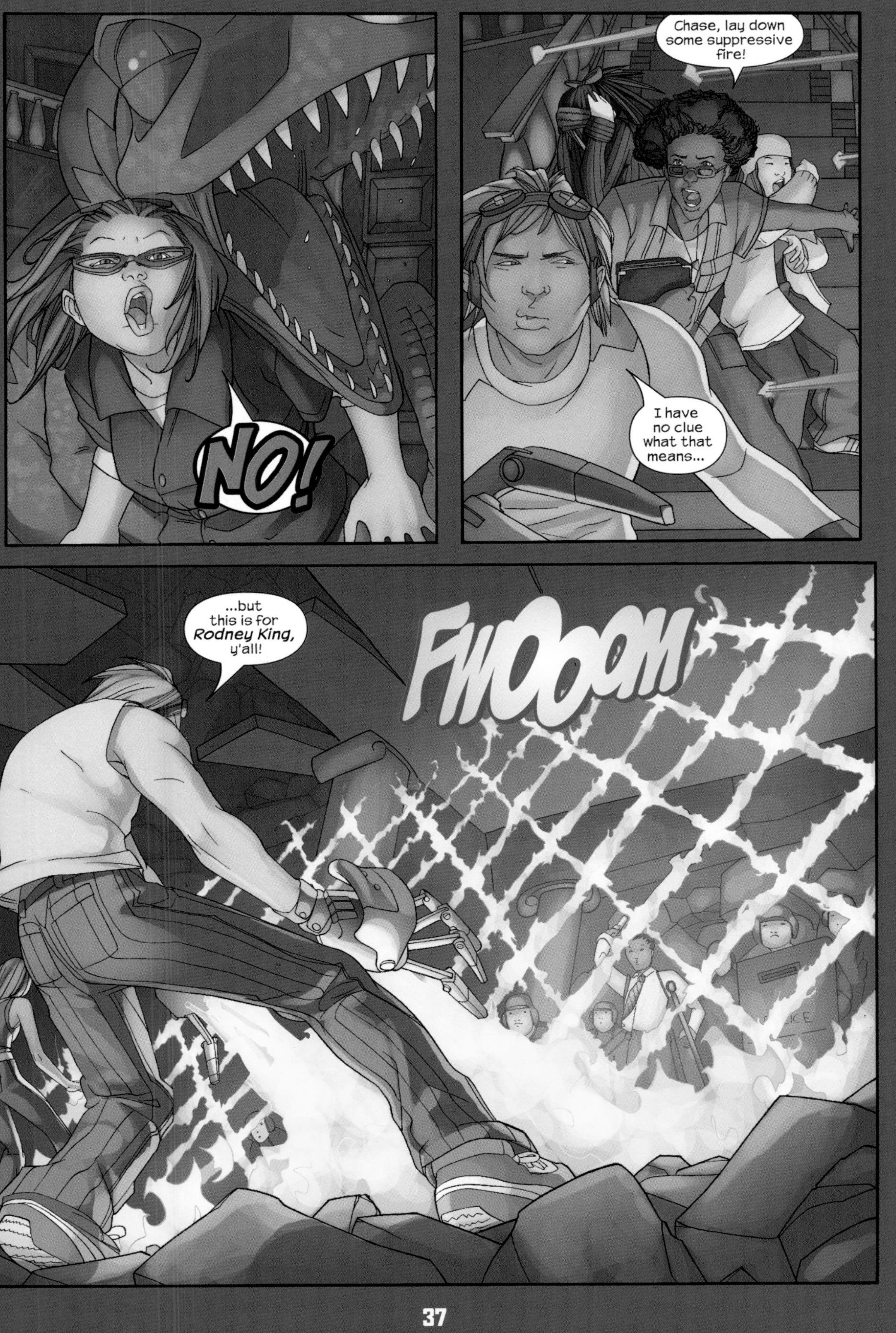
NO!
Chase, lay down some suppressive fire!
I have no clue what that means...
...but this is for Rodney King, y'all!
FWOOOM

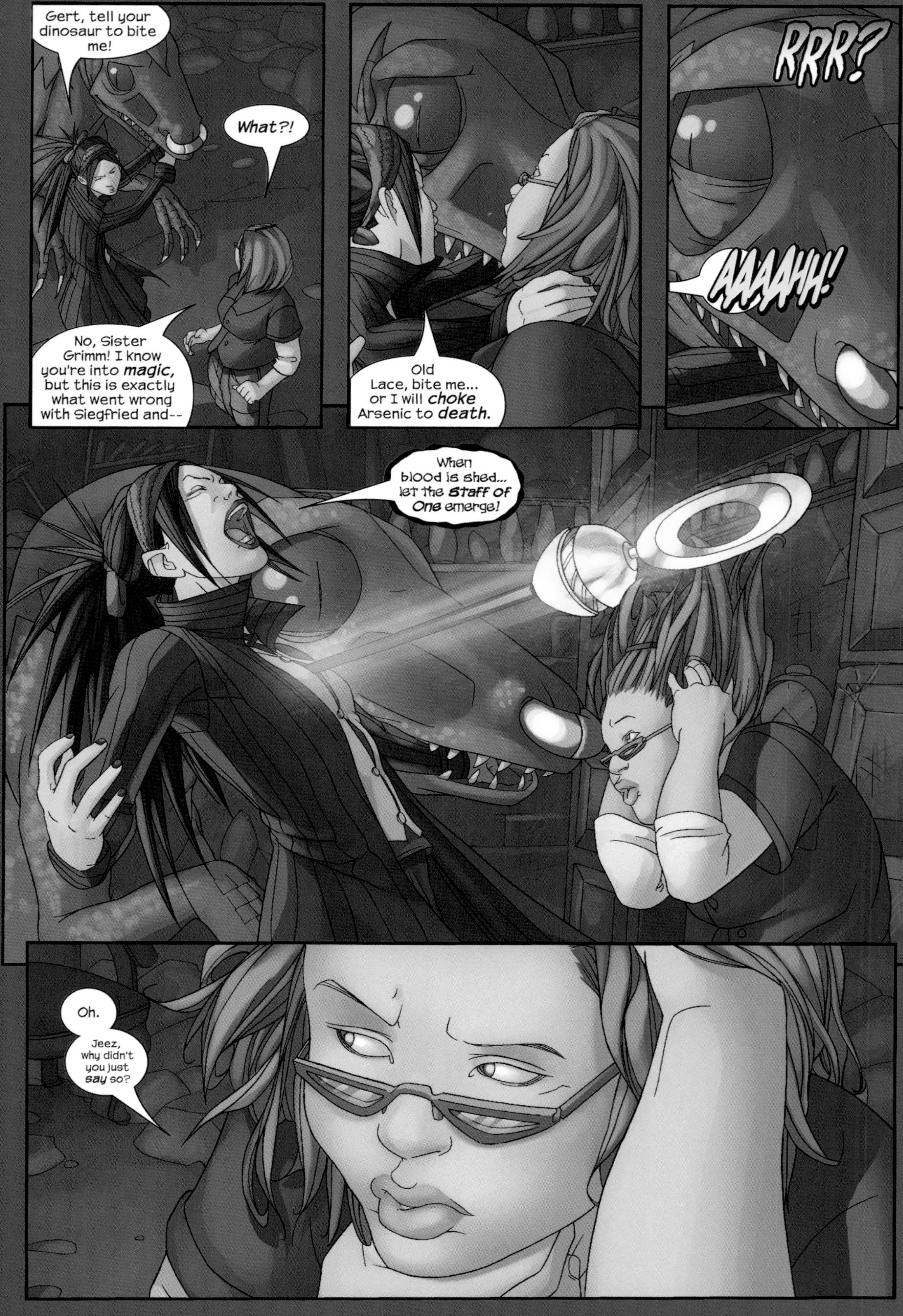

Gert, tell your dinosaur to bite me!
What?!
No, Sister Grimm! I know you're into *magic,* but this is exactly what went wrong with Siegfried and--
Old Lace, bite me... or I will *choke* Arsenic to *death.*
RRR?
AAAAHH!
When blood is shed... let the *Staff of One* emerge!
Oh.
Jeez, why didn't you just *say* so?

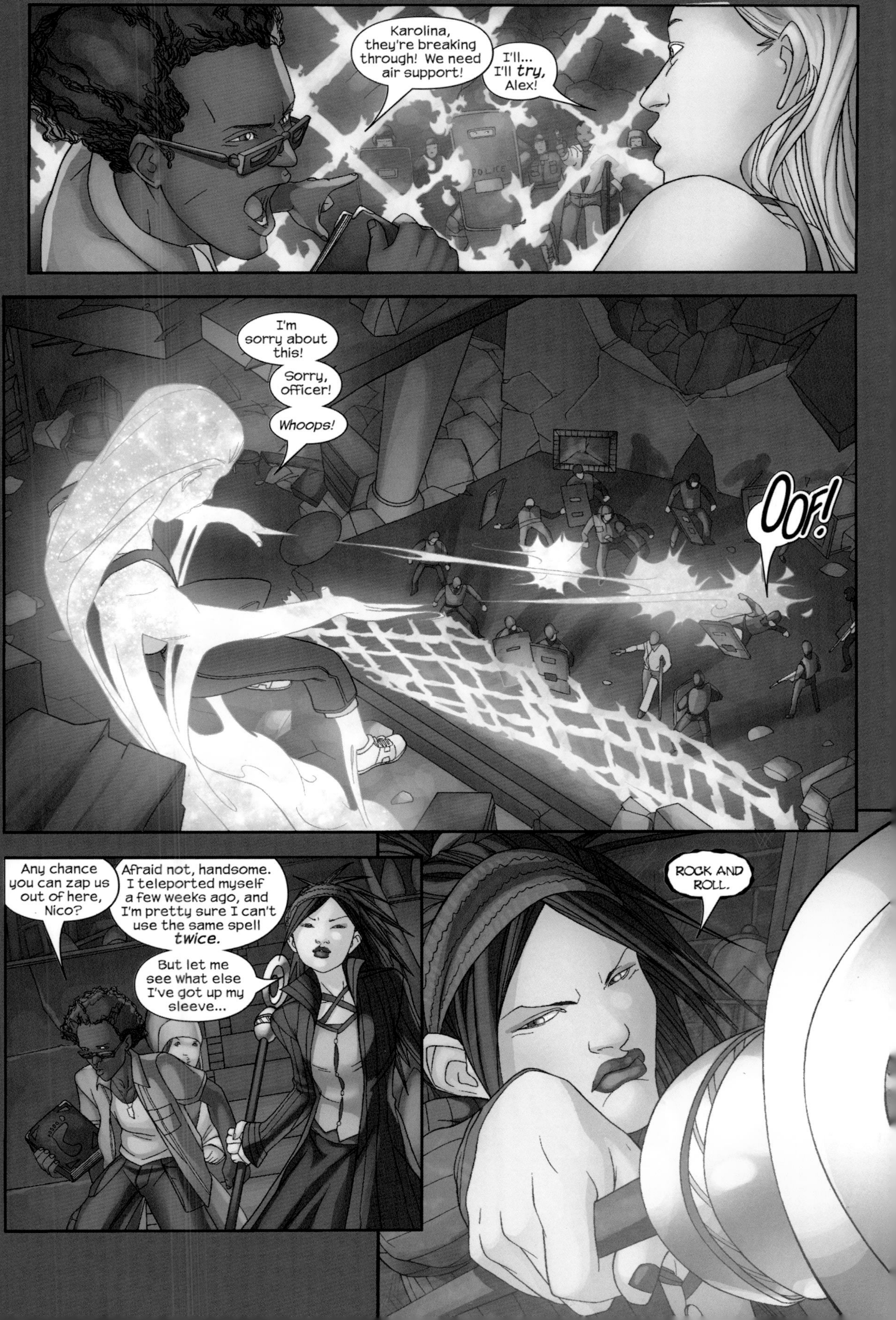
Karolina, they're breaking through! We need air support!
I'll... I'll try, Alex!
POLICE
I'm sorry about this!
Sorry, officer!
Whoops!
OOF!
Any chance you can zap us out of here, Nico?
Afraid not, handsome. I teleported myself a few weeks ago, and I'm pretty sure I can't use the same spell twice.
But let me see what else I've got up my sleeve...
ROCK AND ROLL.

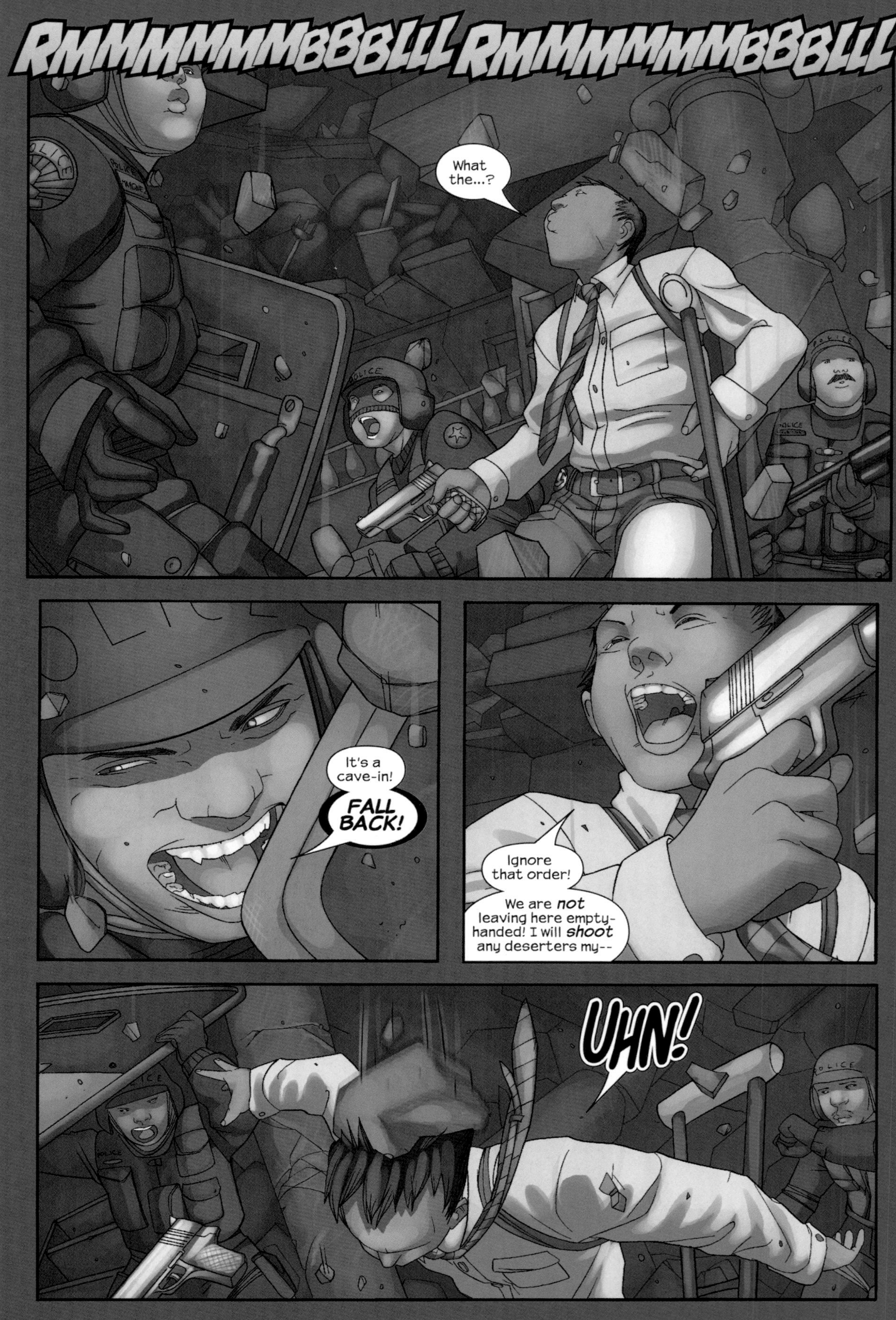
RMMMMMMBBBLLL RMMMMMMMBBBLLL
What the...?
It's a cave-in!
FALL BACK!
Ignore that order!
We are not leaving here empty-handed! I will shoot any deserters my--
UHN!

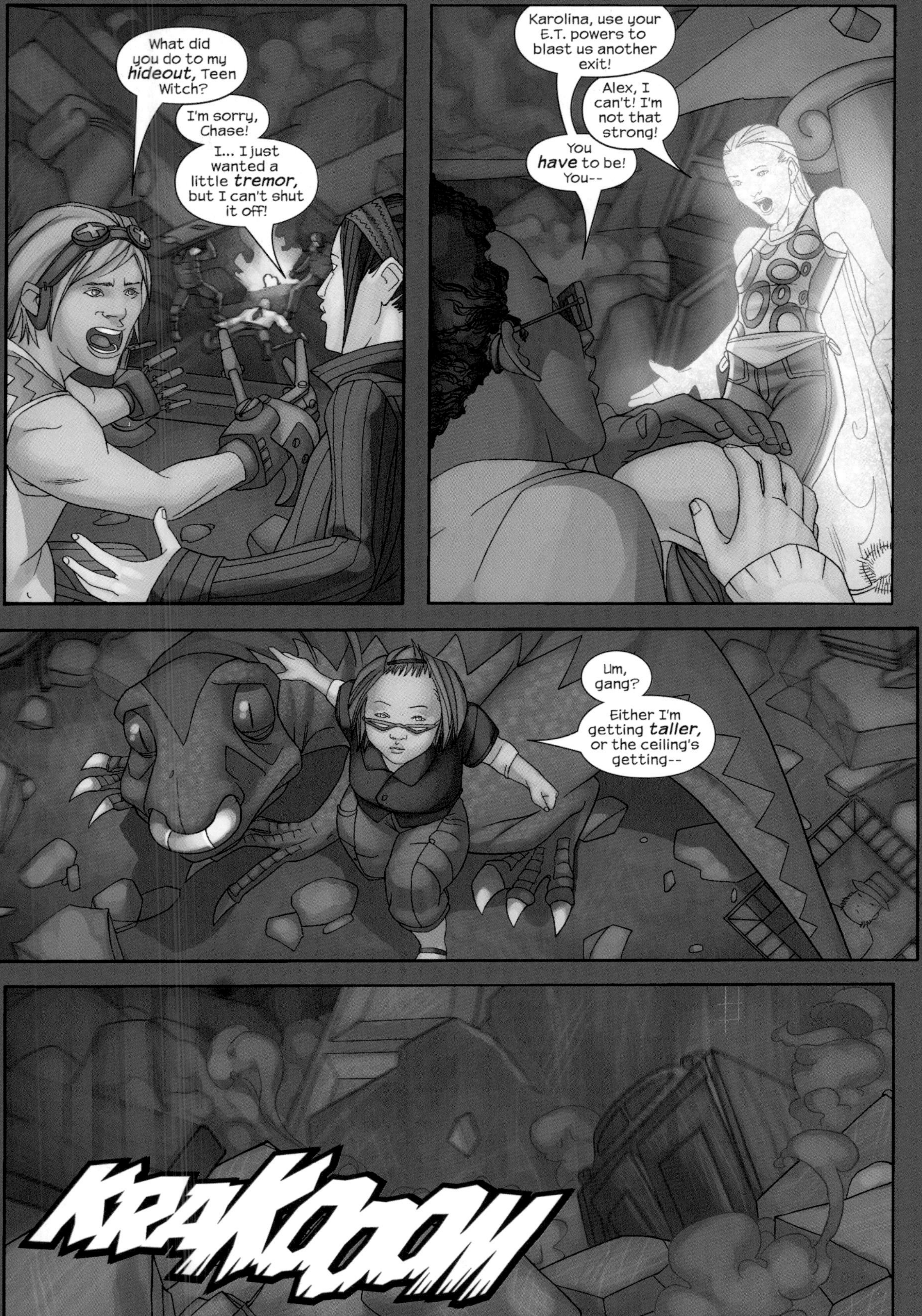
What did you do to my *hideout,* Teen Witch?
I'm sorry, Chase!
I... I just wanted a little *tremor,* but I can't shut it off!
Karolina, use your E.T. powers to blast us another exit!
Alex, I can't! I'm not that strong!
You *have* to be! You--
Um, gang?
Either I'm getting *taller,* or the ceiling's getting--
KRAKOOOM

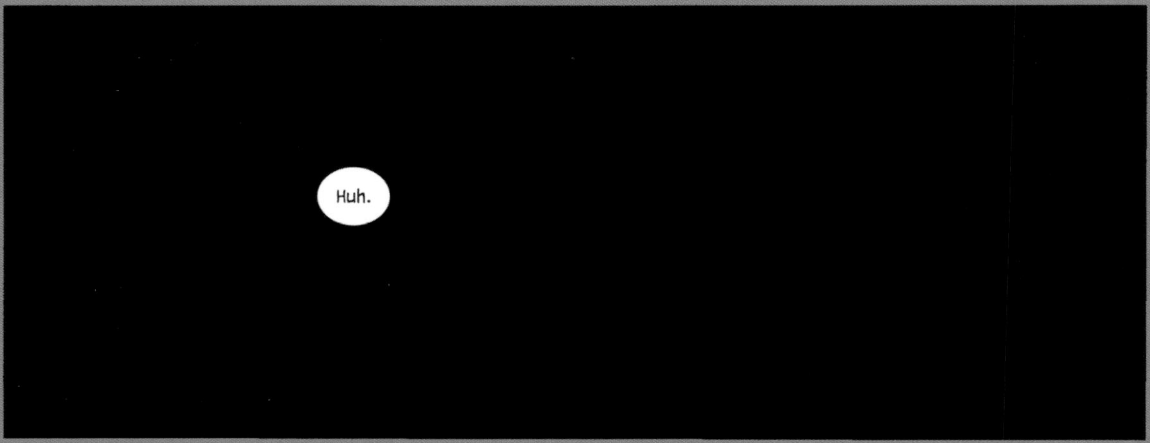
Huh.

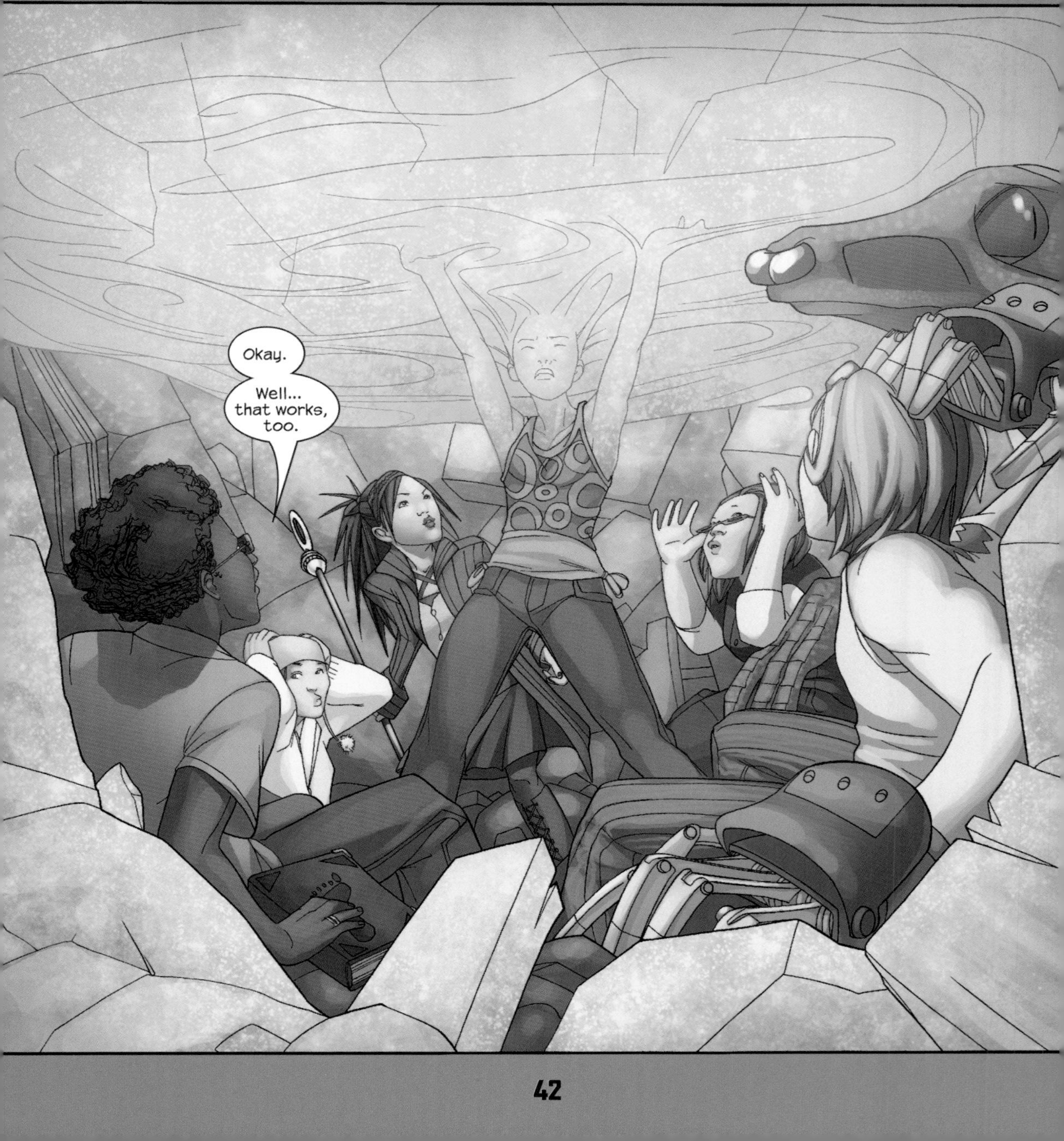
Okay.
Well... that works, too.

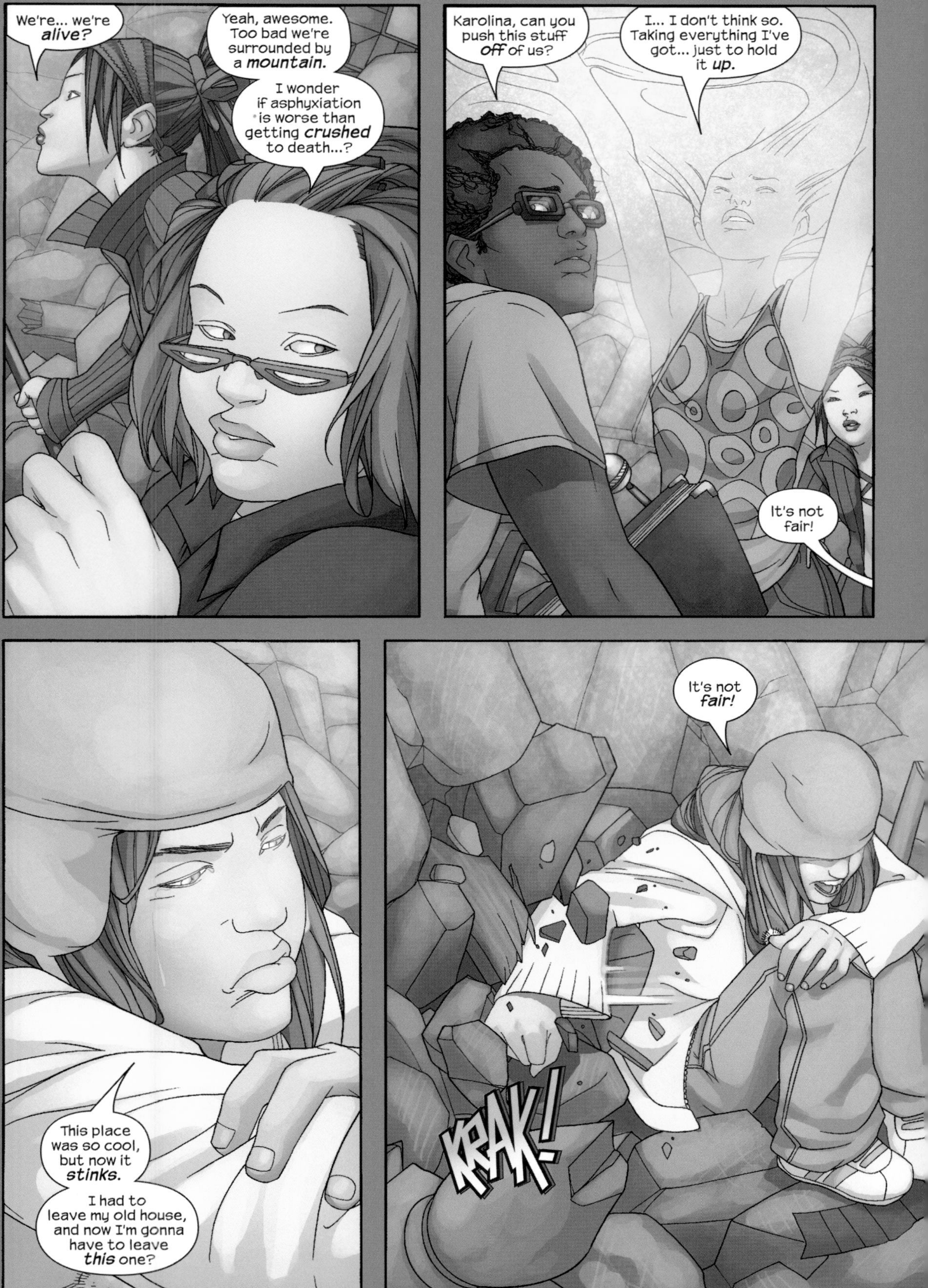
We're... we're *alive?*
Yeah, awesome. Too bad we're surrounded by a *mountain.*
I wonder if asphyxiation is worse than getting *crushed* to death...?
Karolina, can you push this stuff *off* of us?
I... I don't think so. Taking everything I've got... just to hold it *up.*
It's not fair!
This place was so cool, but now it *stinks.*
I had to leave my old house, and now I'm gonna have to leave *this* one?
It's not *fair!*
KRAK!

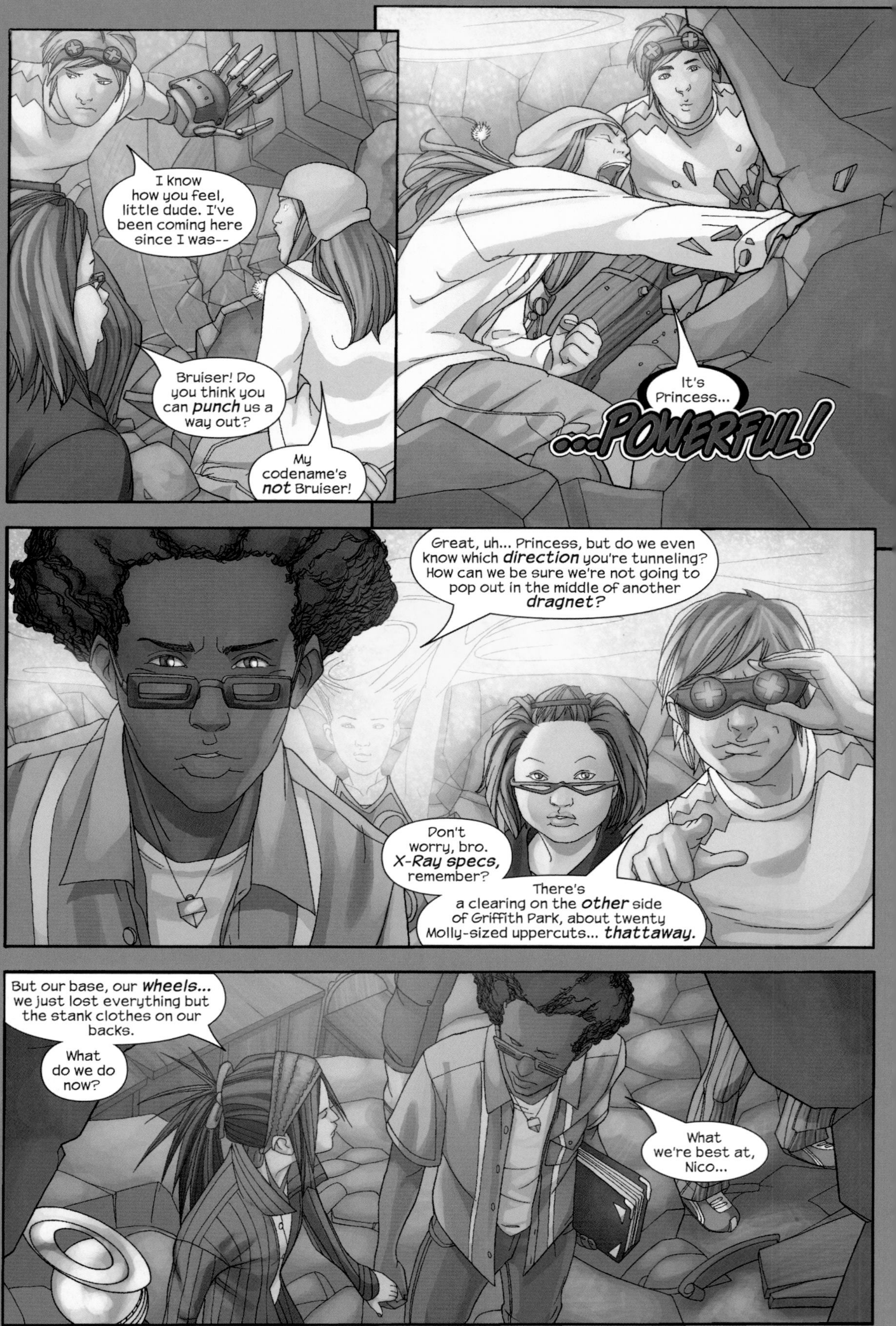

I know how you feel, little dude. I've been coming here since I was--
Bruiser! Do you think you can punch us a way out?
My codename's not Bruiser!
It's Princess...
...POWERFUL!
Great, uh... Princess, but do we even know which direction you're tunneling? How can we be sure we're not going to pop out in the middle of another dragnet?
Don't worry, bro. X-Ray specs, remember?
There's a clearing on the other side of Griffith Park, about twenty Molly-sized uppercuts... thattaway.
But our base, our wheels... we just lost everything but the stank clothes on our backs.
What do we do now?
What we're best at, Nico...

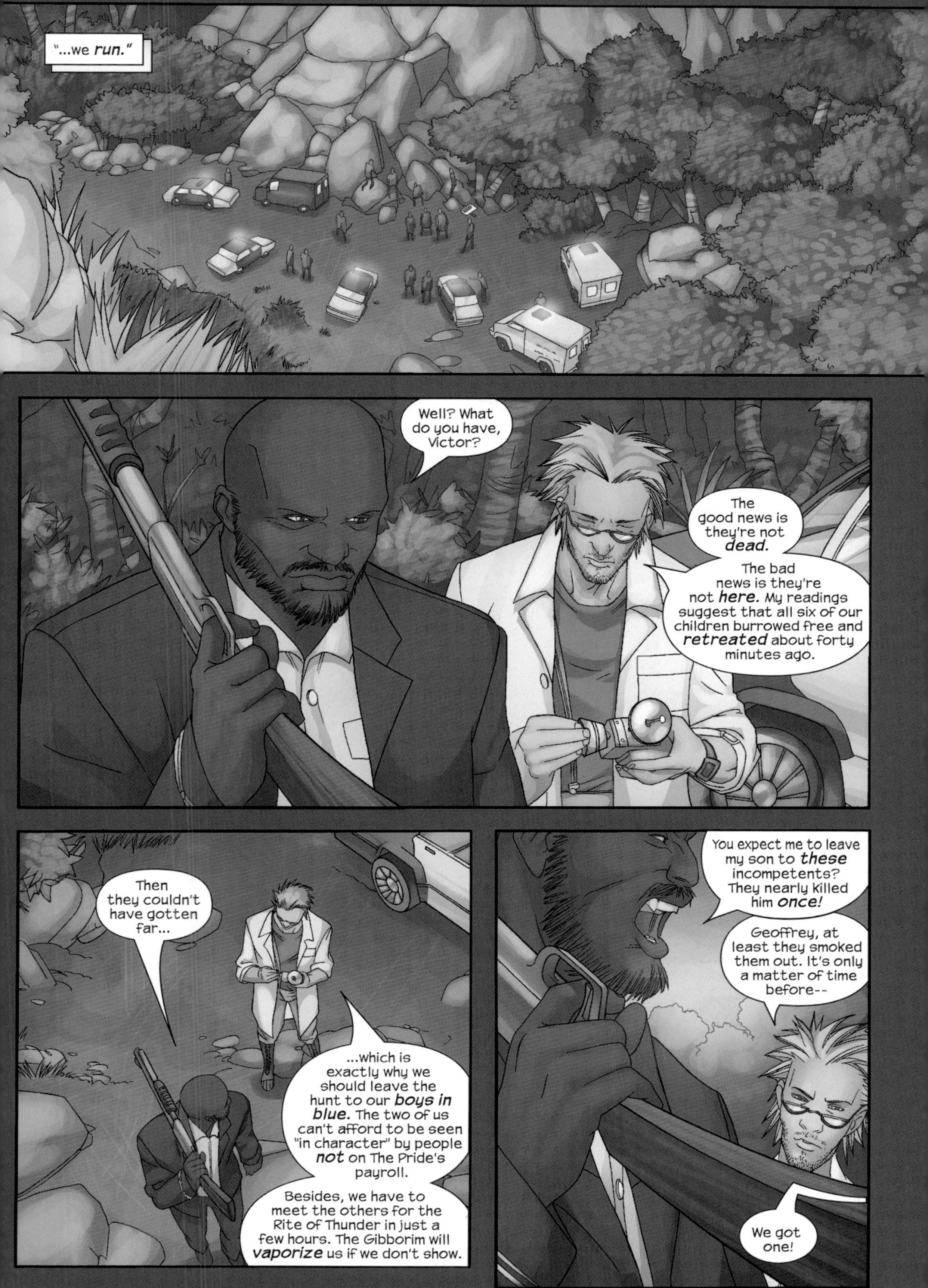
"...we run."
Well? What do you have, Victor?
The good news is they're not dead.
The bad news is they're not here. My readings suggest that all six of our children burrowed free and retreated about forty minutes ago.
Then they couldn't have gotten far...
...which is exactly why we should leave the hunt to our boys in blue. The two of us can't afford to be seen "in character" by people not on The Pride's payroll.
Besides, we have to meet the others for the Rite of Thunder in just a few hours. The Gibborim will vaporize us if we don't show.
You expect me to leave my son to these incompetents? They nearly killed him once!
Geoffrey, at least they smoked them out. It's only a matter of time before--
We got one!

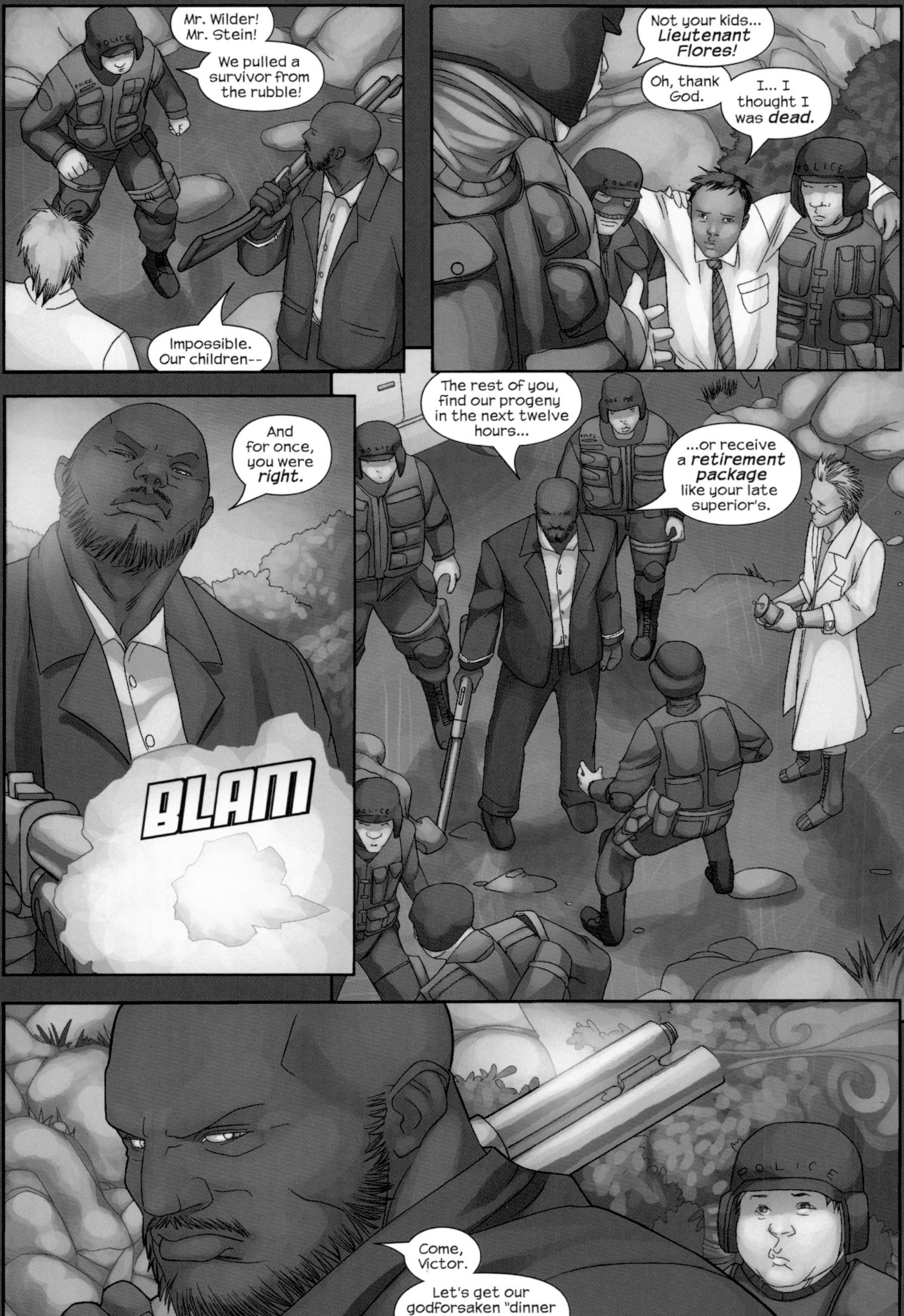
Mr. Wilder! Mr. Stein!
We pulled a survivor from the rubble!
Impossible. Our children--
Not your kids... Lieutenant Flores!
Oh, thank God.
I... I thought I was dead.
And for once, you were right.
BLAM
The rest of you, find our progeny in the next twelve hours...
...or receive a retirement package like your late superior's.
Come, Victor.
Let's get our godforsaken "dinner meeting" over with...

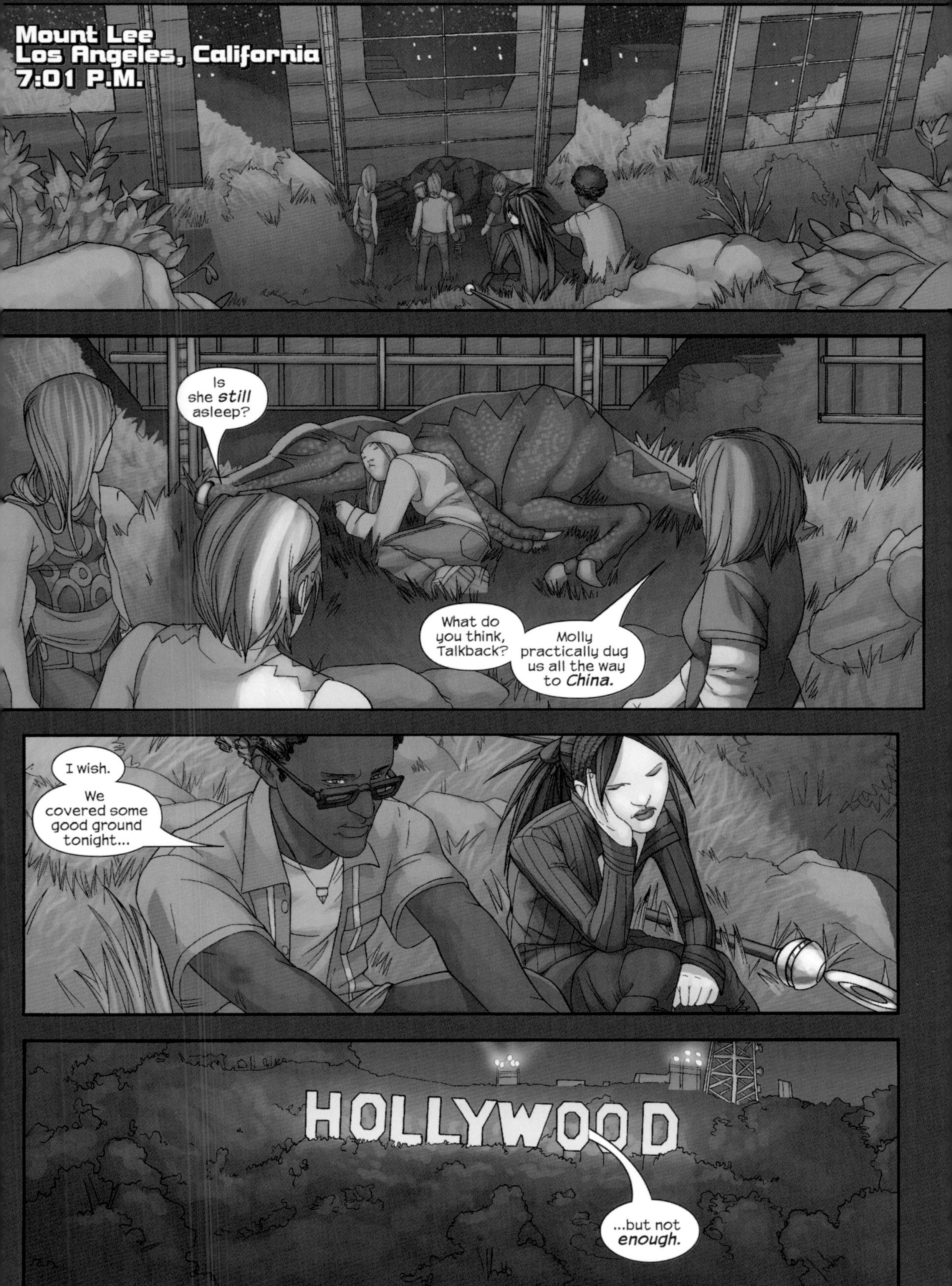

Mount Lee
Los Angeles, California
7:01 P.M.
Is she *still* asleep?
What do you think, Talkback?
Molly practically dug us all the way to *China.*
I wish.
We covered some good ground tonight...
HOLLYWOOD
...but not *enough.*

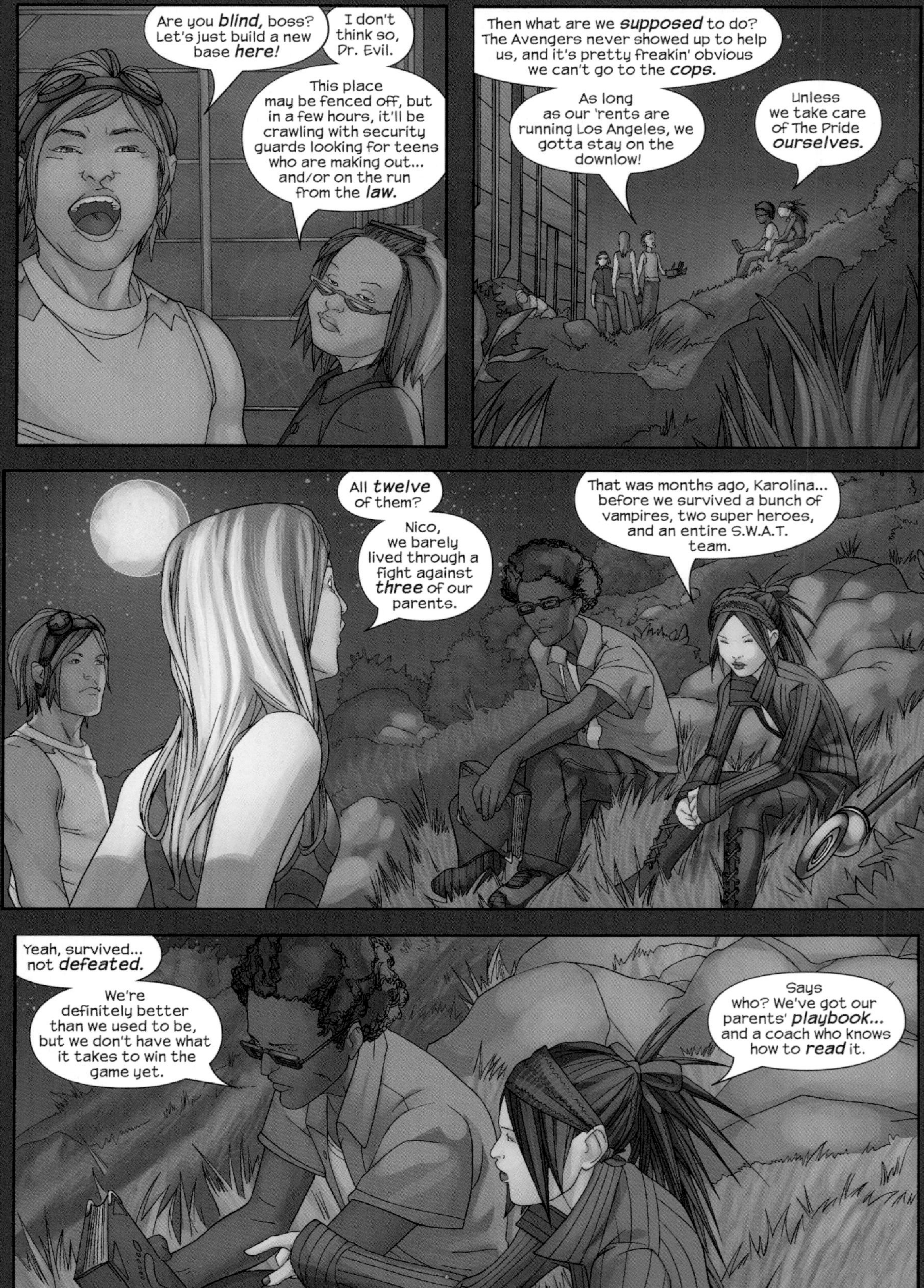
Are you *blind,* boss? Let's just build a new base *here!*
I don't think so, Dr. Evil.
This place may be fenced off, but in a few hours, it'll be crawling with security guards looking for teens who are making out... and/or on the run from the *law.*
Then what are we *supposed* to do? The Avengers never showed up to help us, and it's pretty freakin' obvious we can't go to the *cops.*
As long as our 'rents are running Los Angeles, we gotta stay on the downlow!
Unless we take care of The Pride *ourselves.*
All *twelve* of them?
Nico, we barely lived through a fight against *three* of our parents.
That was months ago, Karolina... before we survived a bunch of vampires, two super heroes, and an entire S.W.A.T. team.
Yeah, survived... not *defeated.*
We're definitely better than we used to be, but we don't have what it takes to win the game yet.
Says who? We've got our parents' *playbook...* and a coach who knows how to *read* it.

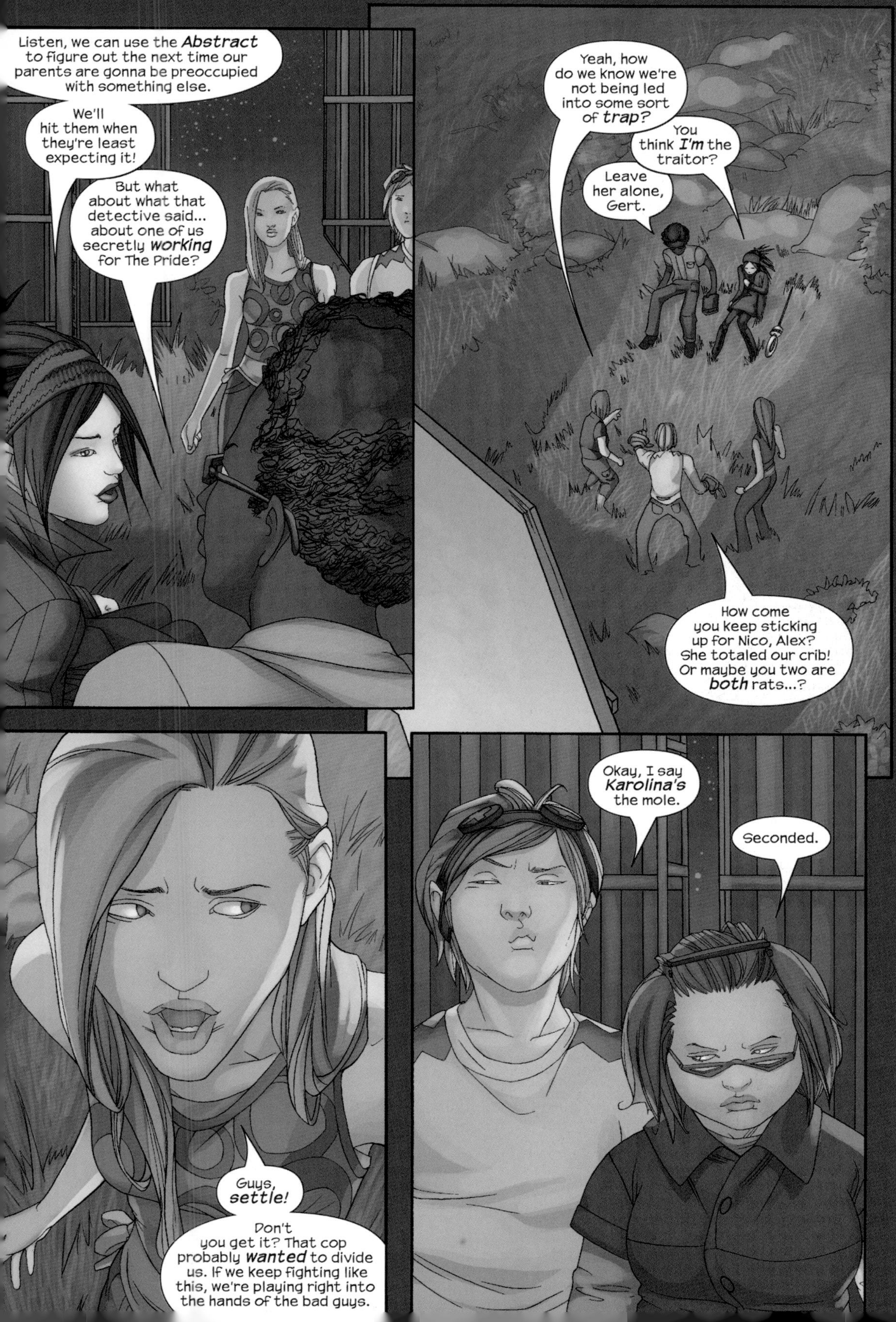
Listen, we can use the Abstract to figure out the next time our parents are gonna be preoccupied with something else.
We'll hit them when they're least expecting it!
But what about what that detective said... about one of us secretly working for The Pride?
Yeah, how do we know we're not being led into some sort of trap?
You think I'm the traitor?
Leave her alone, Gert.
How come you keep sticking up for Nico, Alex? She totaled our crib! Or maybe you two are both rats...?
Guys, settle!
Don't you get it? That cop probably wanted to divide us. If we keep fighting like this, we're playing right into the hands of the bad guys.
Okay, I say Karolina's the mole.
Seconded.

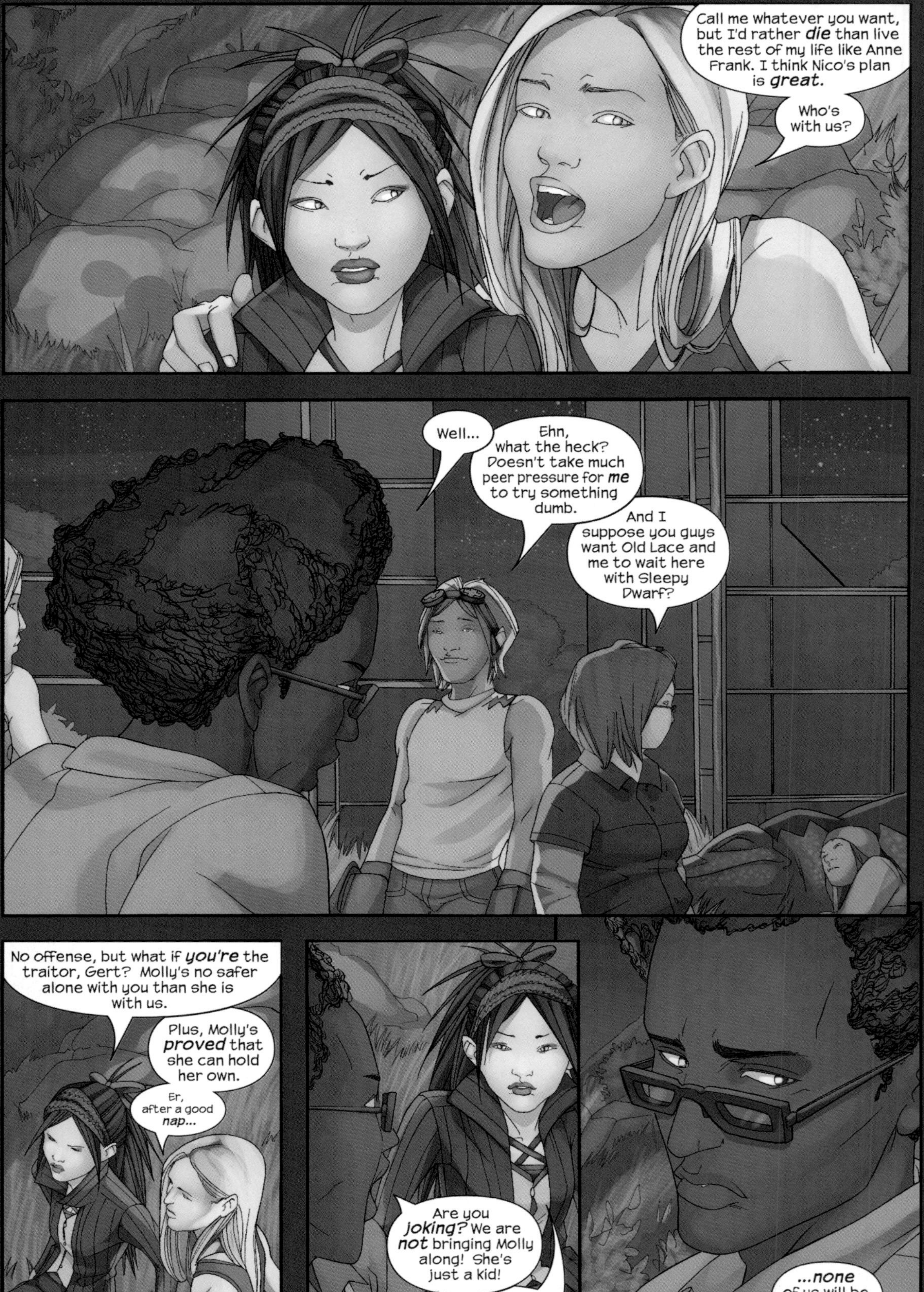

Call me whatever you want, but I'd rather die than live the rest of my life like Anne Frank. I think Nico's plan is great.
Who's with us?
Well...
Ehn, what the heck? Doesn't take much peer pressure for me to try something dumb.
And I suppose you guys want Old Lace and me to wait here with Sleepy Dwarf?
No offense, but what if you're the traitor, Gert? Molly's no safer alone with you than she is with us.
Plus, Molly's proved that she can hold her own.
Er, after a good nap...
Are you joking? We are not bringing Molly along! She's just a kid!
So are we, Alex, and unless we face our parents together...
...none of us will be getting any older.

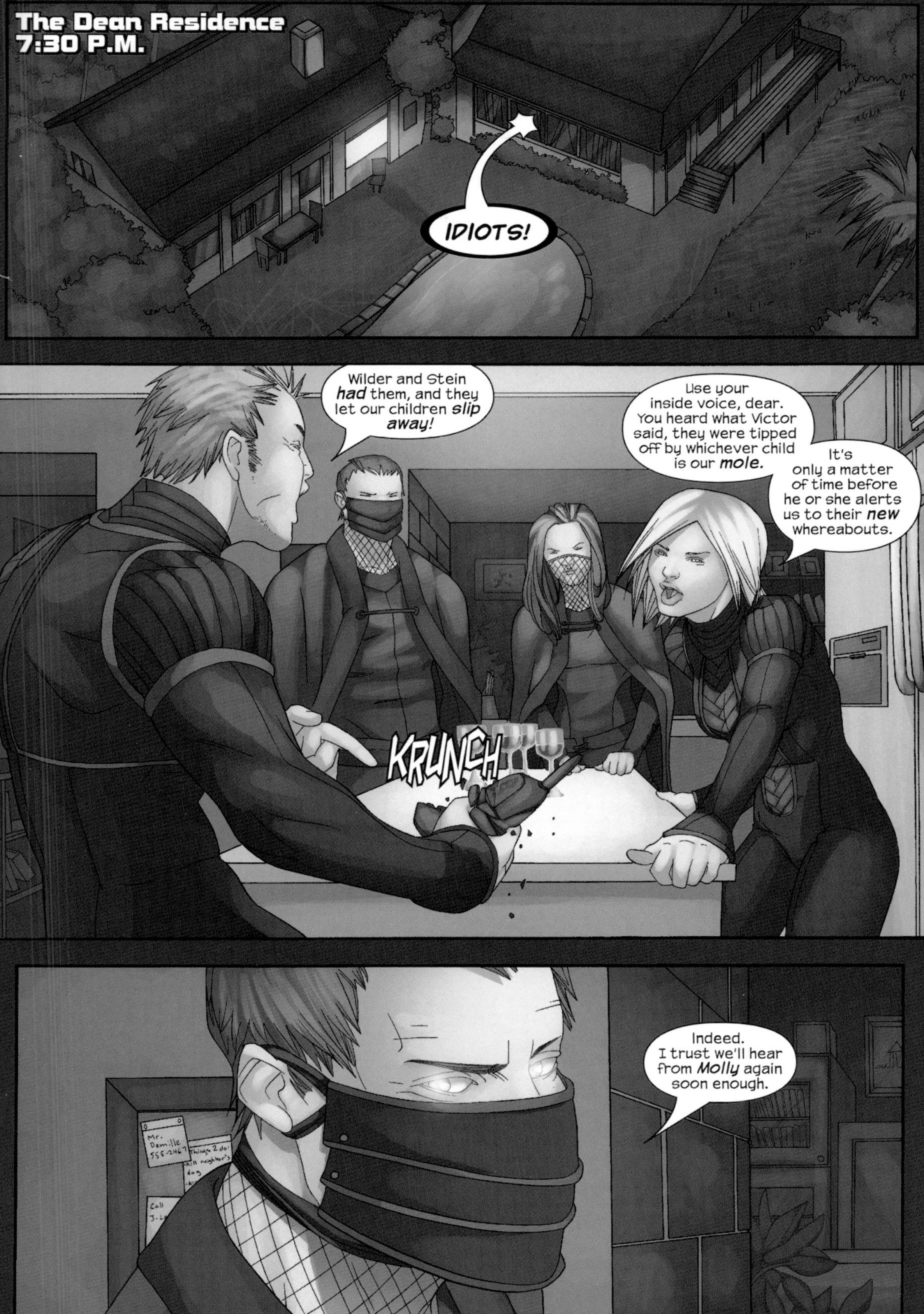
The Dean Residence
7:30 P.M.
IDIOTS!
Wilder and Stein *had* them, and they let our children *slip away!*
Use your inside voice, dear. You heard what Victor said, they were tipped off by whichever child is our *mole.*
It's only a matter of time before he or she alerts us to their *new* whereabouts.
KRUNCH
Indeed. I trust we'll hear from *Molly* again soon enough.

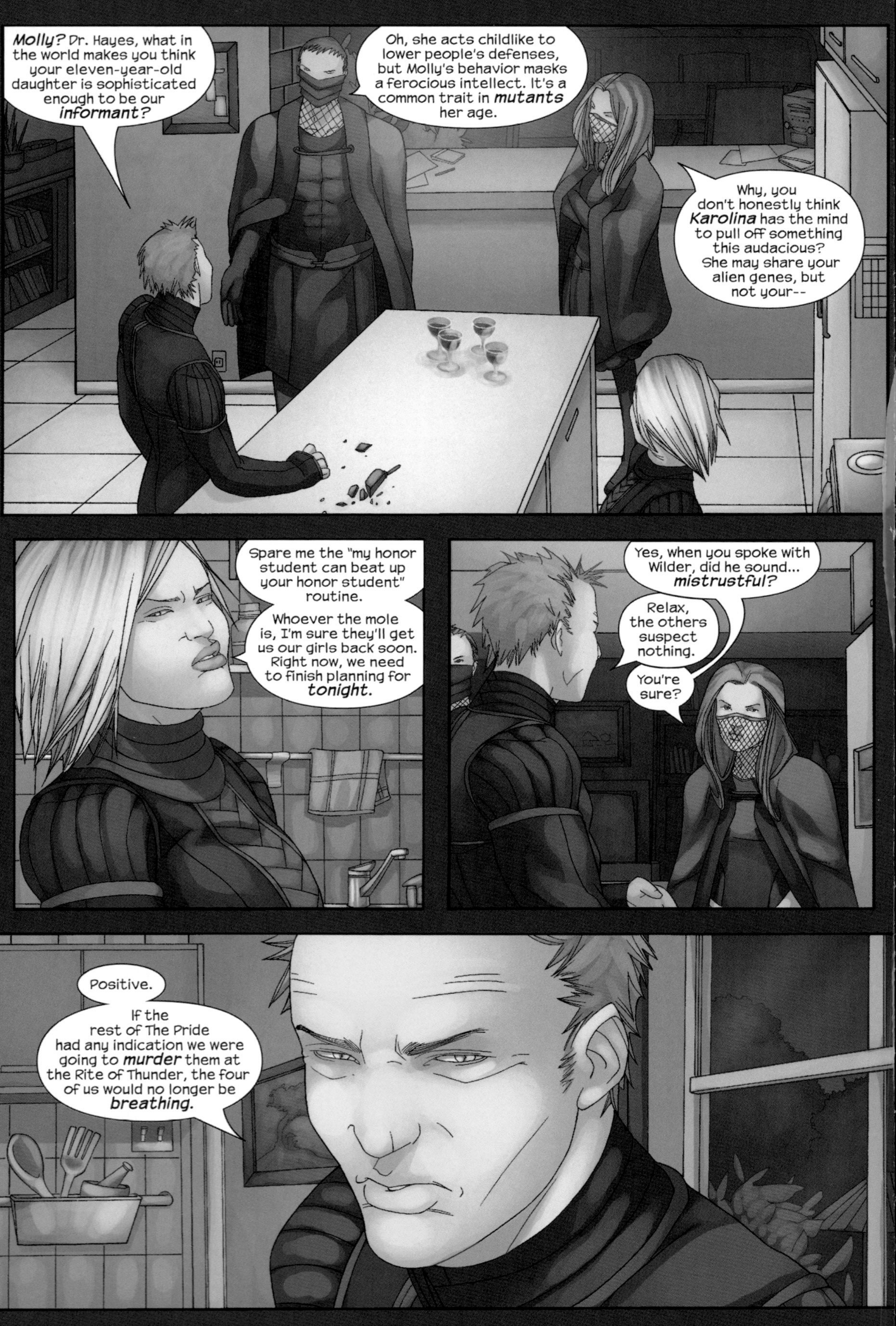
Molly? Dr. Hayes, what in the world makes you think your eleven-year-old daughter is sophisticated enough to be our informant?
Oh, she acts childlike to lower people's defenses, but Molly's behavior masks a ferocious intellect. It's a common trait in mutants her age.
Why, you don't honestly think Karolina has the mind to pull off something this audacious? She may share your alien genes, but not your--
Spare me the "my honor student can beat up your honor student" routine.
Whoever the mole is, I'm sure they'll get us our girls back soon. Right now, we need to finish planning for tonight.
Yes, when you spoke with Wilder, did he sound... mistrustful?
Relax, the others suspect nothing.
You're sure?
Positive.
If the rest of The Pride had any indication we were going to murder them at the Rite of Thunder, the four of us would no longer be breathing.

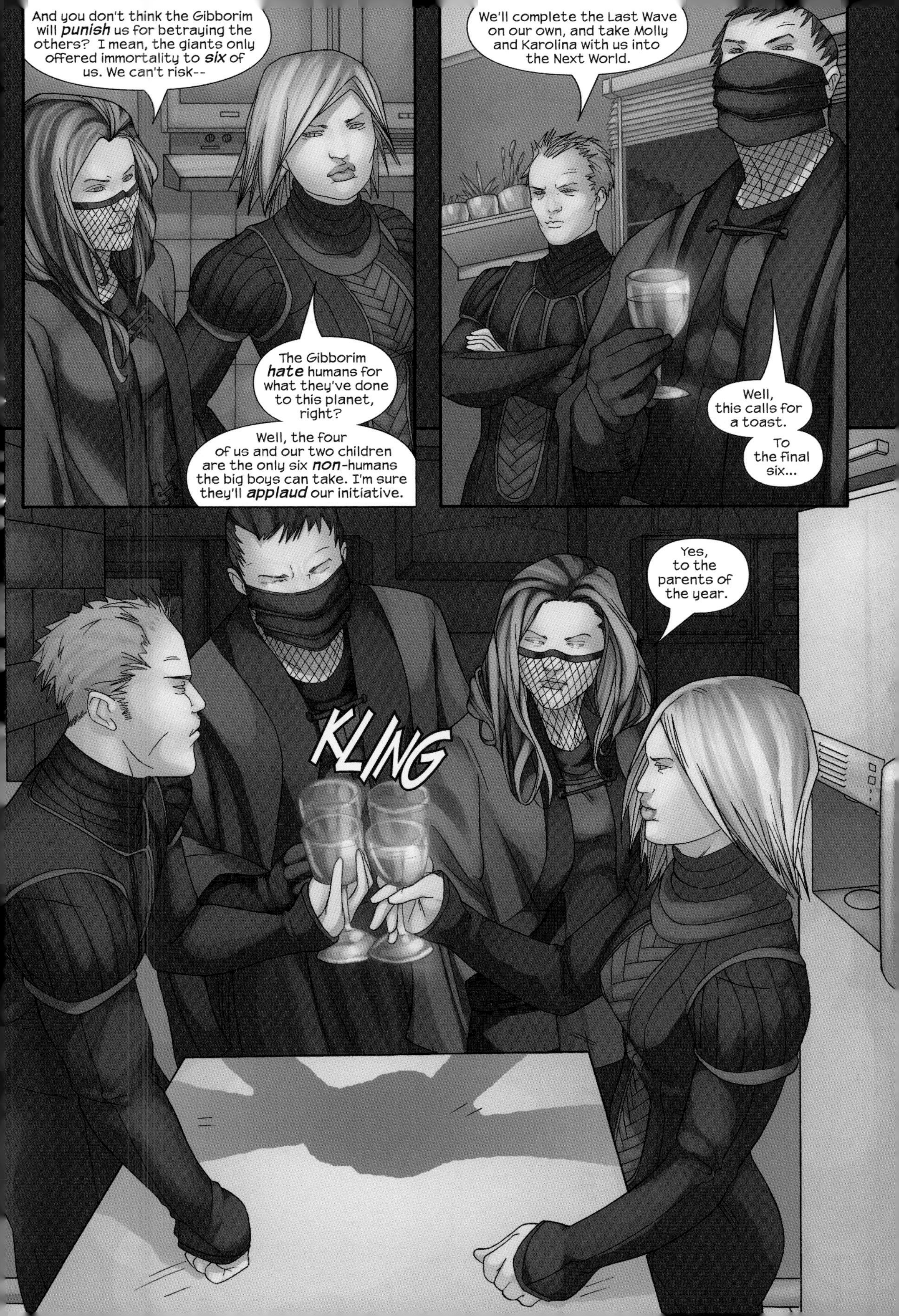
And you don't think the Gibborim will punish us for betraying the others? I mean, the giants only offered immortality to six of us. We can't risk--
The Gibborim hate humans for what they've done to this planet, right?
Well, the four of us and our two children are the only six non-humans the big boys can take. I'm sure they'll applaud our initiative.
We'll complete the Last Wave on our own, and take Molly and Karolina with us into the Next World.
Well, this calls for a toast.
To the final six...
Yes, to the parents of the year.
KLING

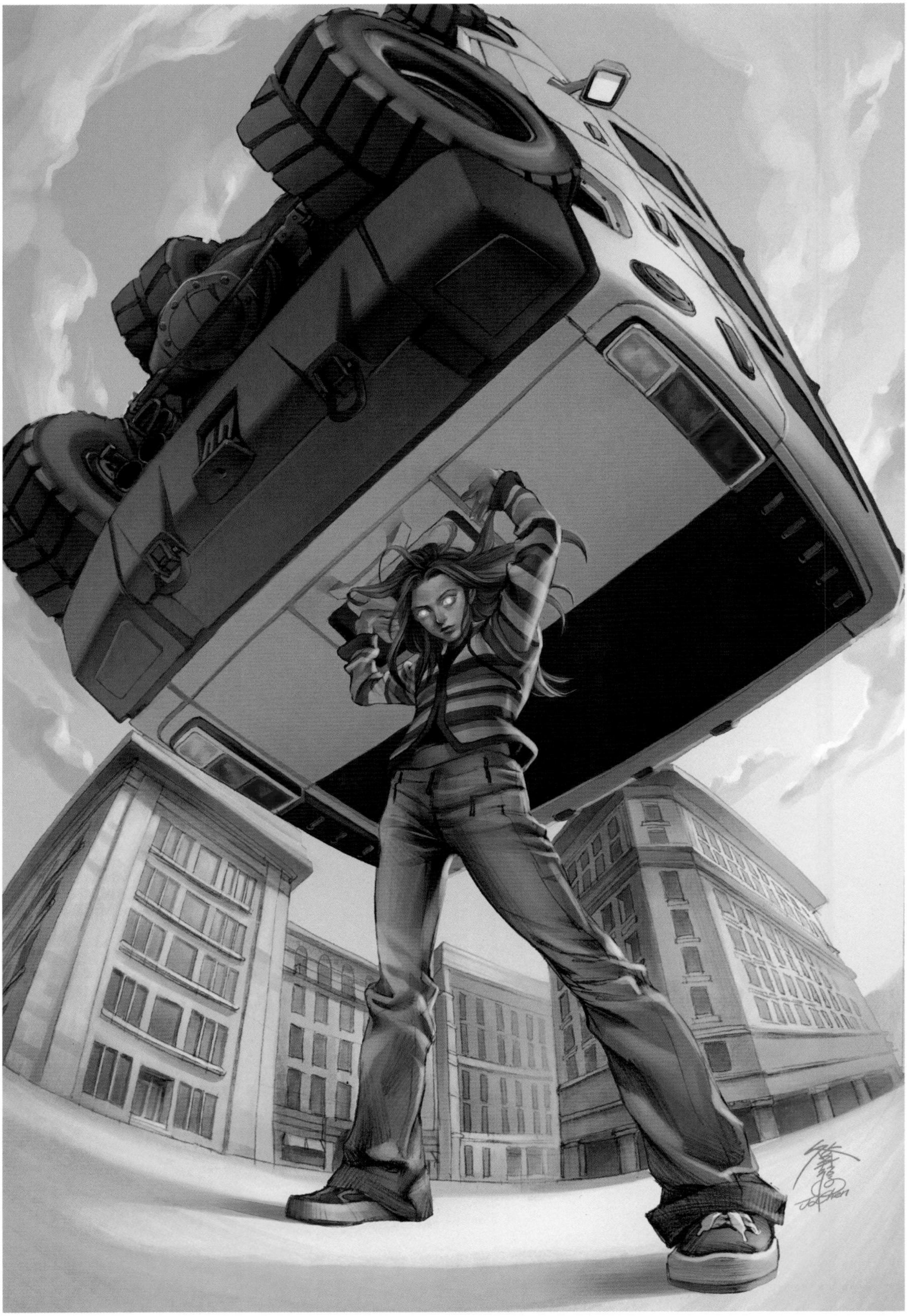

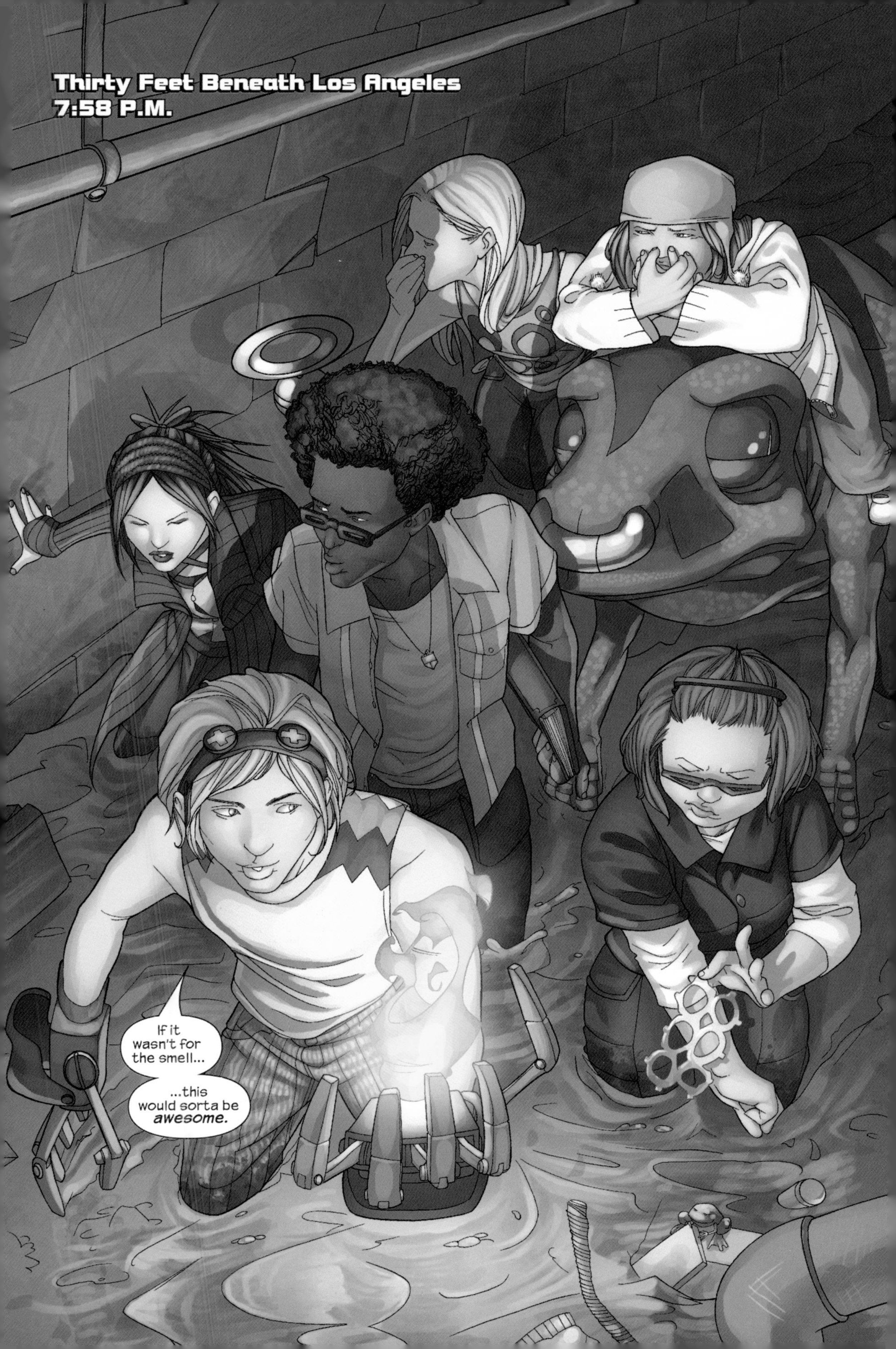
Thirty Feet Beneath Los Angeles
7:58 P.M.
If it wasn't for the smell...
...this would sorta be *awesome.*

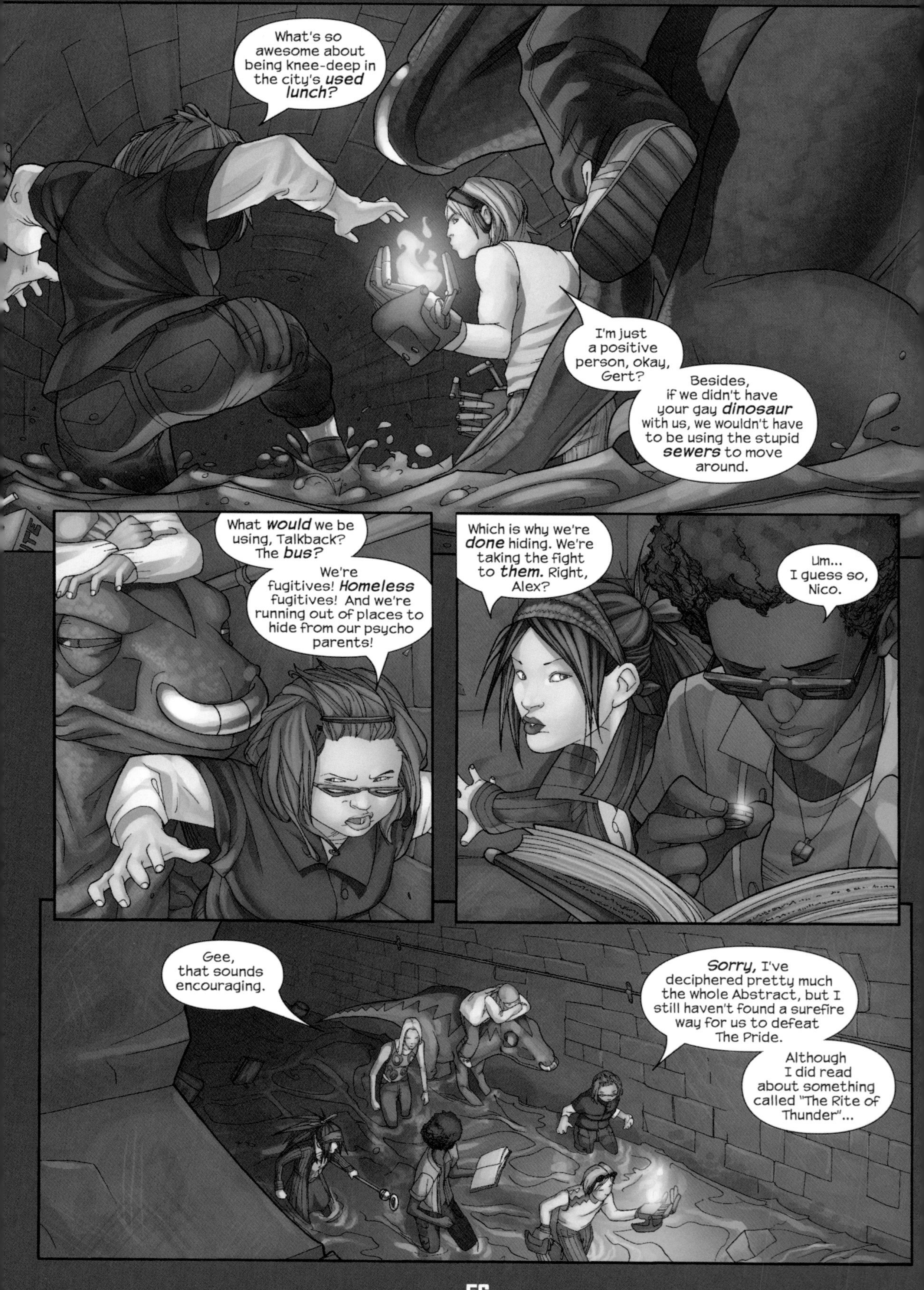
What's so awesome about being knee-deep in the city's *used lunch*?
I'm just a positive person, okay, Gert?
Besides, if we didn't have your gay *dinosaur* with us, we wouldn't have to be using the stupid *sewers* to move around.
What *would* we be using, Talkback? The *bus?*
We're fugitives! *Homeless* fugitives! And we're running out of places to hide from our psycho parents!
Which is why we're *done* hiding. We're taking the fight to *them.* Right, Alex?
Um... I guess so, Nico.
Gee, that sounds encouraging.
Sorry, I've deciphered pretty much the whole Abstract, but I still haven't found a surefire way for us to defeat The Pride.
Although I did read about something called "The Rite of Thunder"...

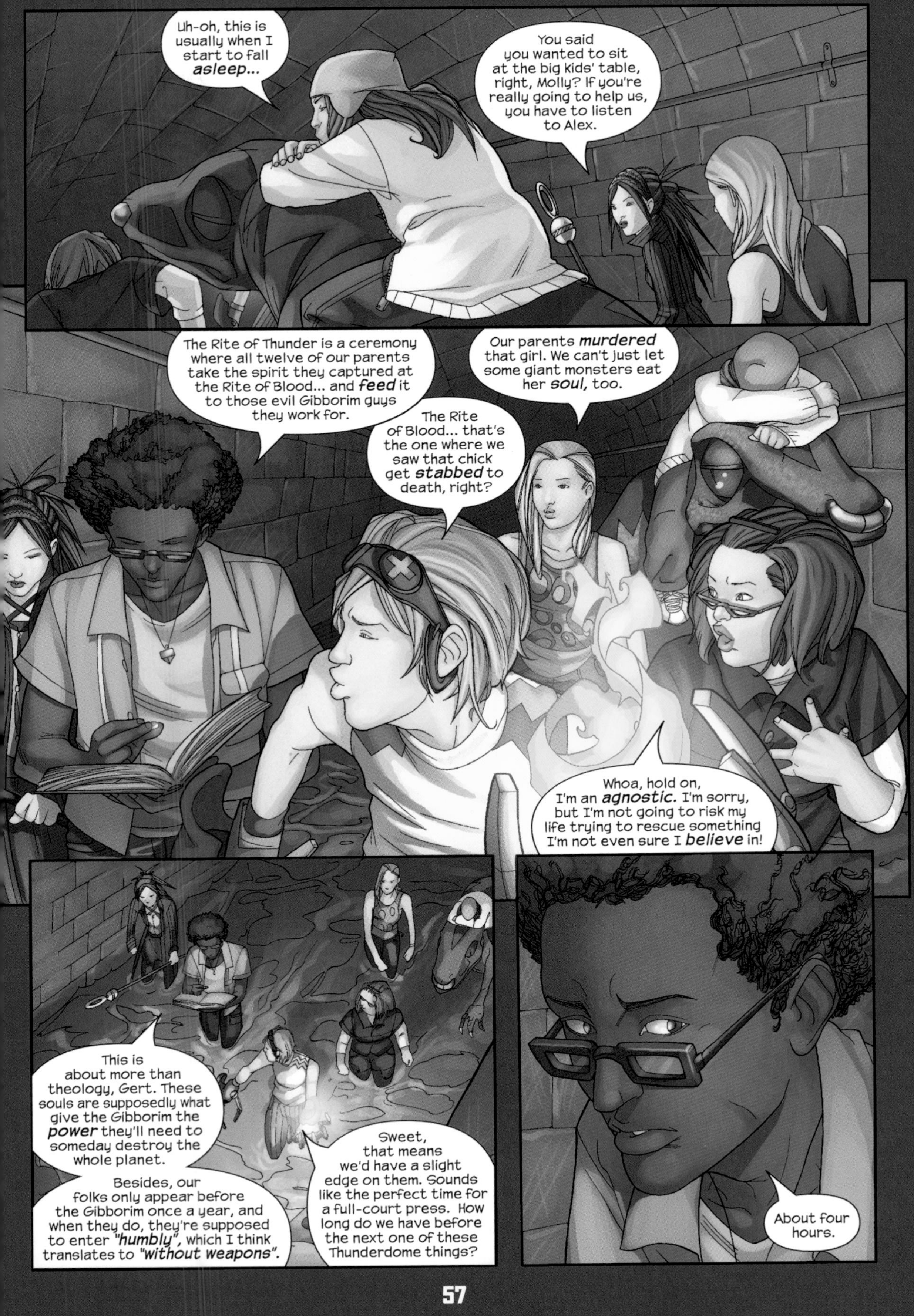
Uh-oh, this is usually when I start to fall *asleep...*
You said you wanted to sit at the big kids' table, right, Molly? If you're really going to help us, you have to listen to Alex.
The Rite of Thunder is a ceremony where all twelve of our parents take the spirit they captured at the Rite of Blood... and *feed* it to those evil Gibborim guys they work for.
The Rite of Blood... that's the one where we saw that chick get *stabbed* to death, right?
Our parents *murdered* that girl. We can't just let some giant monsters eat her *soul,* too.
Whoa, hold on, I'm an *agnostic.* I'm sorry, but I'm not going to risk my life trying to rescue something I'm not even sure I *believe* in!
This is about more than theology, Gert. These souls are supposedly what give the Gibborim the *power* they'll need to someday destroy the whole planet.
Besides, our folks only appear before the Gibborim once a year, and when they do, they're supposed to enter *"humbly"*, which I think translates to *"without weapons"*.
Sweet, that means we'd have a slight edge on them. Sounds like the perfect time for a full-court press. How long do we have before the next one of these Thunderdome things?
About four hours.

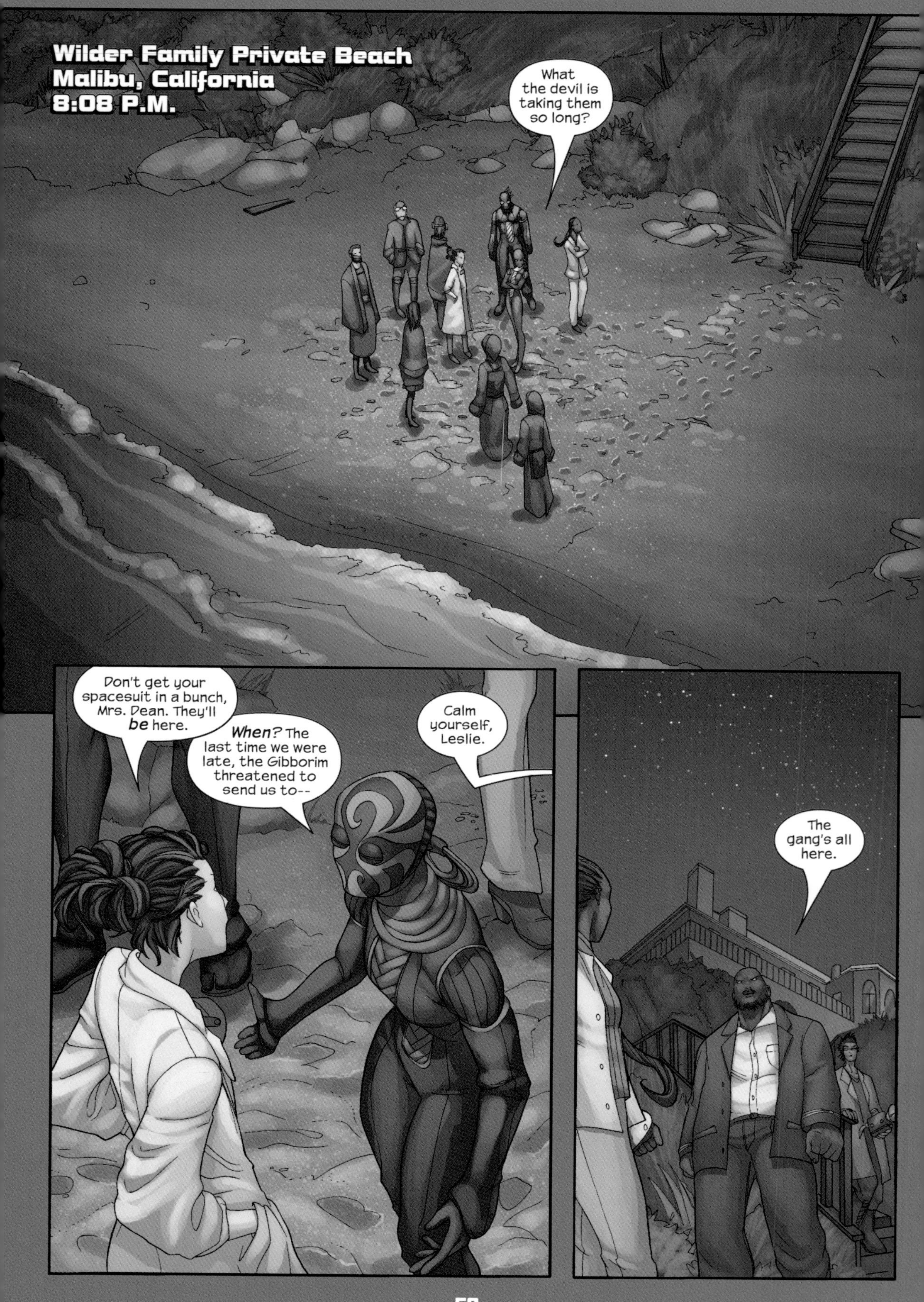
Wilder Family Private Beach
Malibu, California
8:08 P.M.
What the devil is taking them so long?
Don't get your spacesuit in a bunch, Mrs. Dean. They'll *be* here.
When? The last time we were late, the Gibborim threatened to send us to--
Calm yourself, Leslie.
The gang's all here.

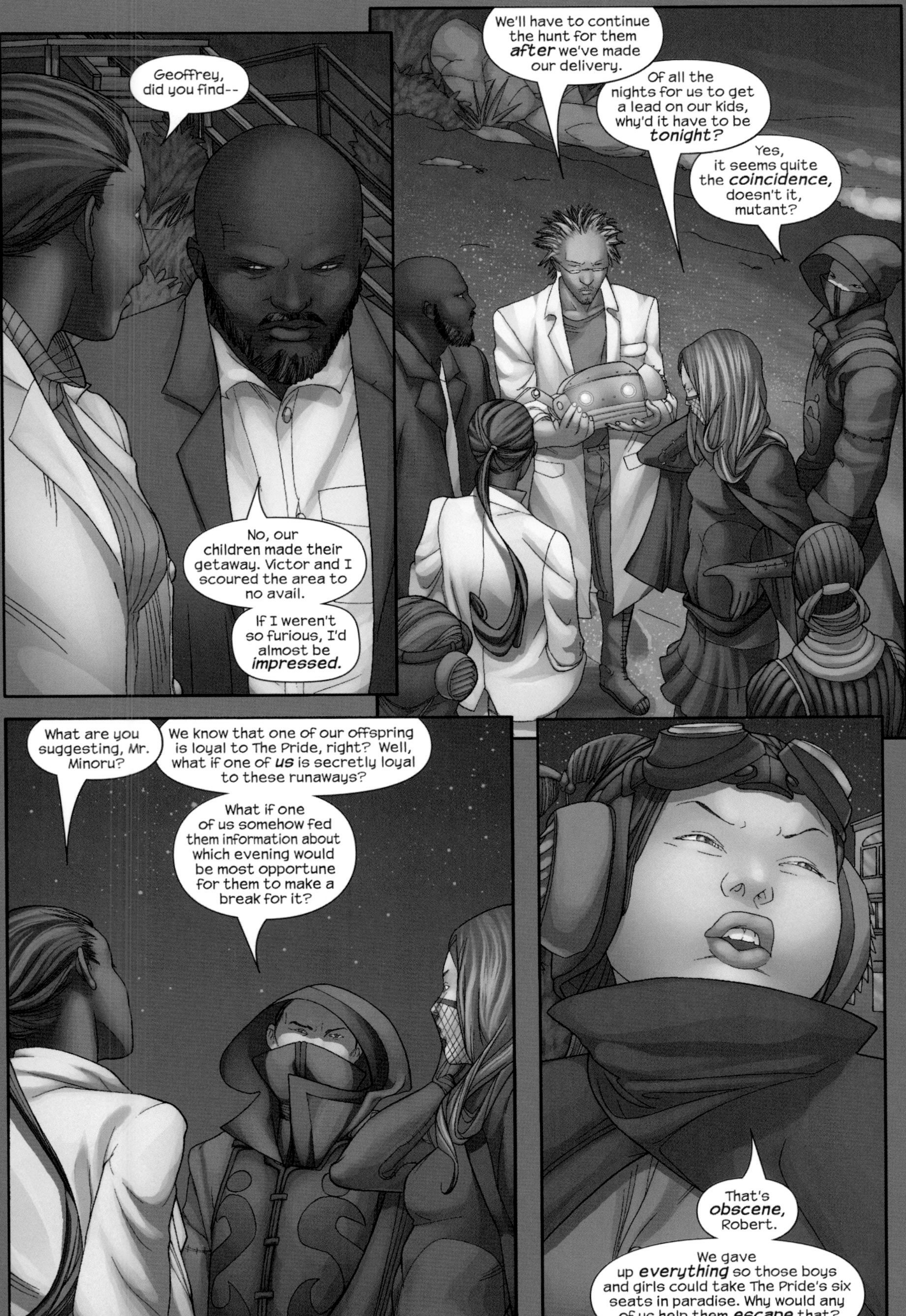
Geoffrey, did you find--
No, our children made their getaway. Victor and I scoured the area to no avail.
If I weren't so furious, I'd almost be *impressed.*
We'll have to continue the hunt for them *after* we've made our delivery.
Of all the nights for us to get a lead on our kids, why'd it have to be *tonight?*
Yes, it seems quite the *coincidence,* doesn't it, mutant?
What are you suggesting, Mr. Minoru?
We know that one of our offspring is loyal to The Pride, right? Well, what if one of *us* is secretly loyal to these runaways?
What if one of us somehow fed them information about which evening would be most opportune for them to make a break for it?
That's *obscene,* Robert.
We gave up *everything* so those boys and girls could take The Pride's six seats in paradise. Why would any of us help them *escape* that?

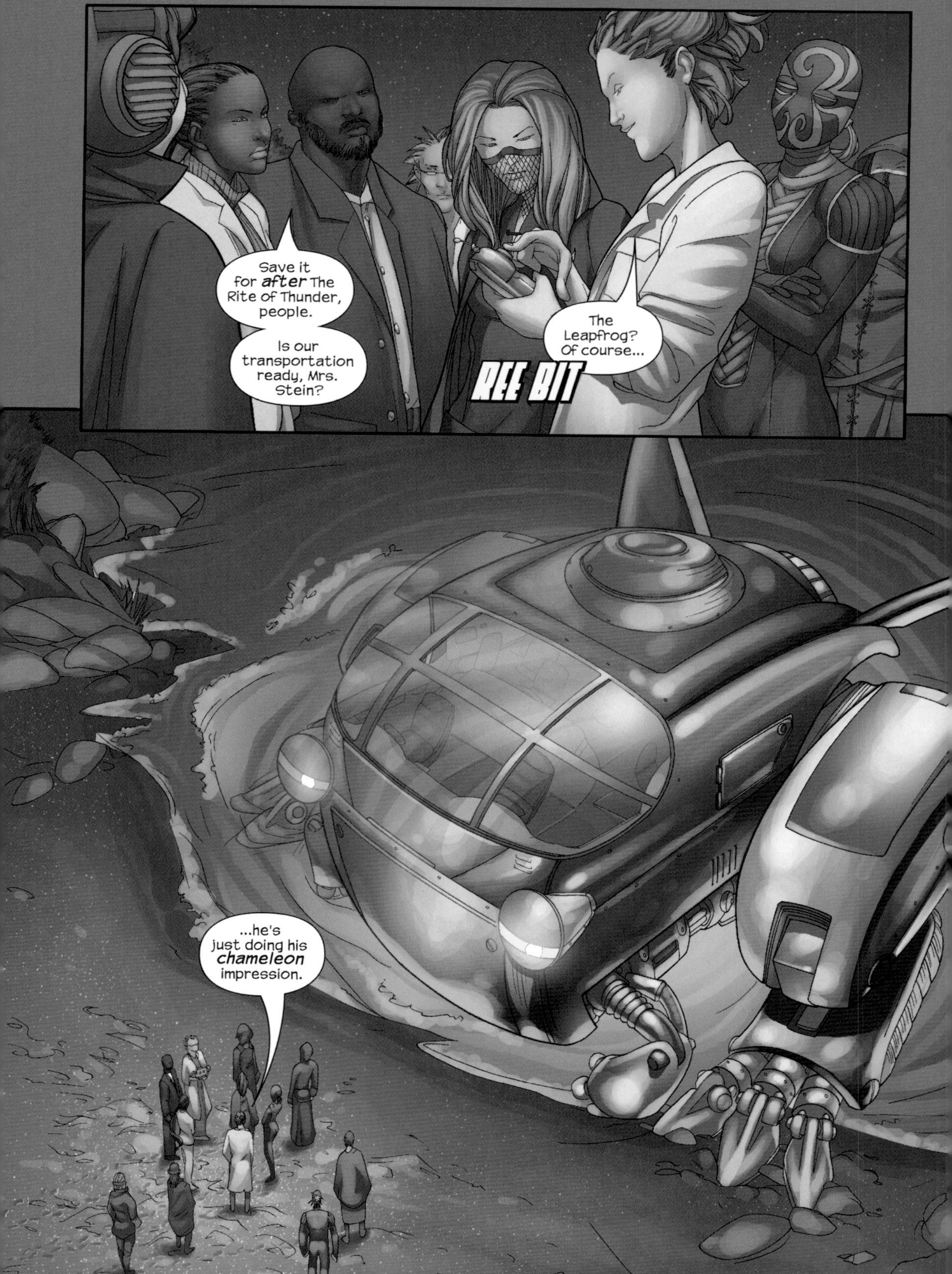
Save it for *after* The Rite of Thunder, people.
Is our transportation ready, Mrs. Stein?
REE BIT
The Leapfrog? Of course...
...he's just doing his *chameleon* impression.

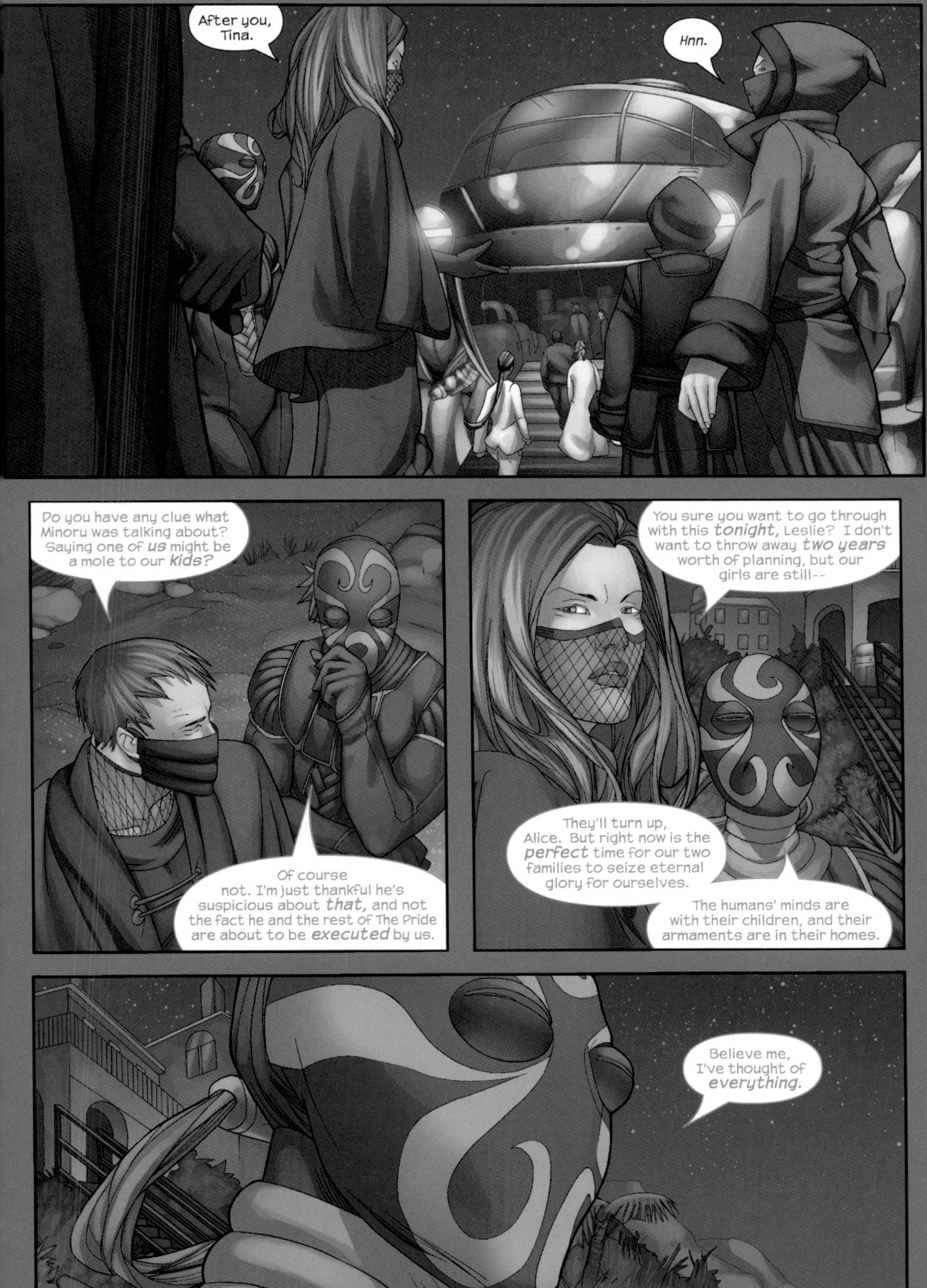
After you, Tina.
Hnn.
Do you have any clue what Minoru was talking about? Saying one of us might be a mole to our kids?
Of course not. I'm just thankful he's suspicious about that, and not the fact he and the rest of The Pride are about to be executed by us.
You sure you want to go through with this tonight, Leslie? I don't want to throw away two years worth of planning, but our girls are still--
They'll turn up, Alice. But right now is the perfect time for our two families to seize eternal glory for ourselves.
The humans' minds are with their children, and their armaments are in their homes.
Believe me, I've thought of everything.

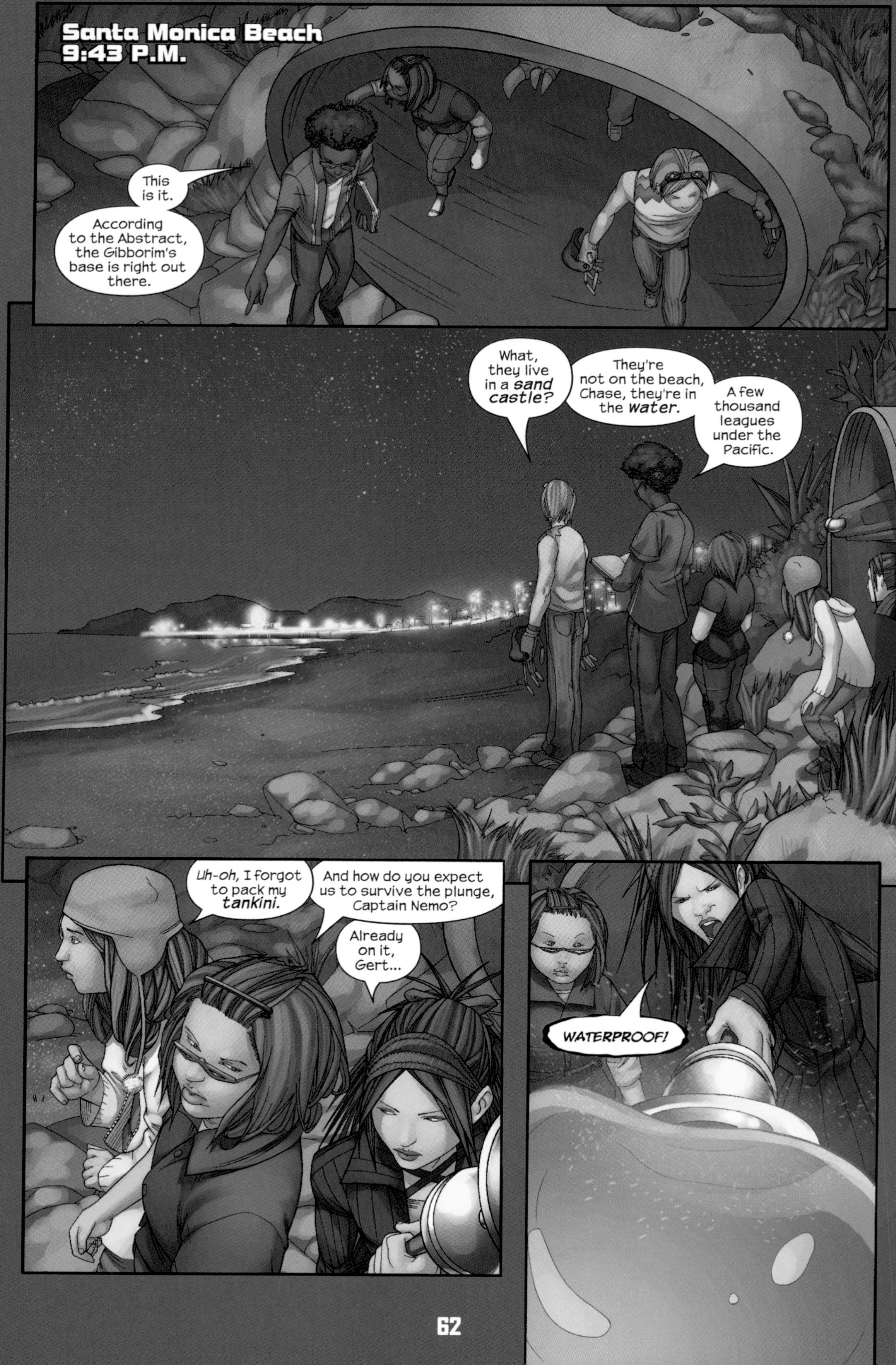
Santa Monica Beach
9:43 P.M.
This is it.
According to the Abstract, the Gibborim's base is right out there.
What, they live in a *sand castle?*
They're not on the beach, Chase, they're in the *water.*
A few thousand leagues under the Pacific.
Uh-oh, I forgot to pack my *tankini.*
And how do you expect us to survive the plunge, Captain Nemo?
Already on it, Gert...
WATERPROOF!

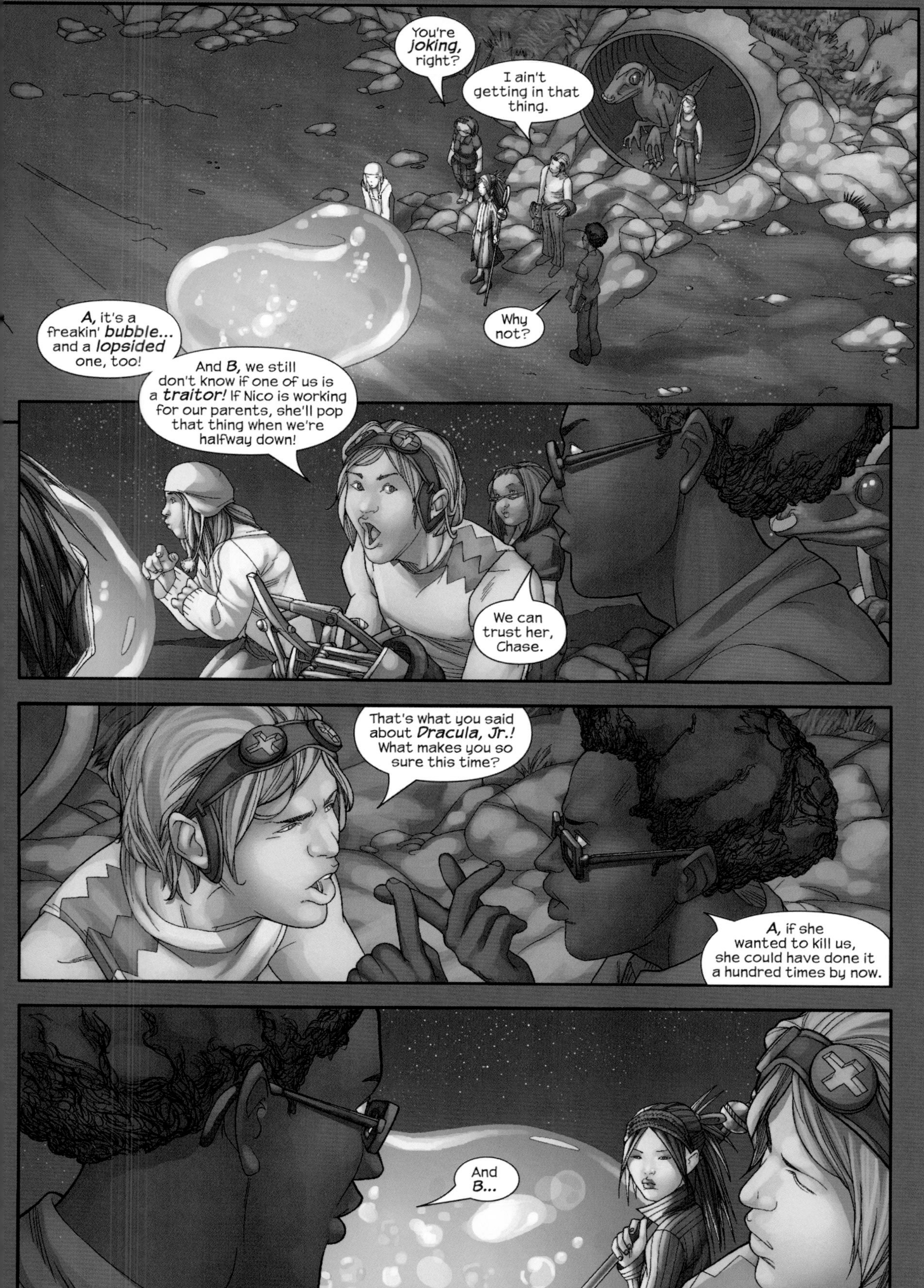
You're *joking,* right?
I ain't getting in that thing.
Why not?
A, it's a freakin' *bubble...* and a *lopsided* one, too!
And *B,* we still don't know if one of us is a *traitor!* If Nico is working for our parents, she'll pop that thing when we're halfway down!
We can trust her, Chase.
That's what you said about *Dracula, Jr.!* What makes you so sure this time?
A, if she wanted to kill us, she could have done it a hundred times by now.
And *B...*

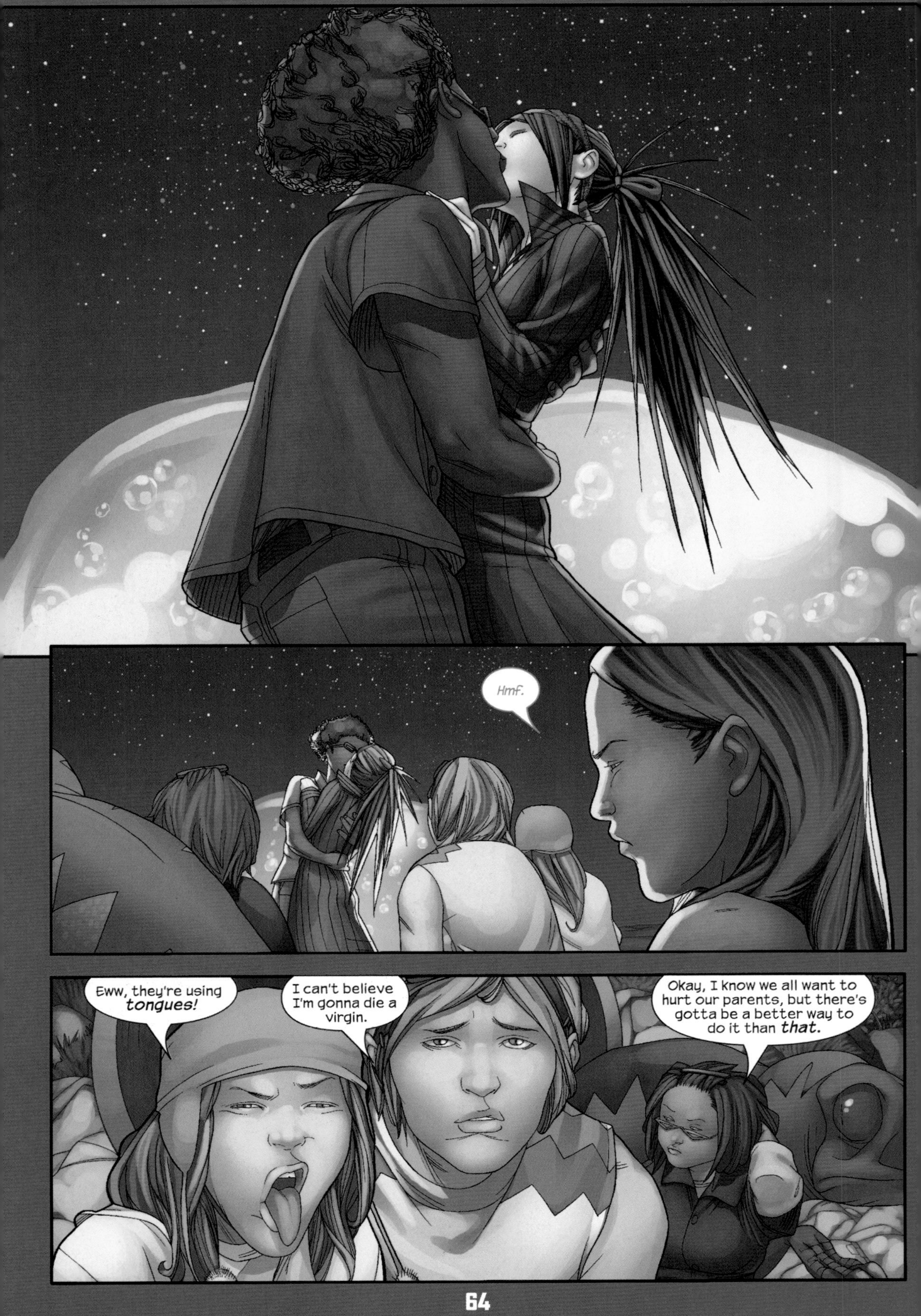
Hmf.
Eww, they're using *tongues!*
I can't believe I'm gonna die a virgin.
Okay, I know we all want to hurt our parents, but there's gotta be a better way to do it than *that.*

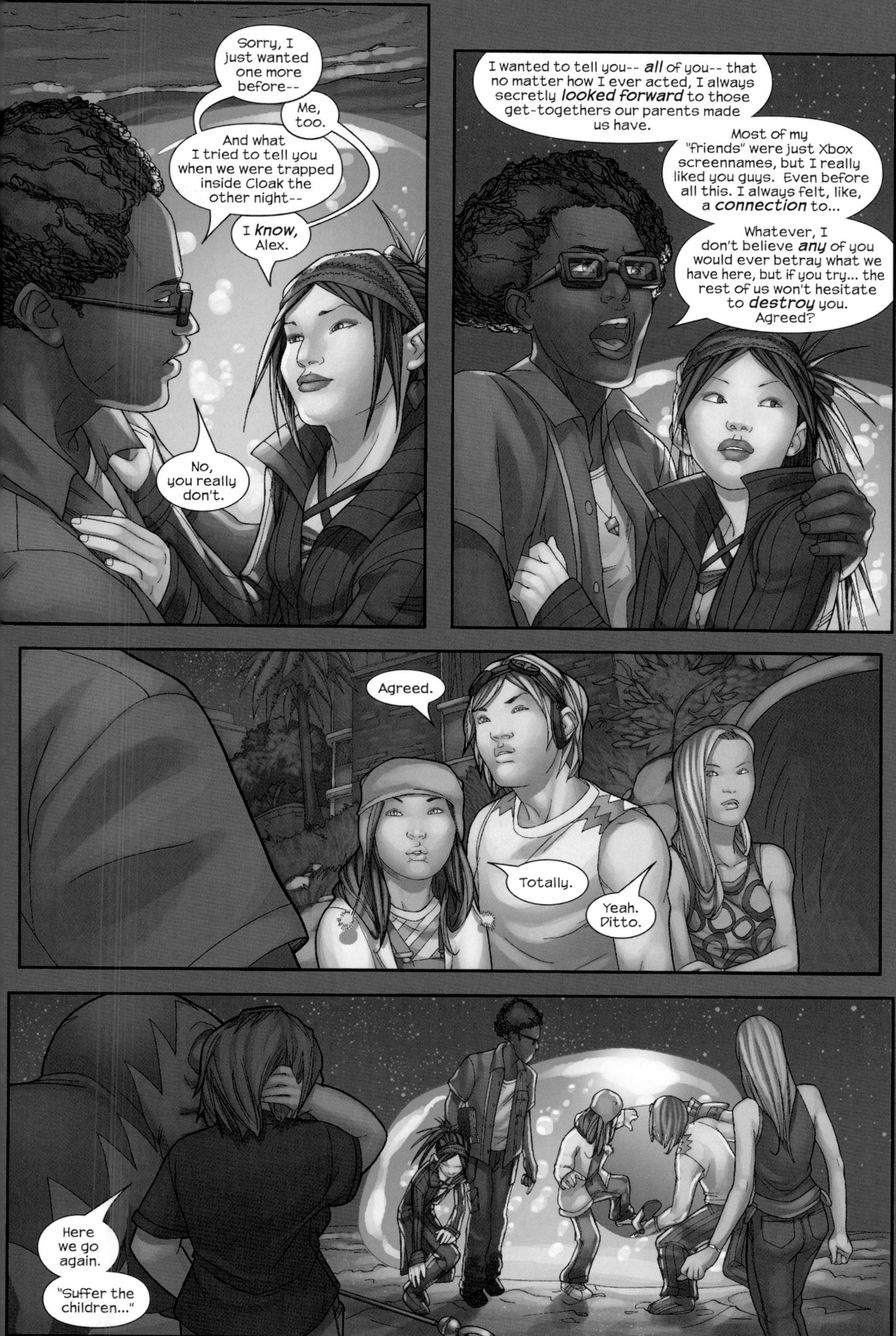

Sorry, I just wanted one more before--
Me, too.
And what I tried to tell you when we were trapped inside Cloak the other night--
I *know,* Alex.
No, you really don't.
I wanted to tell you-- *all* of you-- that no matter how I ever acted, I always secretly *looked forward* to those get-togethers our parents made us have.
Most of my "friends" were just Xbox screennames, but I really liked you guys. Even before all this. I always felt, like, a *connection* to...
Whatever, I don't believe *any* of you would ever betray what we have here, but if you try... the rest of us won't hesitate to *destroy* you. Agreed?
Agreed.
Totally.
Yeah. Ditto.
Here we go again.
"Suffer the children..."

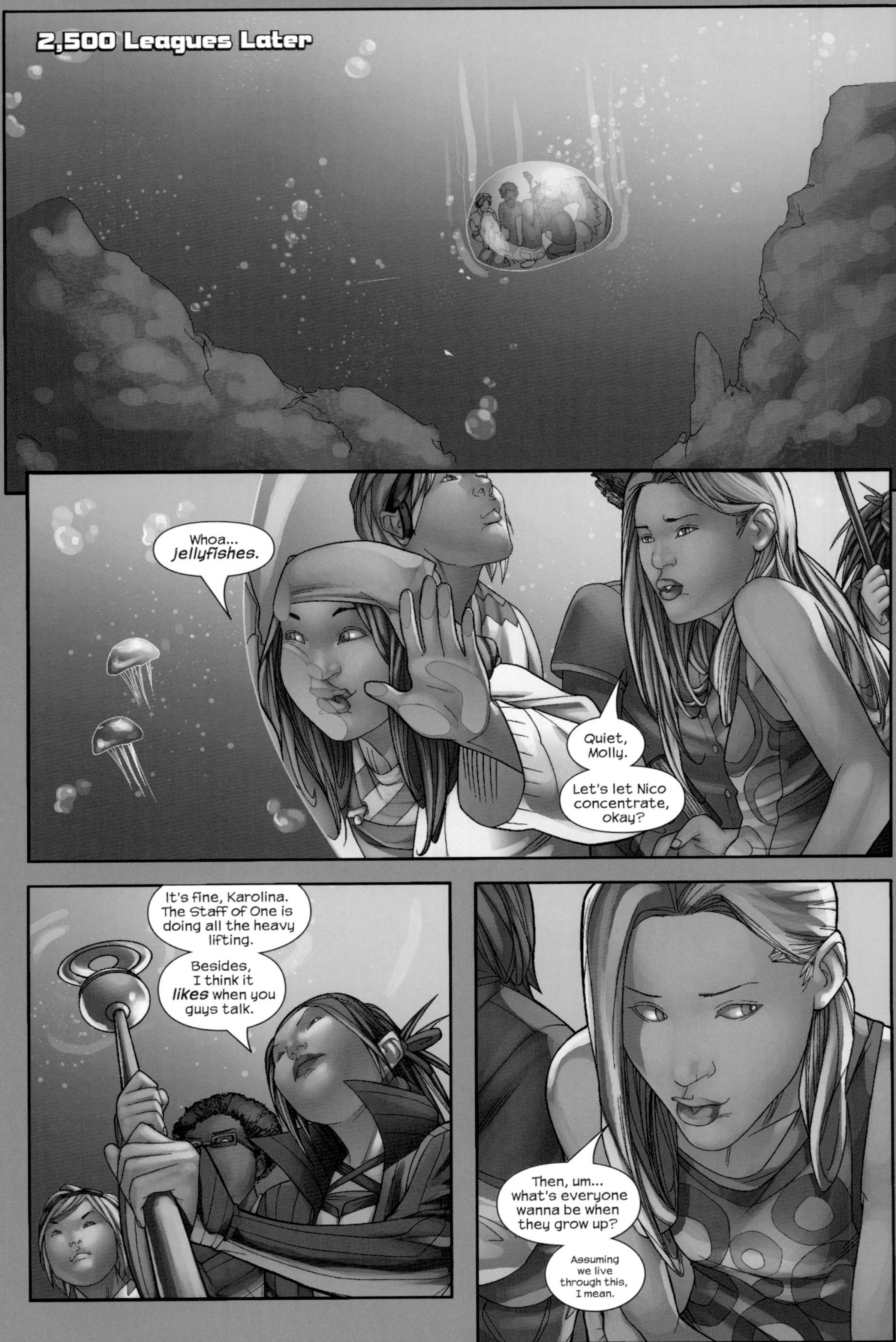
2,500 Leagues Later
Whoa... *jellyfishes.*
Quiet, Molly.
Let's let Nico concentrate, okay?
It's fine, Karolina. The Staff of One is doing all the heavy lifting.
Besides, I think it *likes* when you guys talk.
Then, um... what's everyone wanna be when they grow up?
Assuming we live through this, I mean.

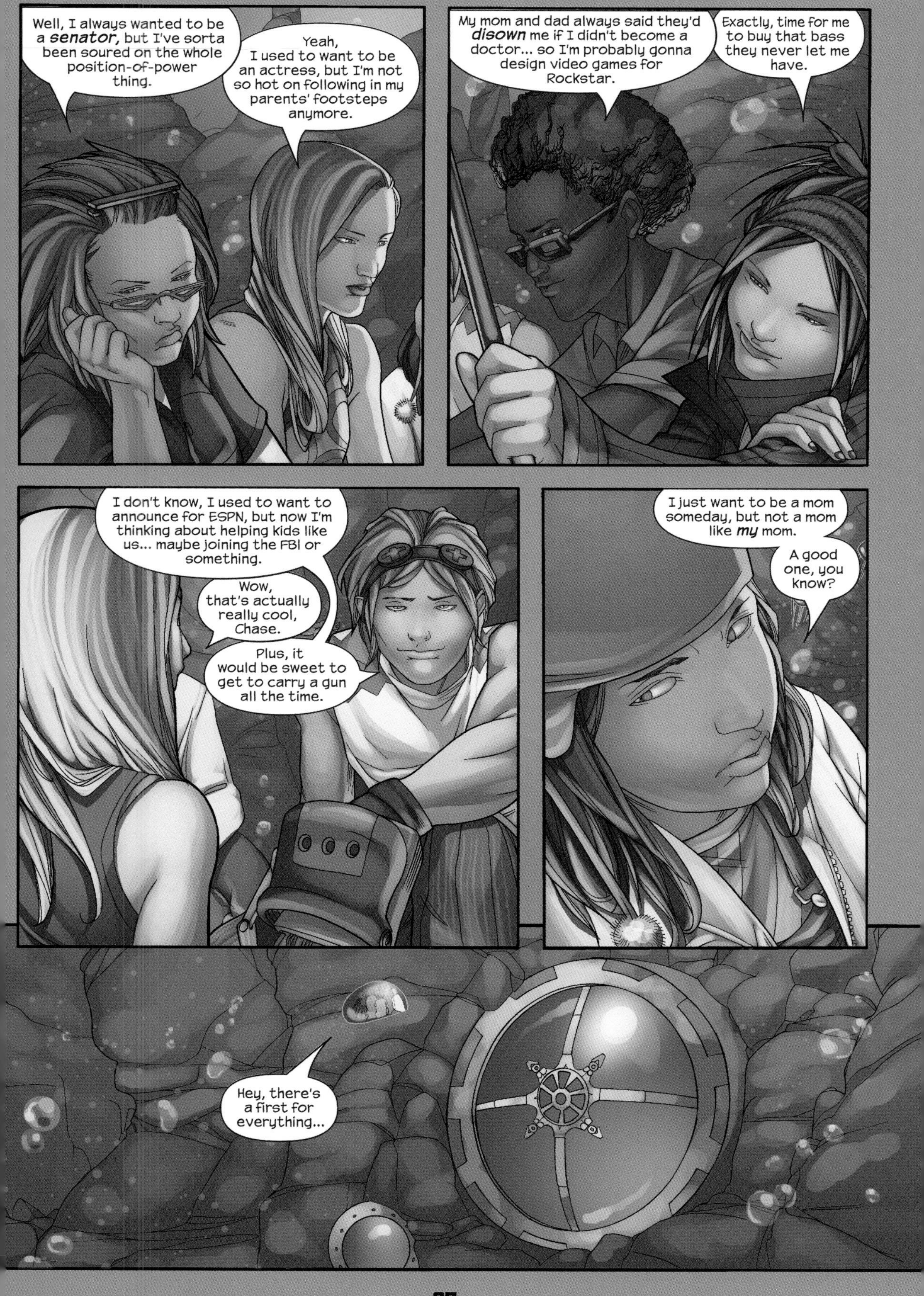
Well, I always wanted to be a senator, but I've sorta been soured on the whole position-of-power thing.
Yeah, I used to want to be an actress, but I'm not so hot on following in my parents' footsteps anymore.
My mom and dad always said they'd disown me if I didn't become a doctor... so I'm probably gonna design video games for Rockstar.
Exactly, time for me to buy that bass they never let me have.
I don't know, I used to want to announce for ESPN, but now I'm thinking about helping kids like us... maybe joining the FBI or something.
Wow, that's actually really cool, Chase.
Plus, it would be sweet to get to carry a gun all the time.
I just want to be a mom someday, but not a mom like my mom.
A good one, you know?
Hey, there's a first for everything...

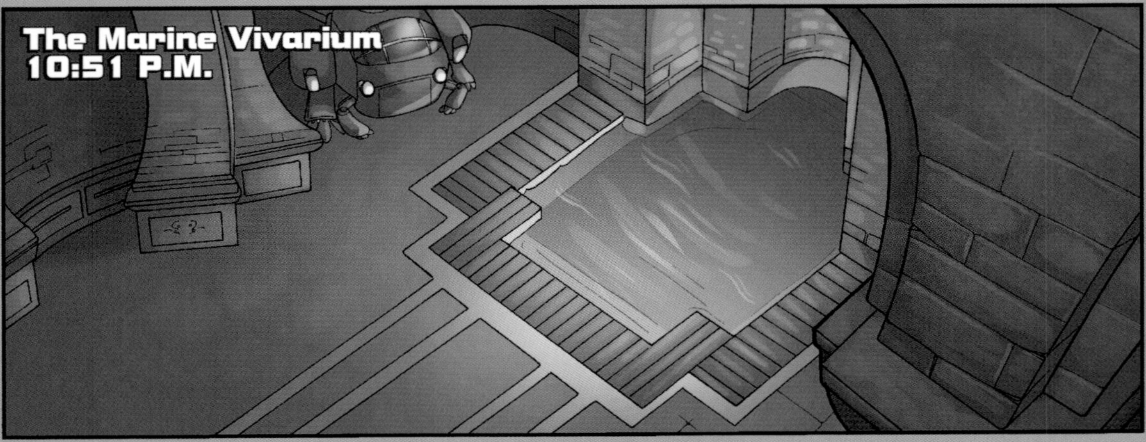
The Marine Vivarium
10:51 P.M.

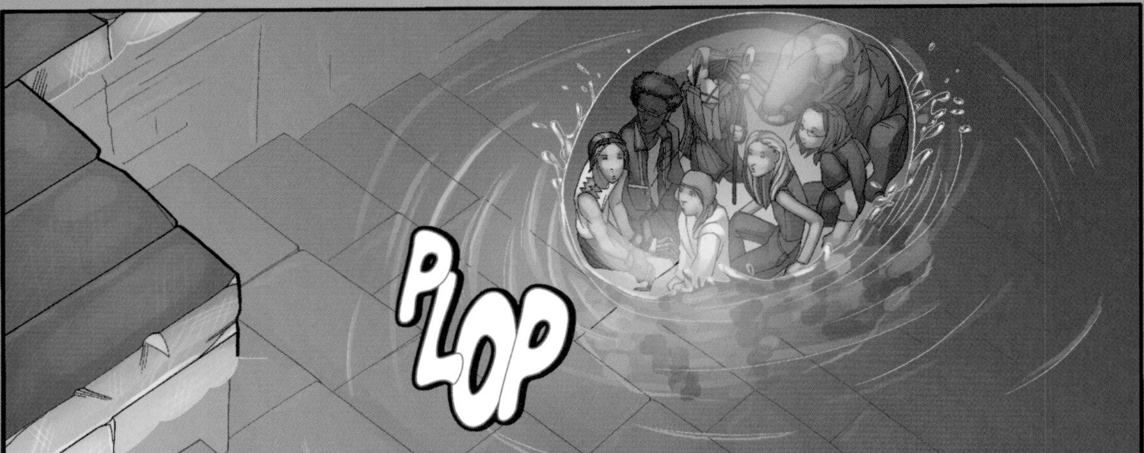
PLOP

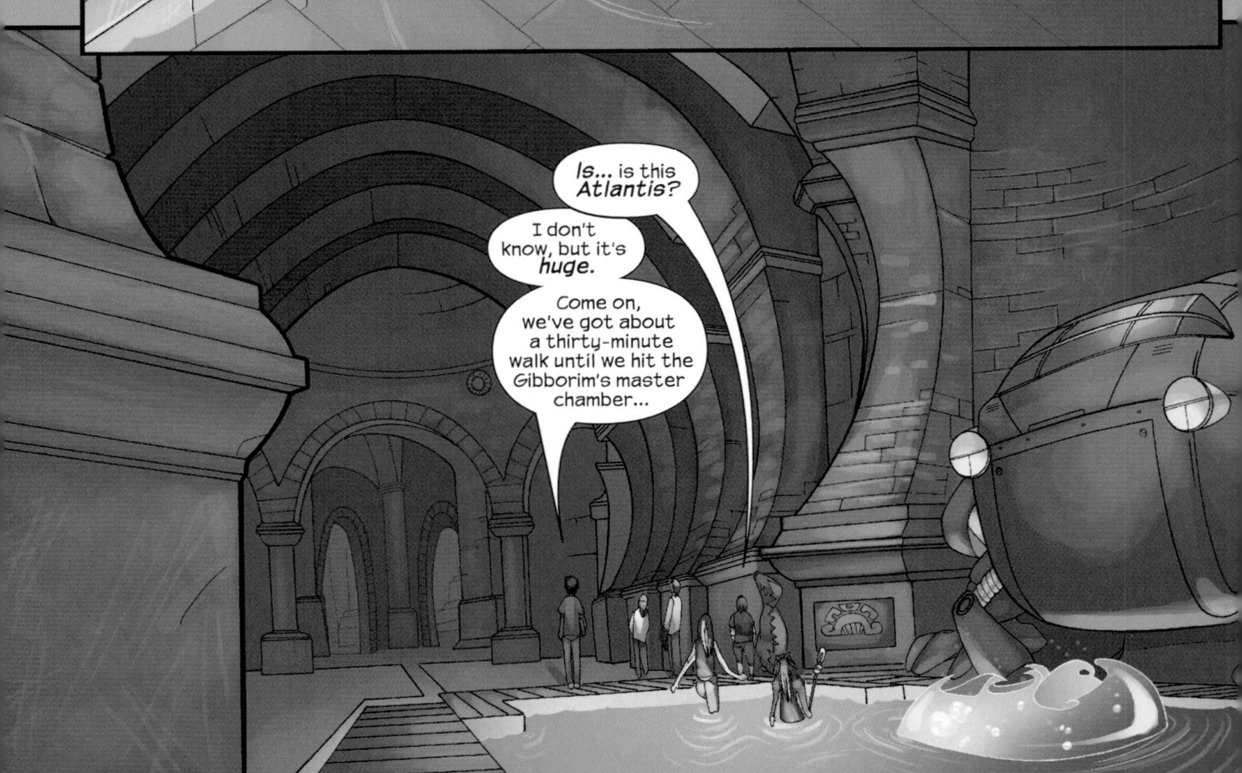
Is... is this Atlantis?
I don't know, but it's huge.
Come on, we've got about a thirty-minute walk until we hit the Gibborim's master chamber...

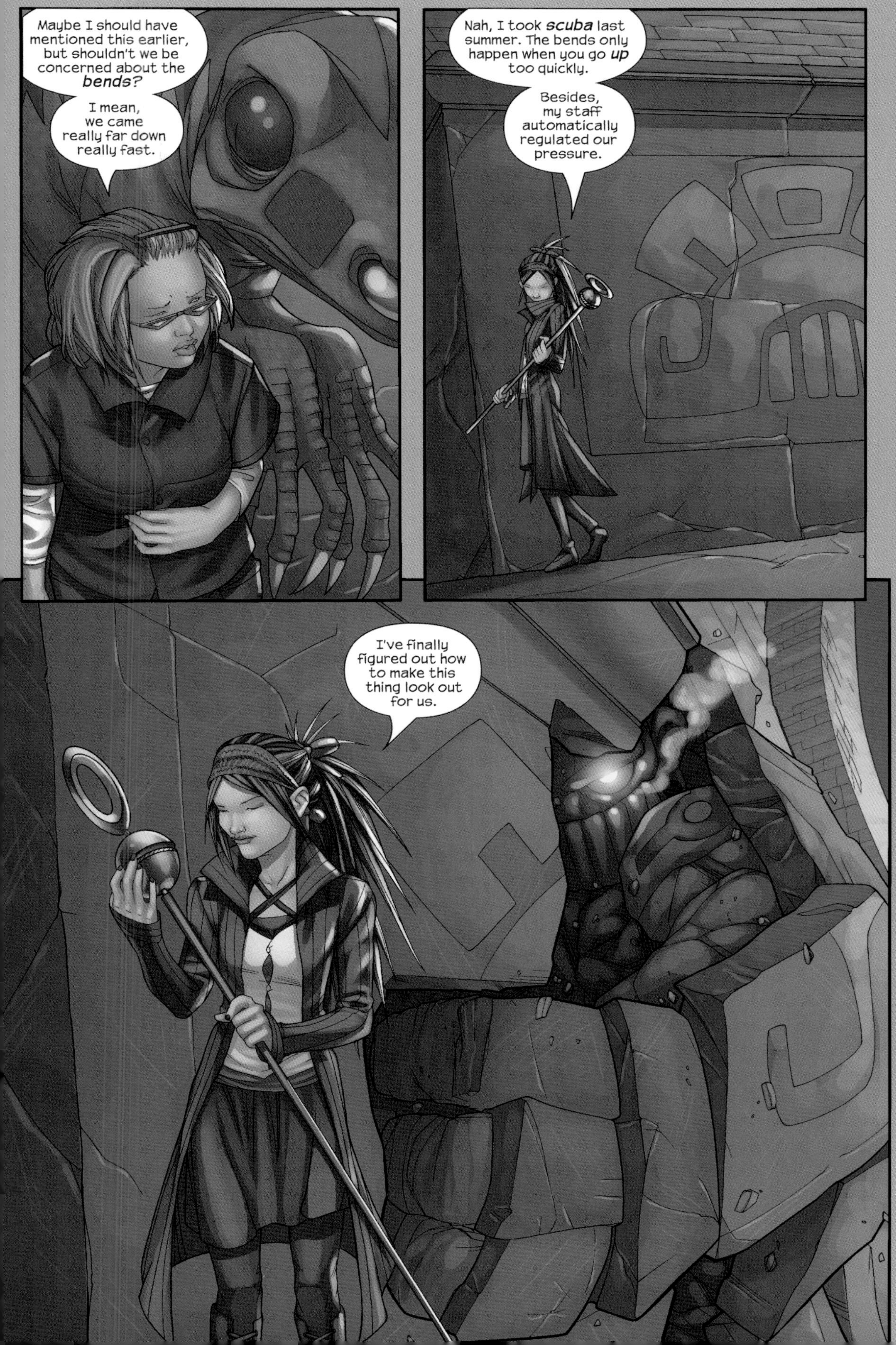

Maybe I should have mentioned this earlier, but shouldn't we be concerned about the *bends*?
I mean, we came really far down really fast.
Nah, I took *scuba* last summer. The bends only happen when you go *up* too quickly.
Besides, my staff automatically regulated our pressure.
I've finally figured out how to make this thing look out for us.

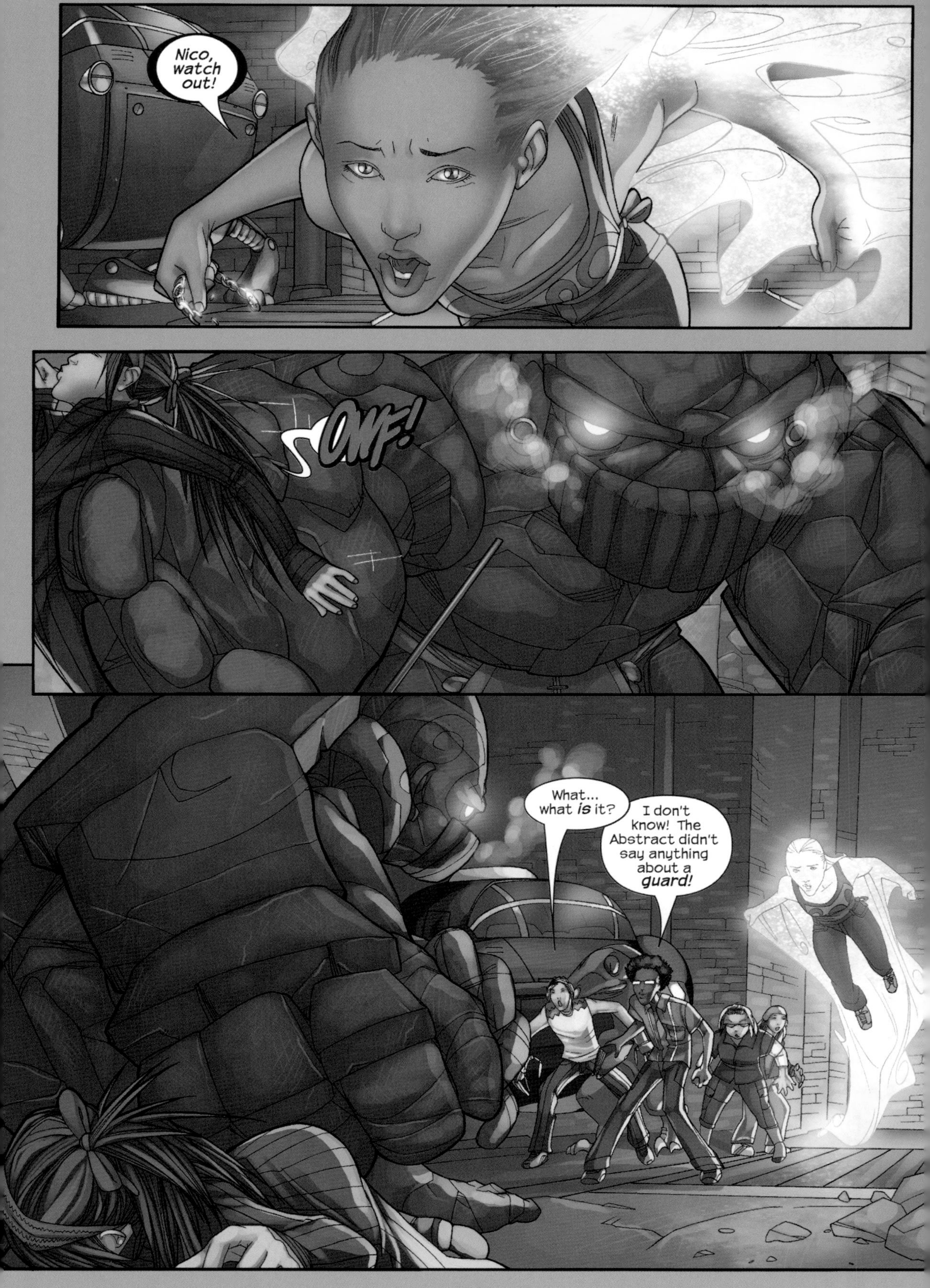
Nico, watch out!
SOWF!
What... what *is* it?
I don't know! The Abstract didn't say anything about a **guard!**

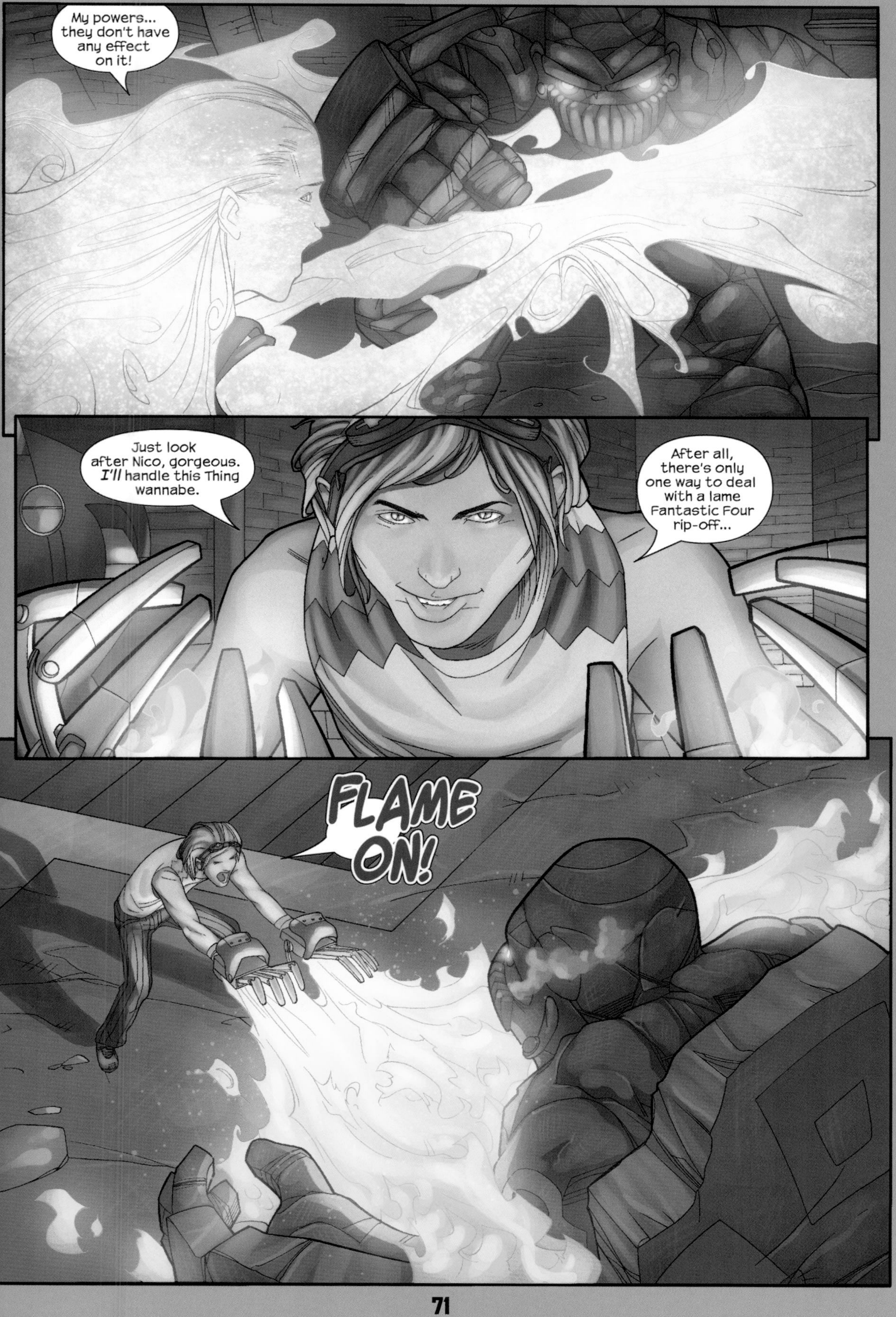
My powers... they don't have any effect on it!
Just look after Nico, gorgeous. *I'll* handle this Thing wannabe.
After all, there's only one way to deal with a lame Fantastic Four rip-off...
FLAME ON!

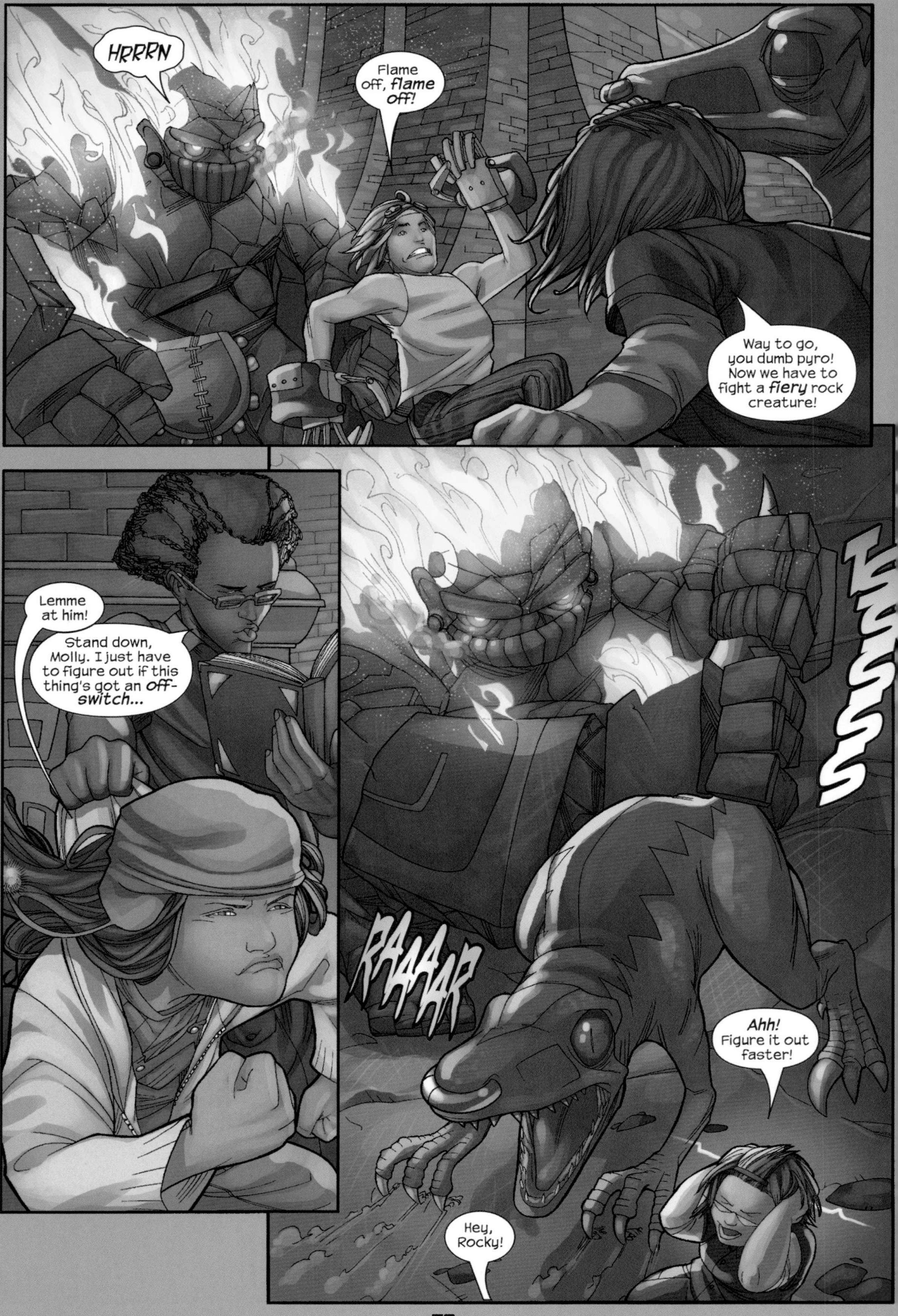
HRRRN
Flame off, *flame off!*
Way to go, you dumb pyro! Now we have to fight a *fiery* rock creature!
Lemme at him!
Stand down, Molly. I just have to figure out if this thing's got an *off-switch...*
TSSSSS
RAAAAR
Ahh! Figure it out faster!
Hey, Rocky!

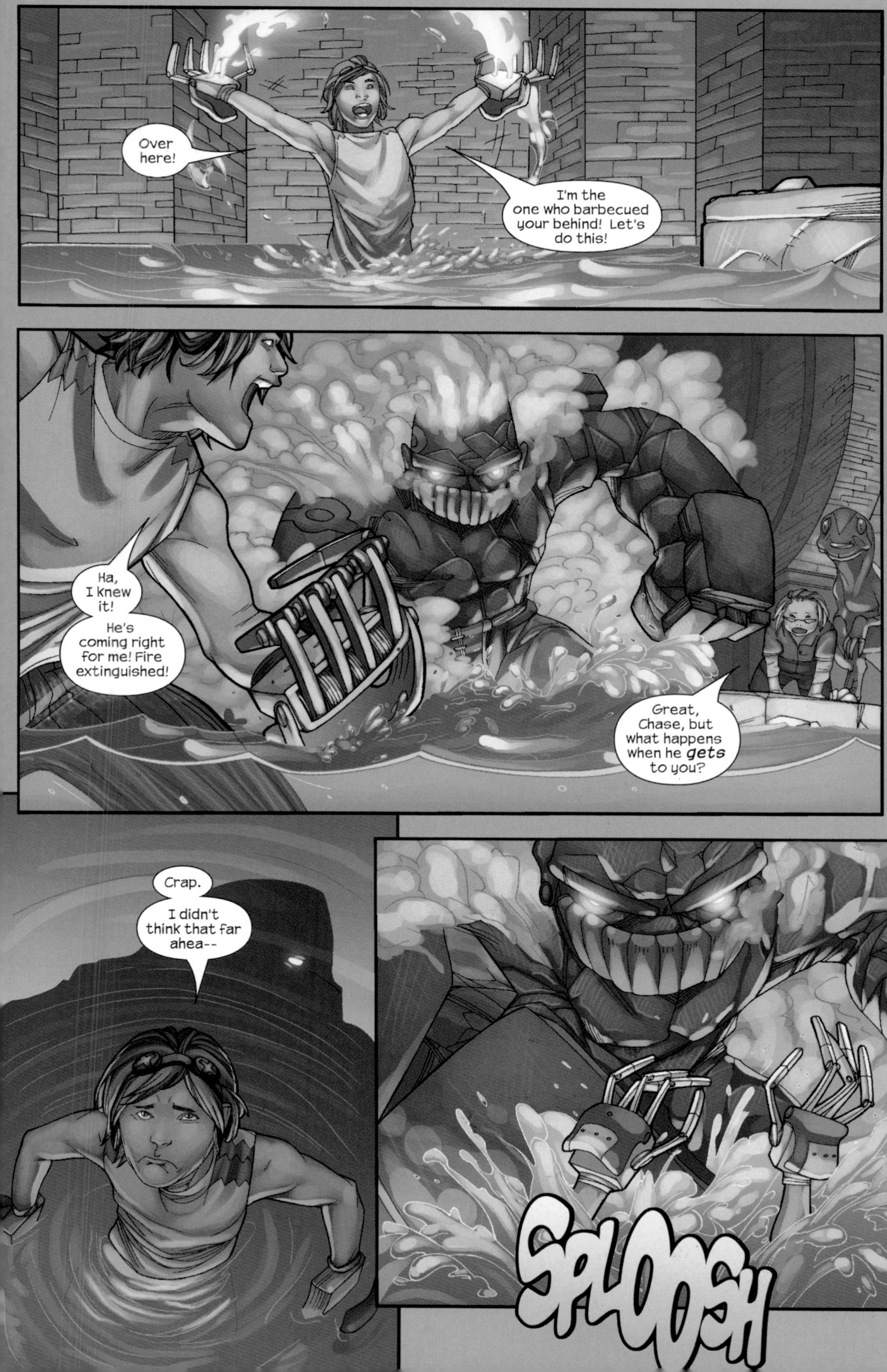
Over here!
I'm the one who barbecued your behind! Let's do this!
Ha, I knew it!
He's coming right for me! Fire extinguished!
Great, Chase, but what happens when he *gets* to you?
Crap.
I didn't think that far ahea--
SPLOOSH

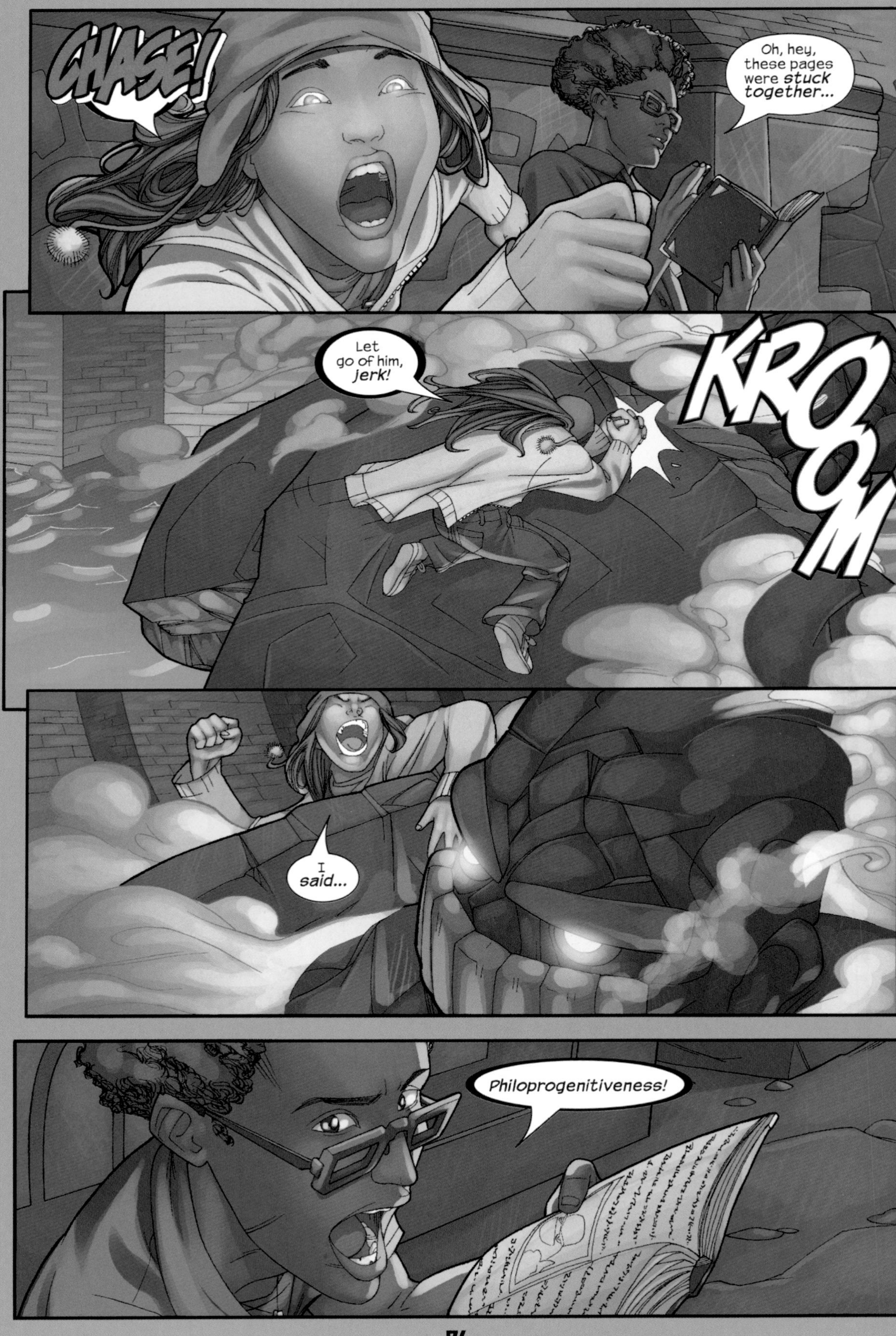
CHASE!
Oh, hey, these pages were *stuck together*...
Let go of him, *jerk!*
KROOM
I said...
Philoprogenitiveness!

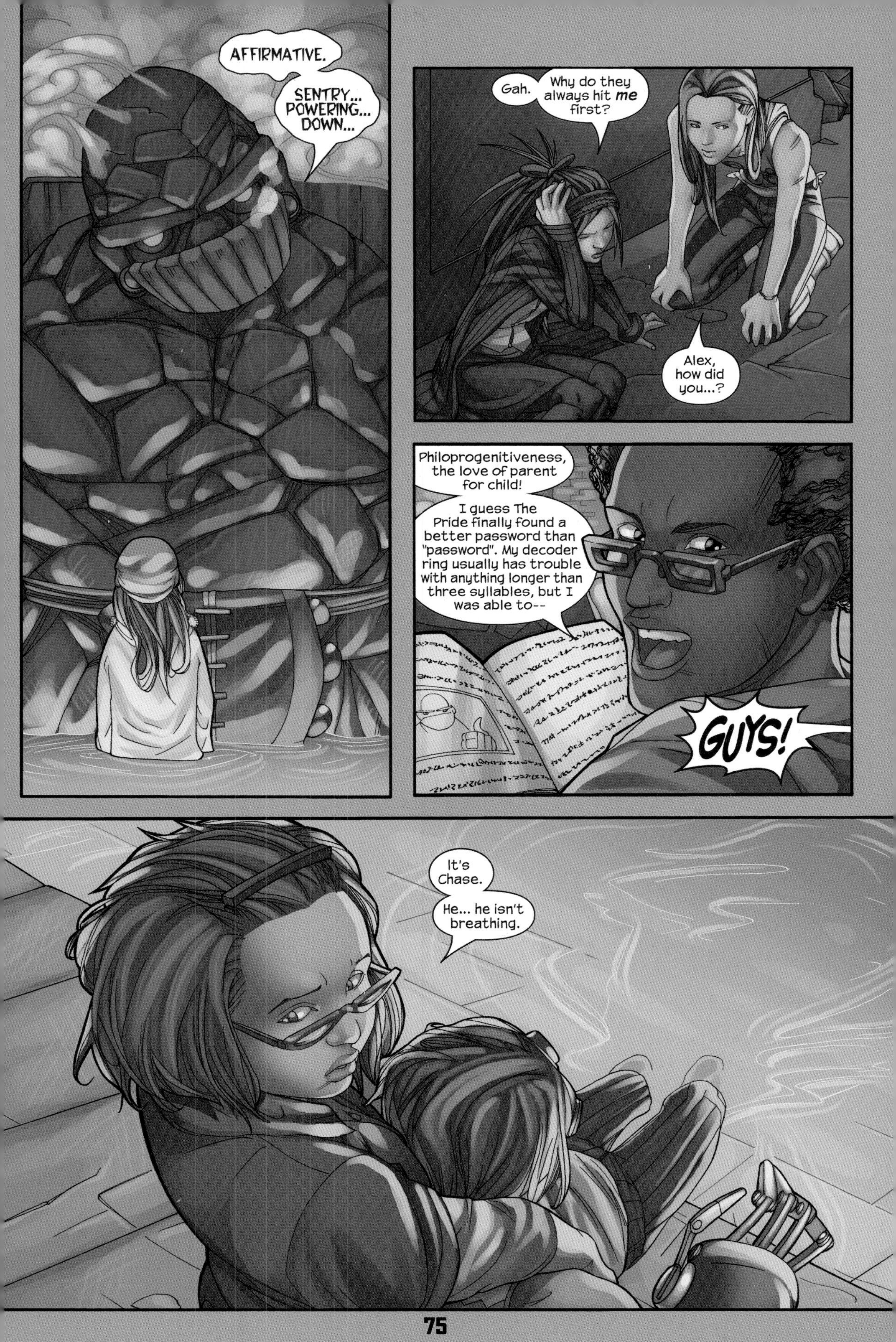
AFFIRMATIVE.
SENTRY... POWERING... DOWN...
Gah.
Why do they always hit *me* first?
Alex, how did you...?
Philoprogenitiveness, the love of parent for child!
I guess The Pride finally found a better password than "password". My decoder ring usually has trouble with anything longer than three syllables, but I was able to--
GUYS!
It's Chase.
He... he isn't breathing.

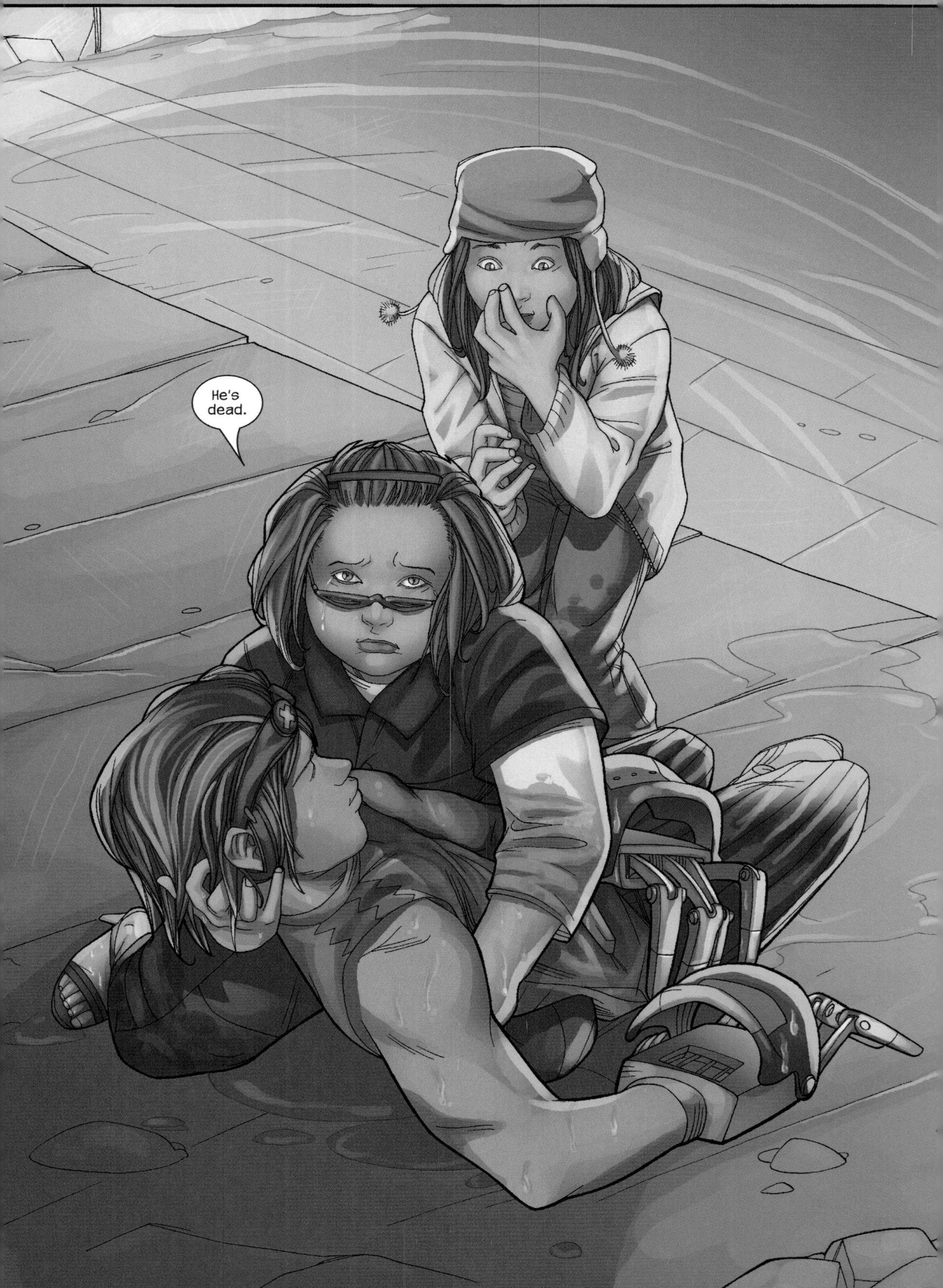
He's dead.

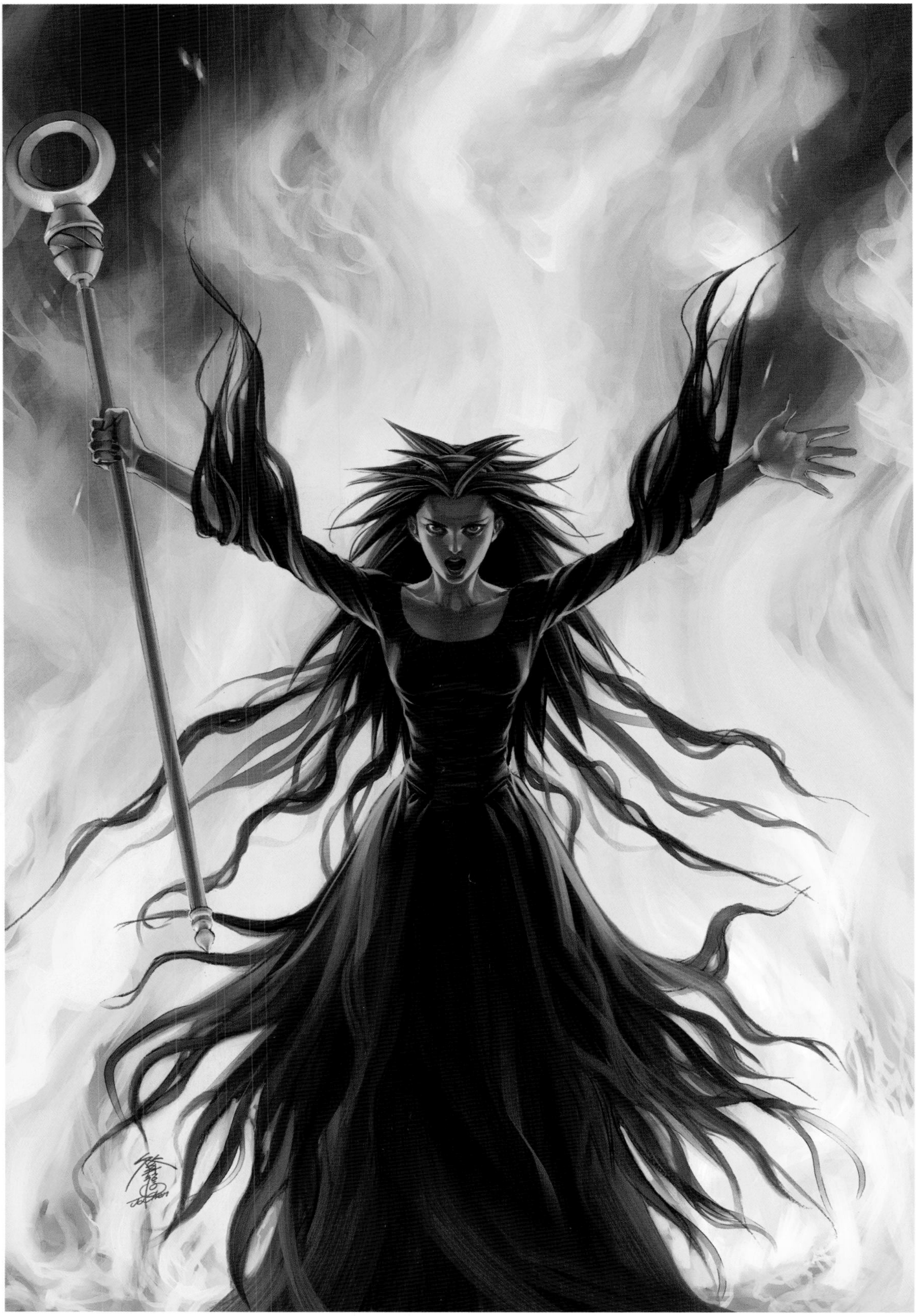

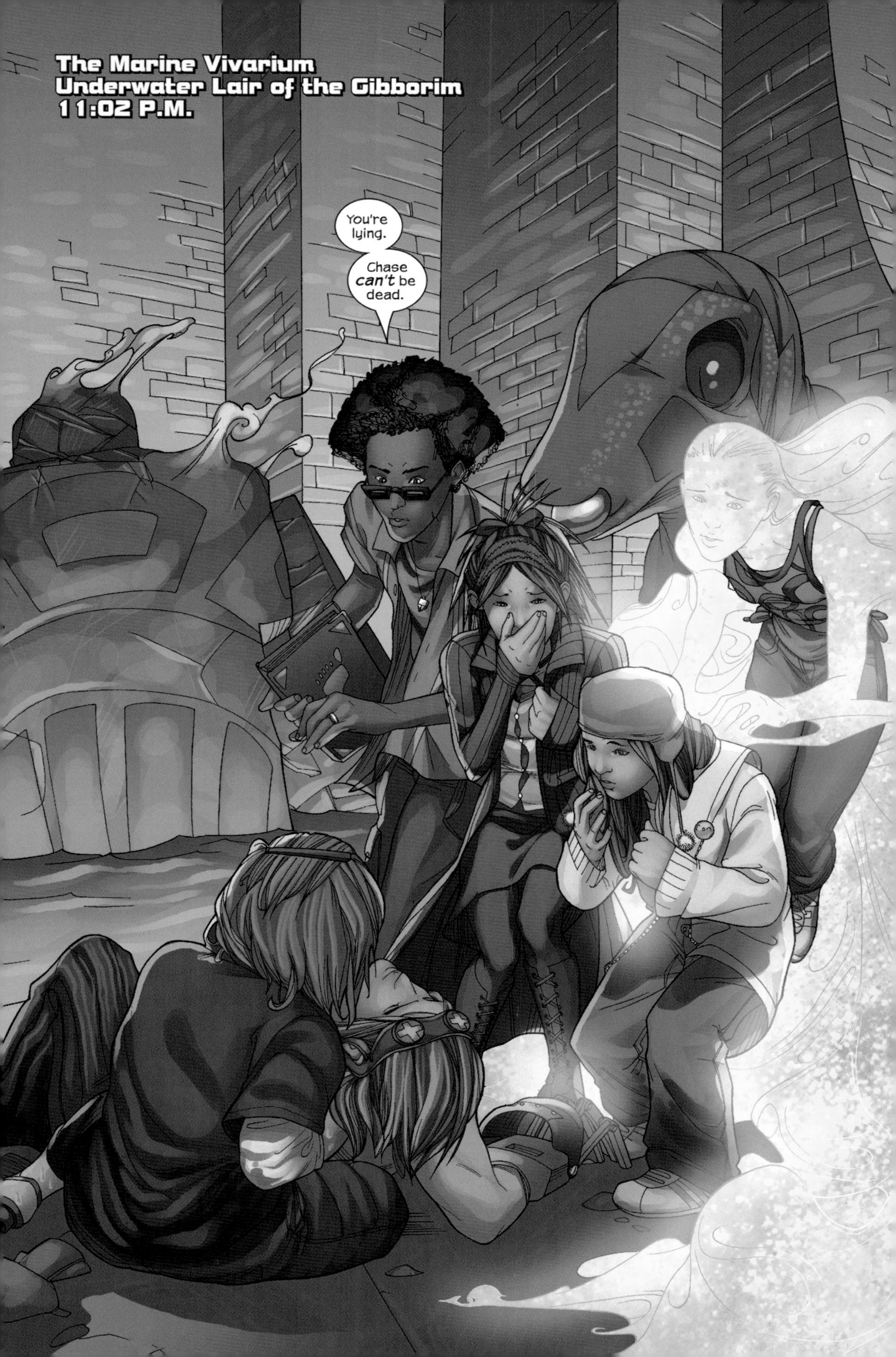
The Marine Vivarium
Underwater Lair of the Gibborim
11:02 P.M.
You're lying.
Chase can't be dead.

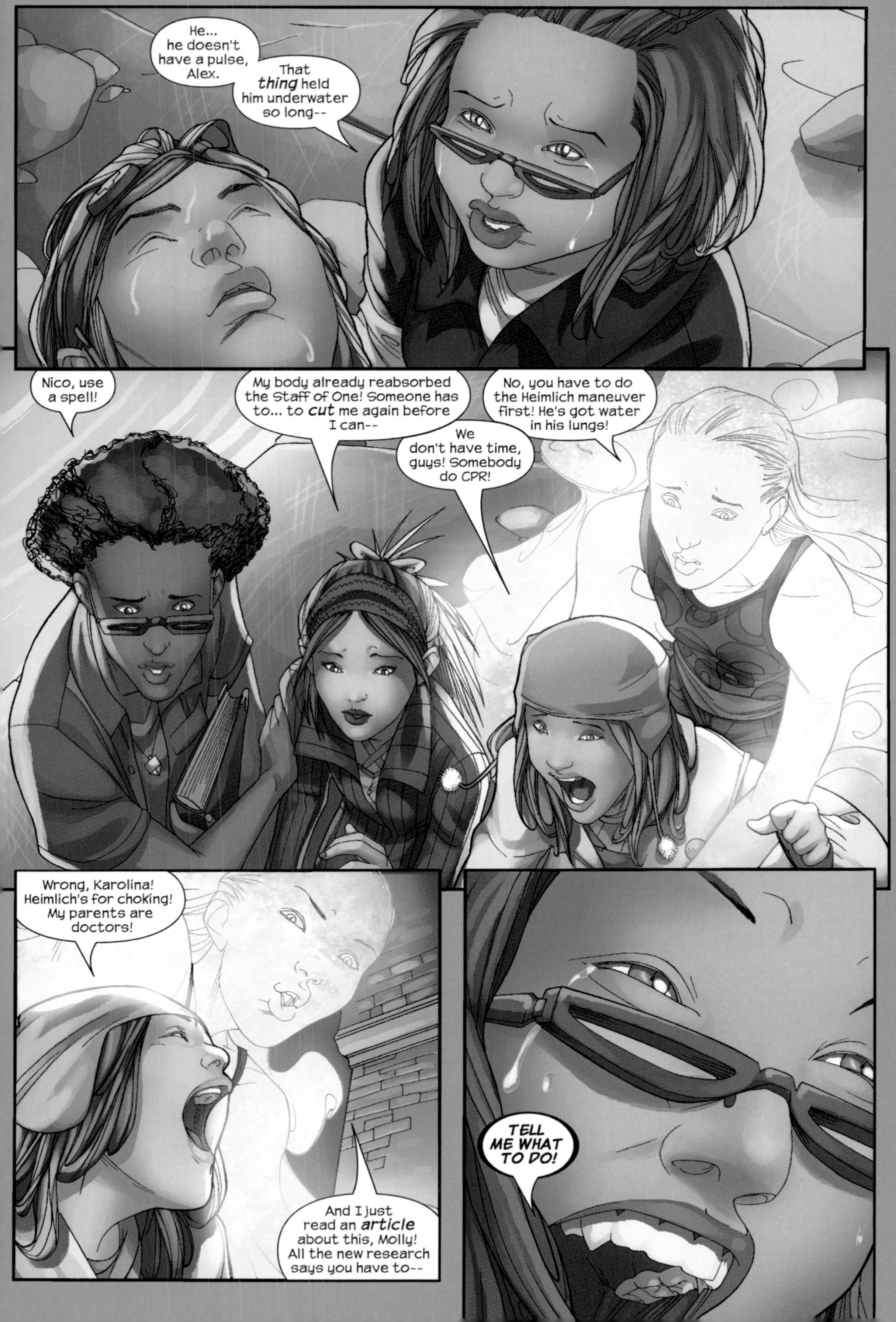
He... he doesn't have a pulse, Alex.
That thing held him underwater so long--
Nico, use a spell!
My body already reabsorbed the Staff of One! Someone has to... to cut me again before I can--
No, you have to do the Heimlich maneuver first! He's got water in his lungs!
We don't have time, guys! Somebody do CPR!
Wrong, Karolina! Heimlich's for choking! My parents are doctors!
And I just read an article about this, Molly! All the new research says you have to--
TELL ME WHAT TO DO!

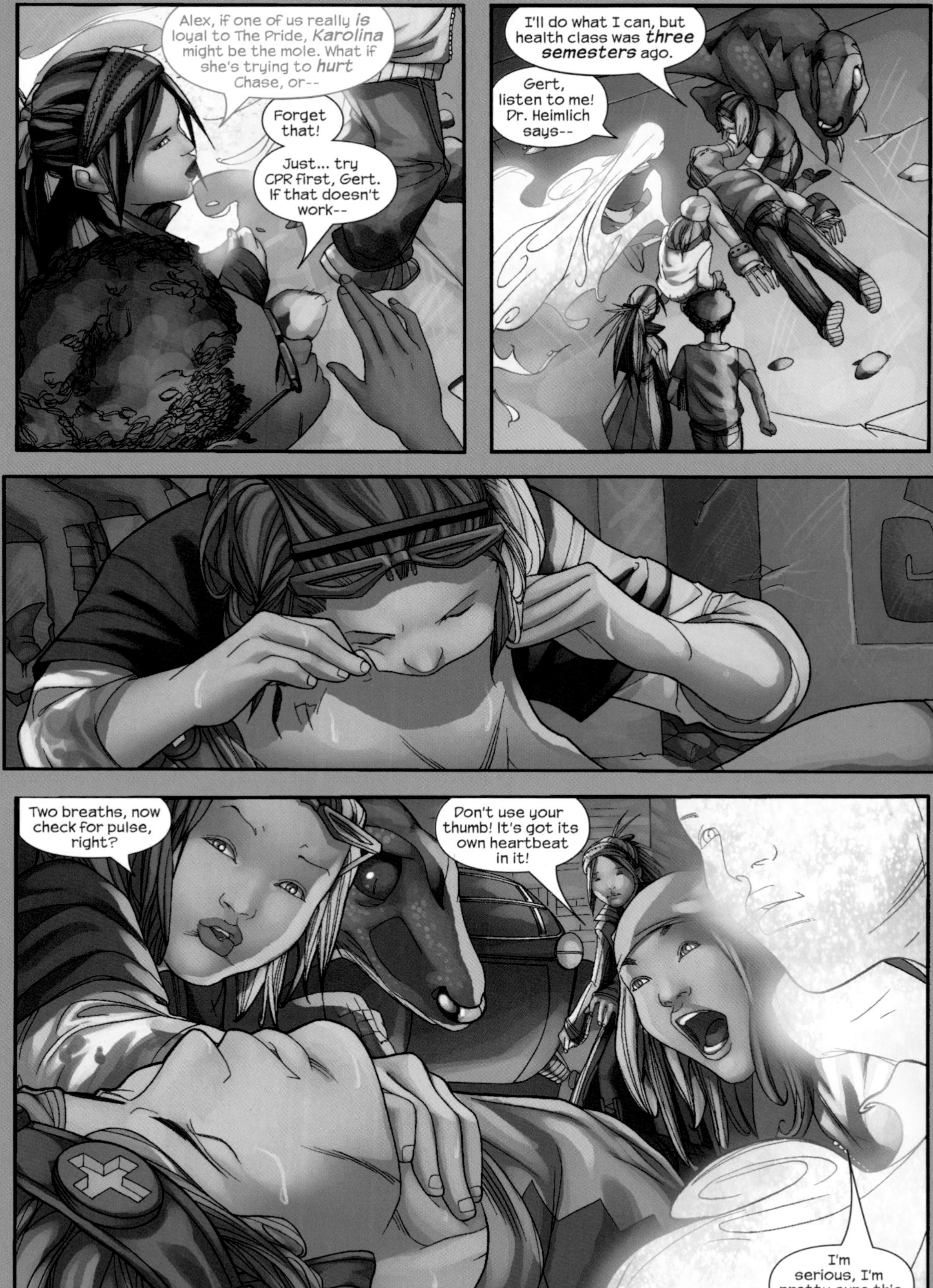
Alex, if one of us really is loyal to The Pride, Karolina might be the mole. What if she's trying to hurt Chase, or--
Forget that!
Just... try CPR first, Gert. If that doesn't work--
I'll do what I can, but health class was three semesters ago.
Gert, listen to me! Dr. Heimlich says--
Two breaths, now check for pulse, right?
Don't use your thumb! It's got its own heartbeat in it!
I'm serious, I'm pretty sure this is wrong!

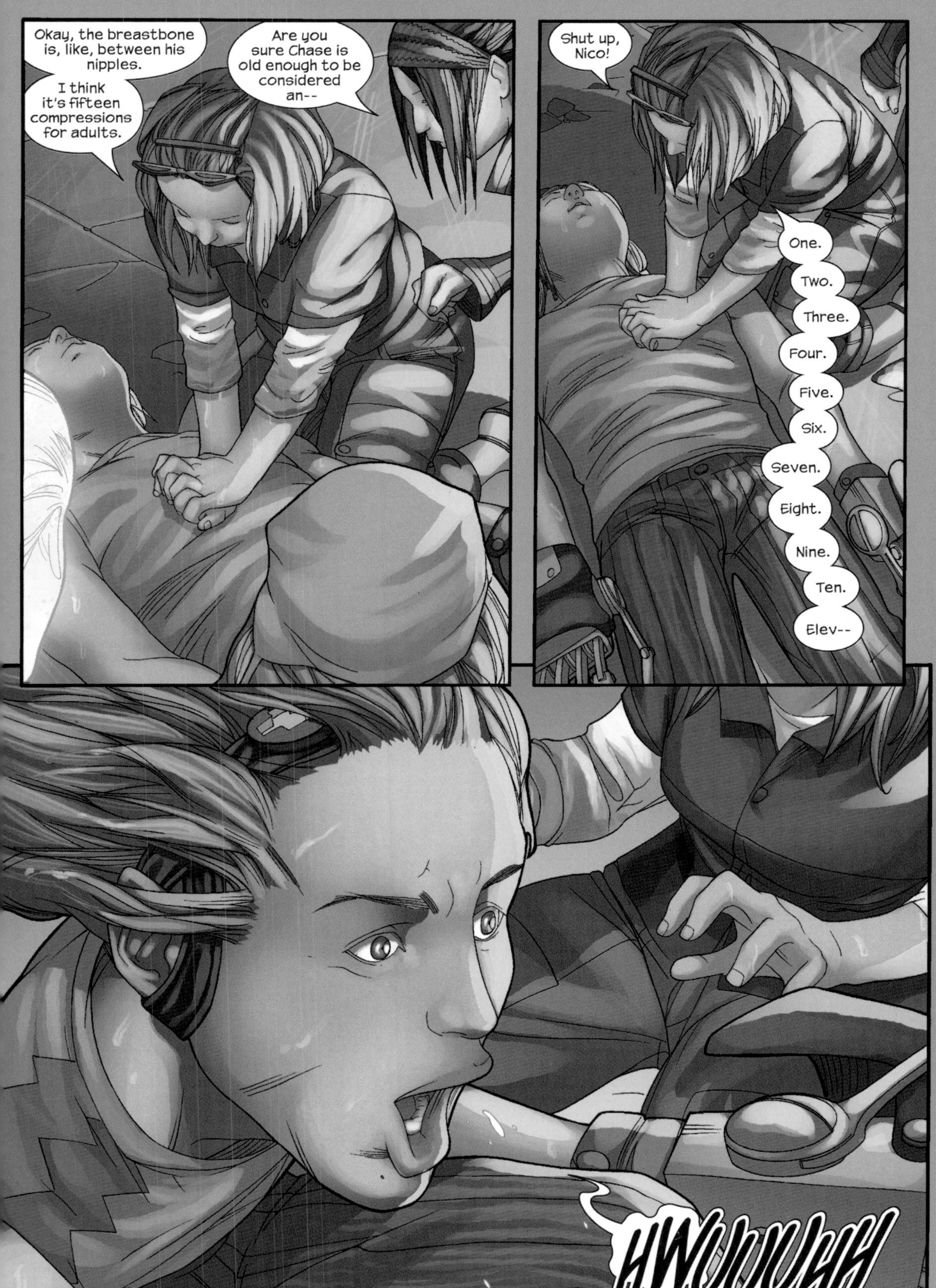
Okay, the breastbone is, like, between his nipples.
I think it's fifteen compressions for adults.
Are you sure Chase is old enough to be considered an--
Shut up, Nico!
One.
Two.
Three.
Four.
Five.
Six.
Seven.
Eight.
Nine.
Ten.
Elev--
HWUUUHH

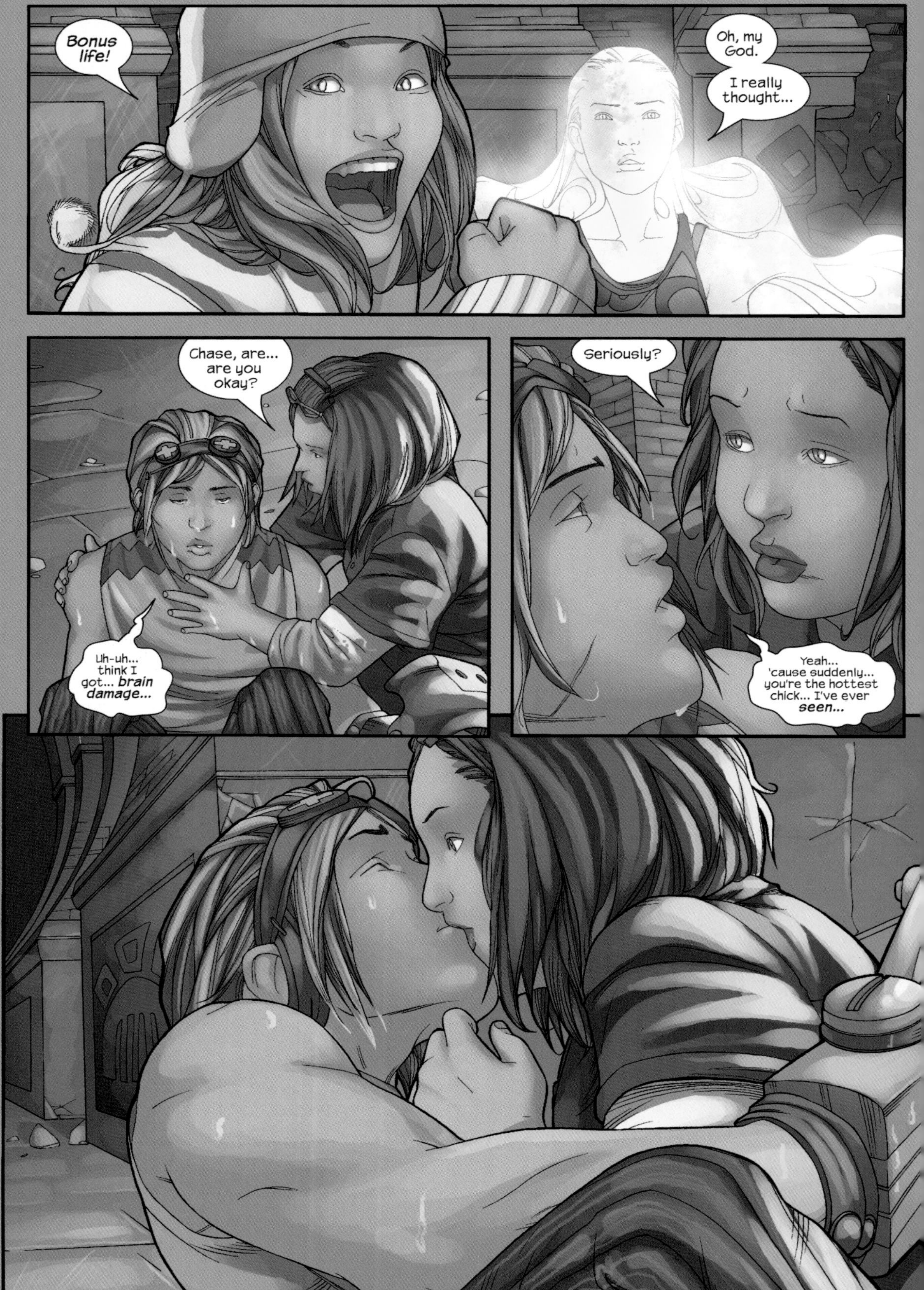
Bonus life!
Oh, my God.
I really thought...
Chase, are... are you okay?
Uh-uh... think I got... *brain damage...*
Seriously?
Yeah... 'cause suddenly... you're the hottest chick... I've ever *seen...*

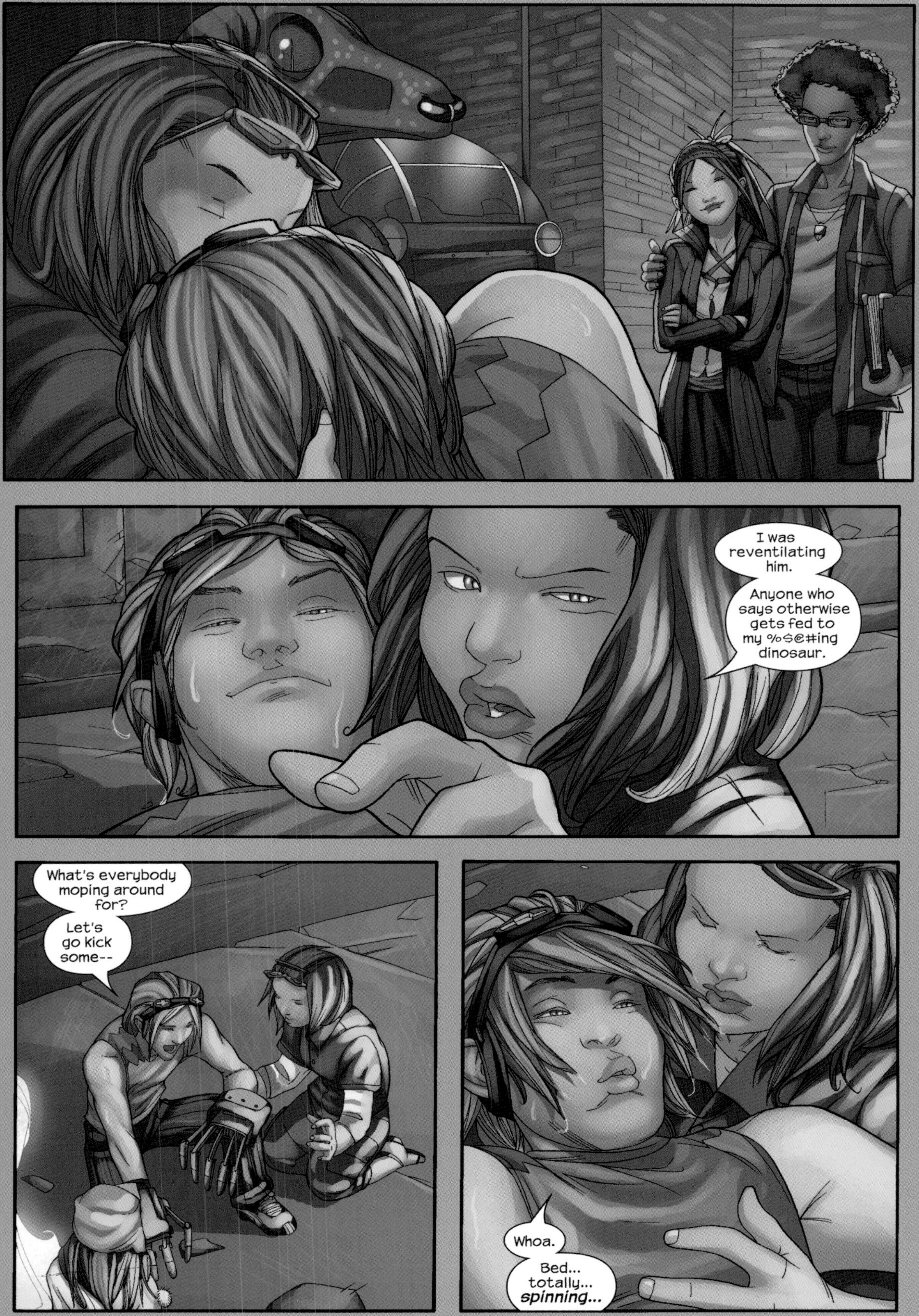
I was reventilating him.
Anyone who says otherwise gets fed to my %$@#ing dinosaur.
What's everybody moping around for?
Let's go kick some--
Whoa.
Bed... totally... *spinning*...

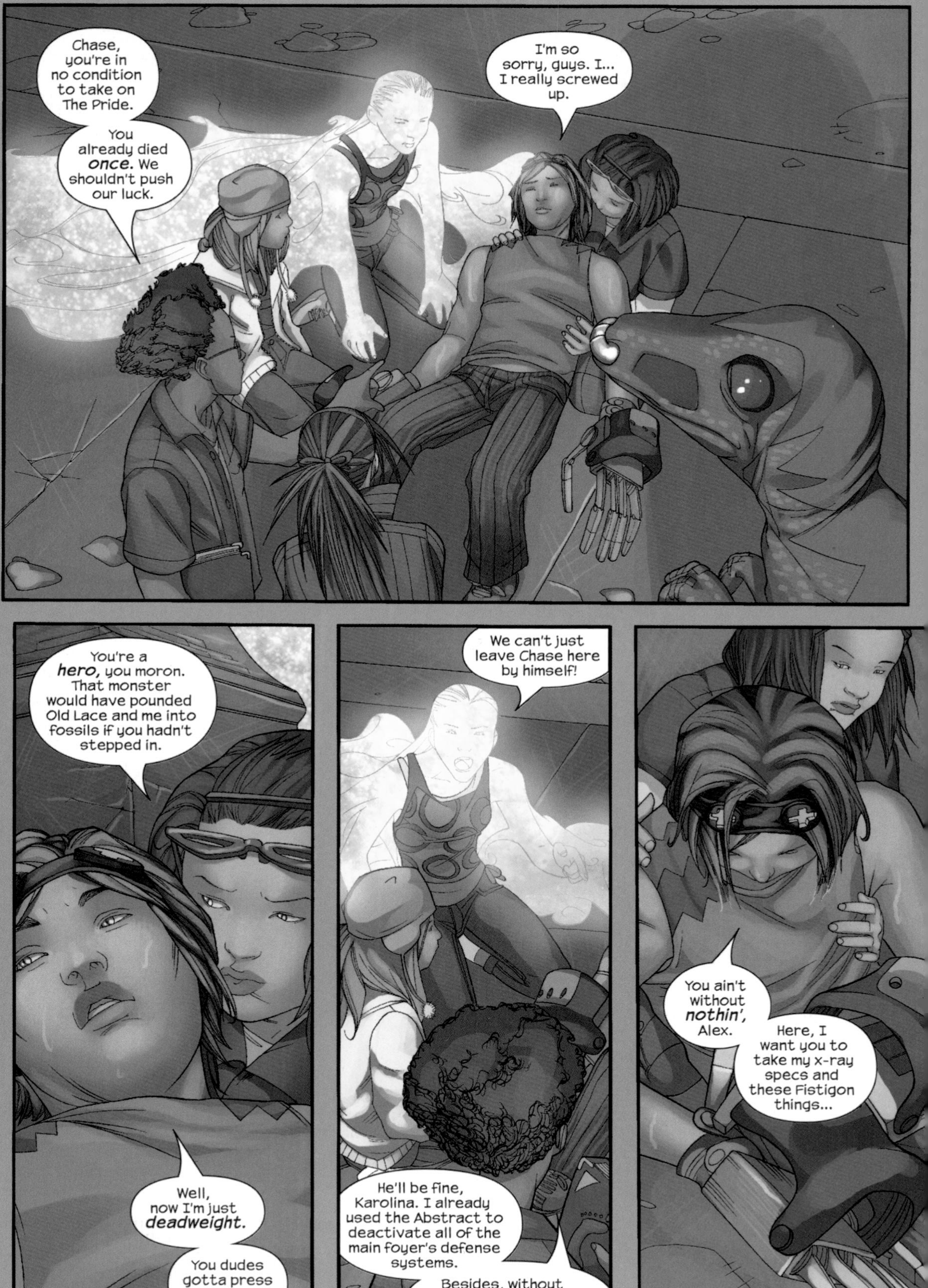
Chase, you're in no condition to take on The Pride.
You already died *once.* We shouldn't push our luck.
I'm so sorry, guys. I... I really screwed up.
You're a *hero,* you moron. That monster would have pounded Old Lace and me into fossils if you hadn't stepped in.
Well, now I'm just *deadweight.*
You dudes gotta press on without me.
We can't just leave Chase here by himself!
He'll be fine, Karolina. I already used the Abstract to deactivate all of the main foyer's defense systems.
Besides, without Chase's firepower, we're gonna need the rest of the team more than ever.
You ain't without *nothin',* Alex.
Here, I want you to take my x-ray specs and these Fistigon things...

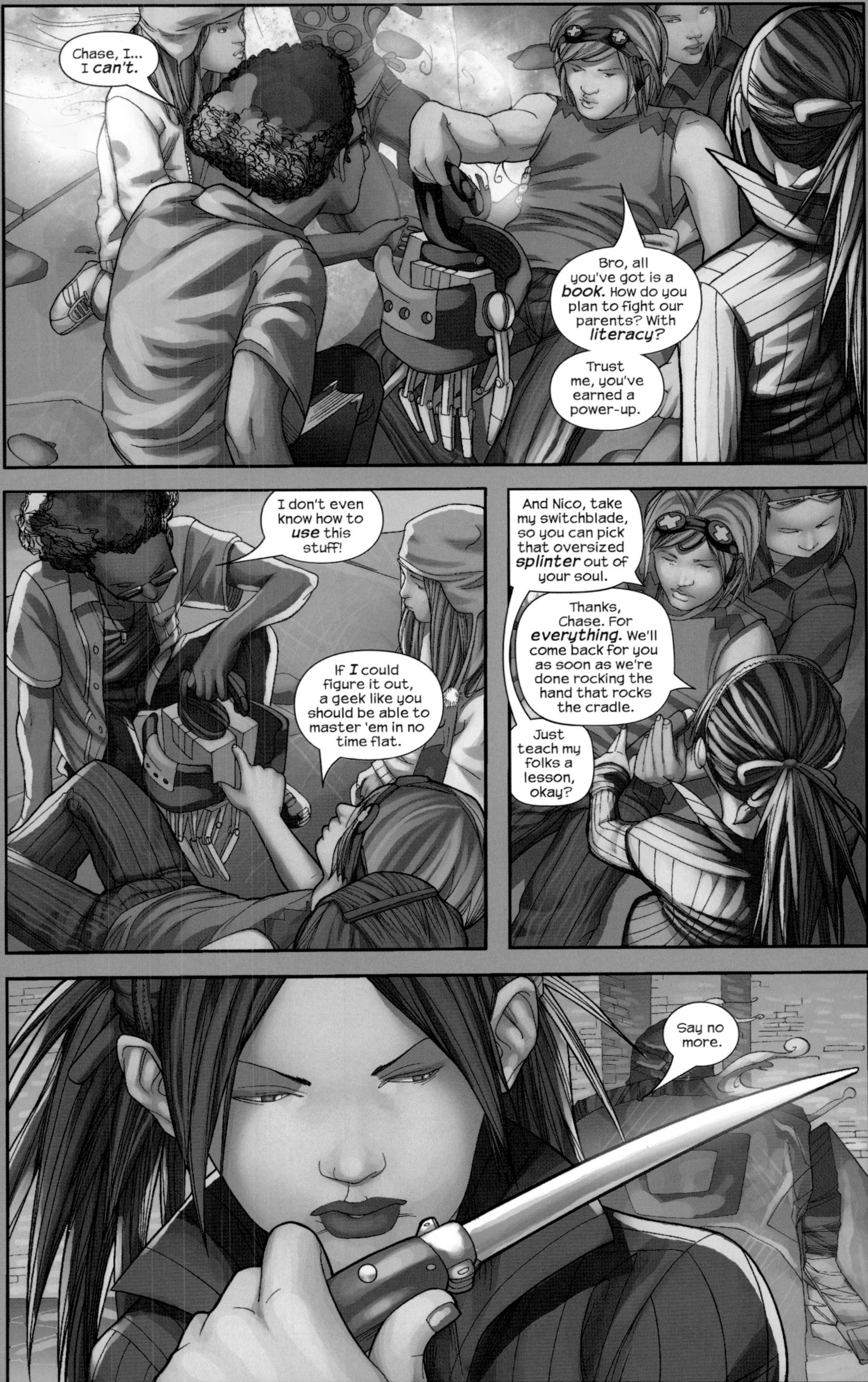
Chase, I... I can't.
Bro, all you've got is a book. How do you plan to fight our parents? With literacy?
Trust me, you've earned a power-up.
I don't even know how to use this stuff!
If I could figure it out, a geek like you should be able to master 'em in no time flat.
And Nico, take my switchblade, so you can pick that oversized splinter out of your soul.
Thanks, Chase. For everything. We'll come back for you as soon as we're done rocking the hand that rocks the cradle.
Just teach my folks a lesson, okay?
Say no more.

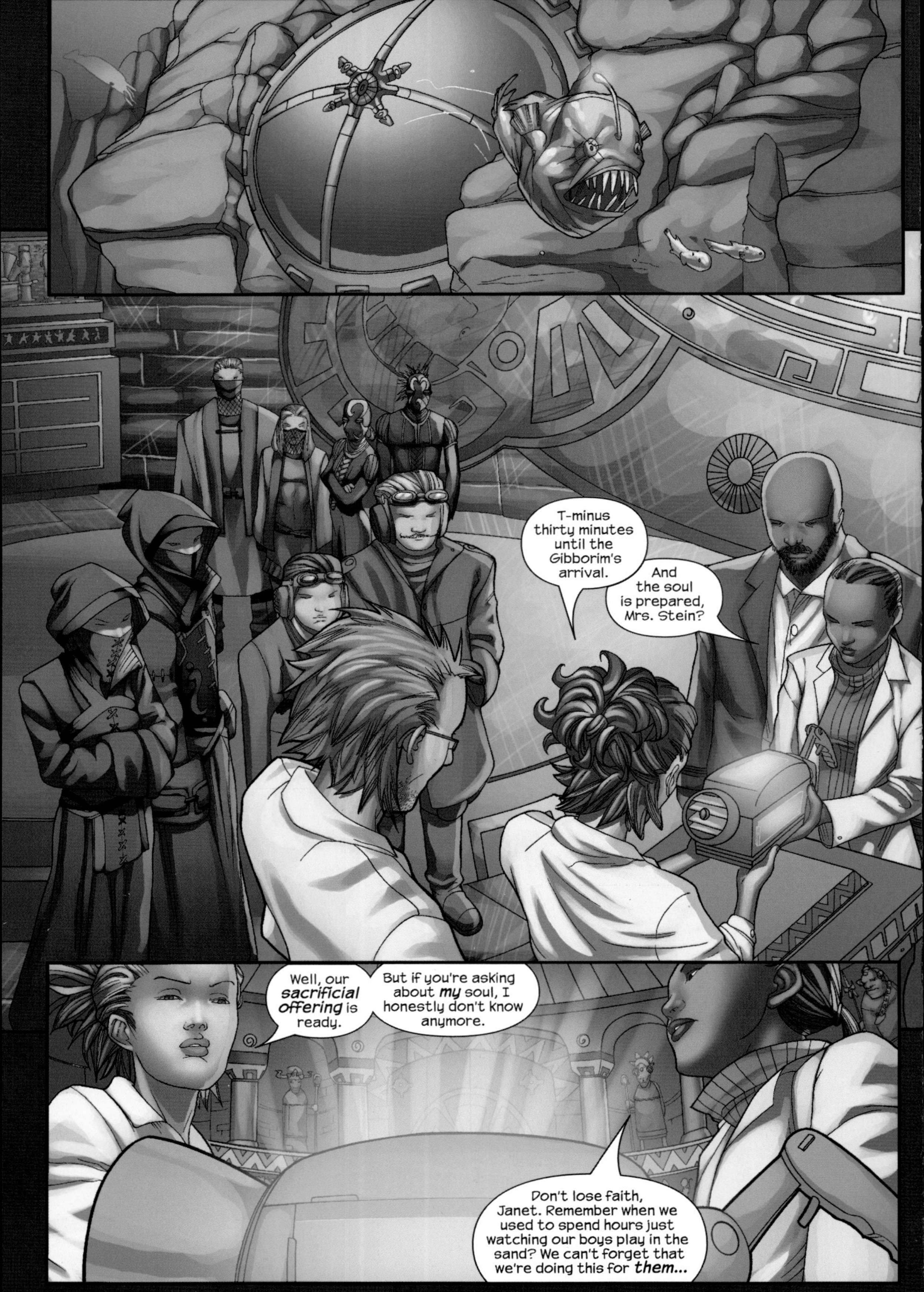

T-minus thirty minutes until the Gibborim's arrival.
And the soul is prepared, Mrs. Stein?
Well, our *sacrificial offering* is ready.
But if you're asking about *my* soul, I honestly don't know anymore.
Don't lose faith, Janet. Remember when we used to spend hours just watching our boys play in the sand? We can't forget that we're doing this for *them*...

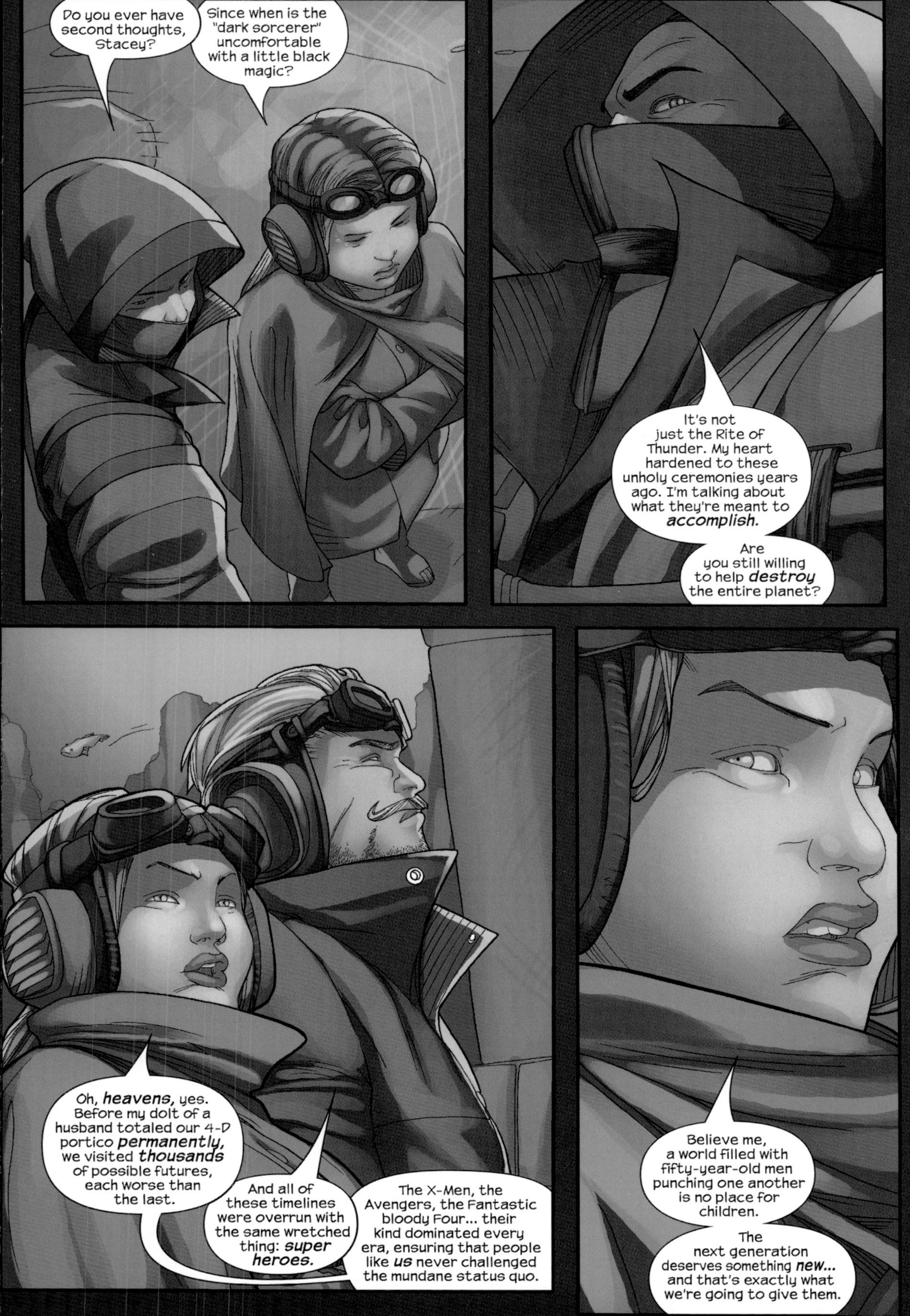
Do you ever have second thoughts, Stacey?
Since when is the "dark sorcerer" uncomfortable with a little black magic?
It's not just the Rite of Thunder. My heart hardened to these unholy ceremonies years ago. I'm talking about what they're meant to accomplish.
Are you still willing to help destroy the entire planet?
Oh, heavens, yes. Before my dolt of a husband totaled our 4-D portico permanently, we visited thousands of possible futures, each worse than the last.
And all of these timelines were overrun with the same wretched thing: super heroes.
The X-Men, the Avengers, the Fantastic bloody Four... their kind dominated every era, ensuring that people like us never challenged the mundane status quo.
Believe me, a world filled with fifty-year-old men punching one another is no place for children.
The next generation deserves something new... and that's exactly what we're going to give them.

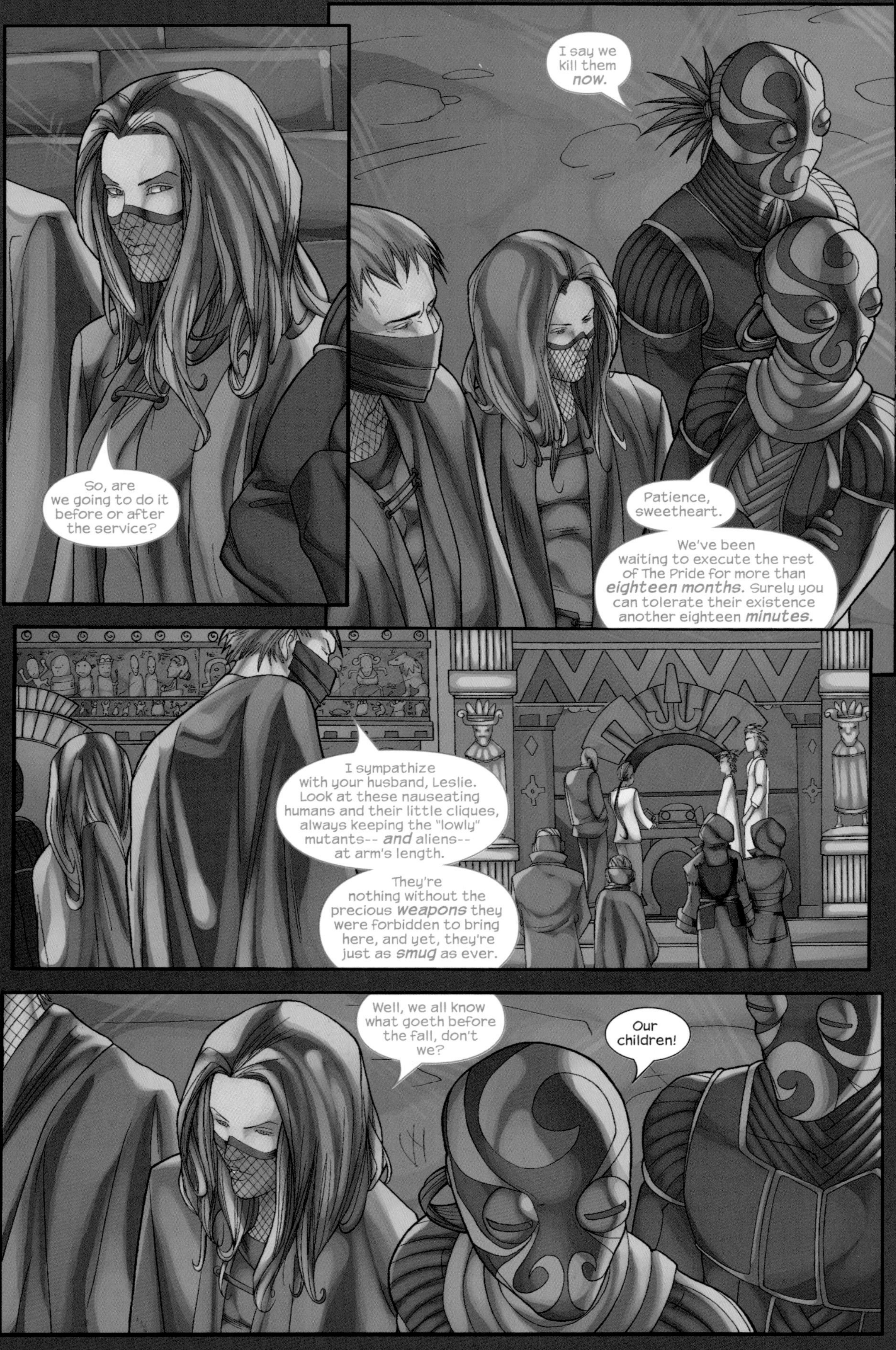
I say we kill them *now.*
So, are we going to do it before or after the service?
Patience, sweetheart.
We've been waiting to execute the rest of The Pride for more than ***eighteen months.*** Surely you can tolerate their existence another eighteen ***minutes.***
I sympathize with your husband, Leslie. Look at these nauseating humans and their little cliques, always keeping the "lowly" mutants-- ***and*** aliens-- at arm's length.
They're nothing without the precious ***weapons*** they were forbidden to bring here, and yet, they're just as ***smug*** as ever.
Well, we all know what goeth before the fall, don't we?
Our children!

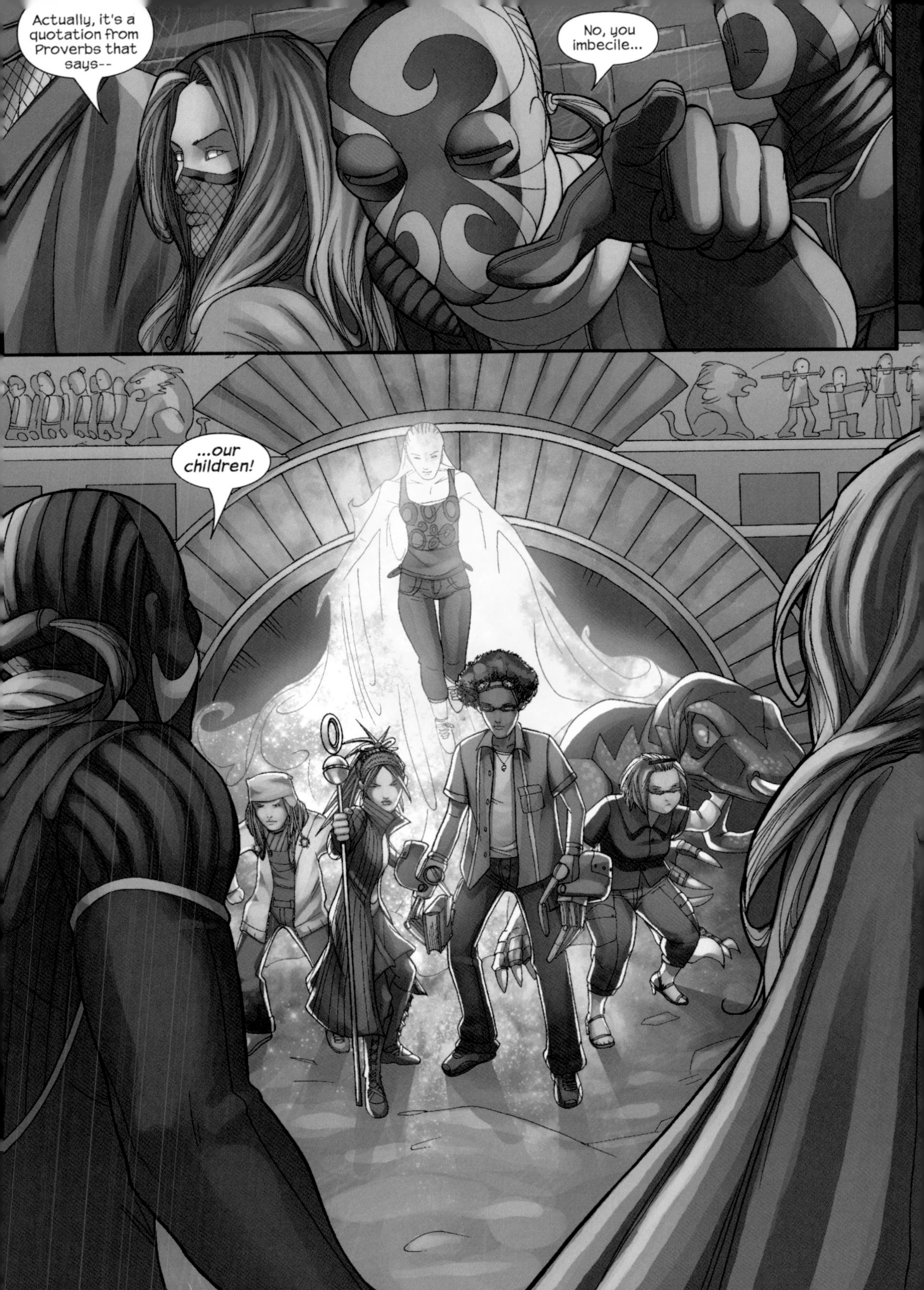
Actually, it's a quotation from Proverbs that says--
No, you imbecile...
...our children!

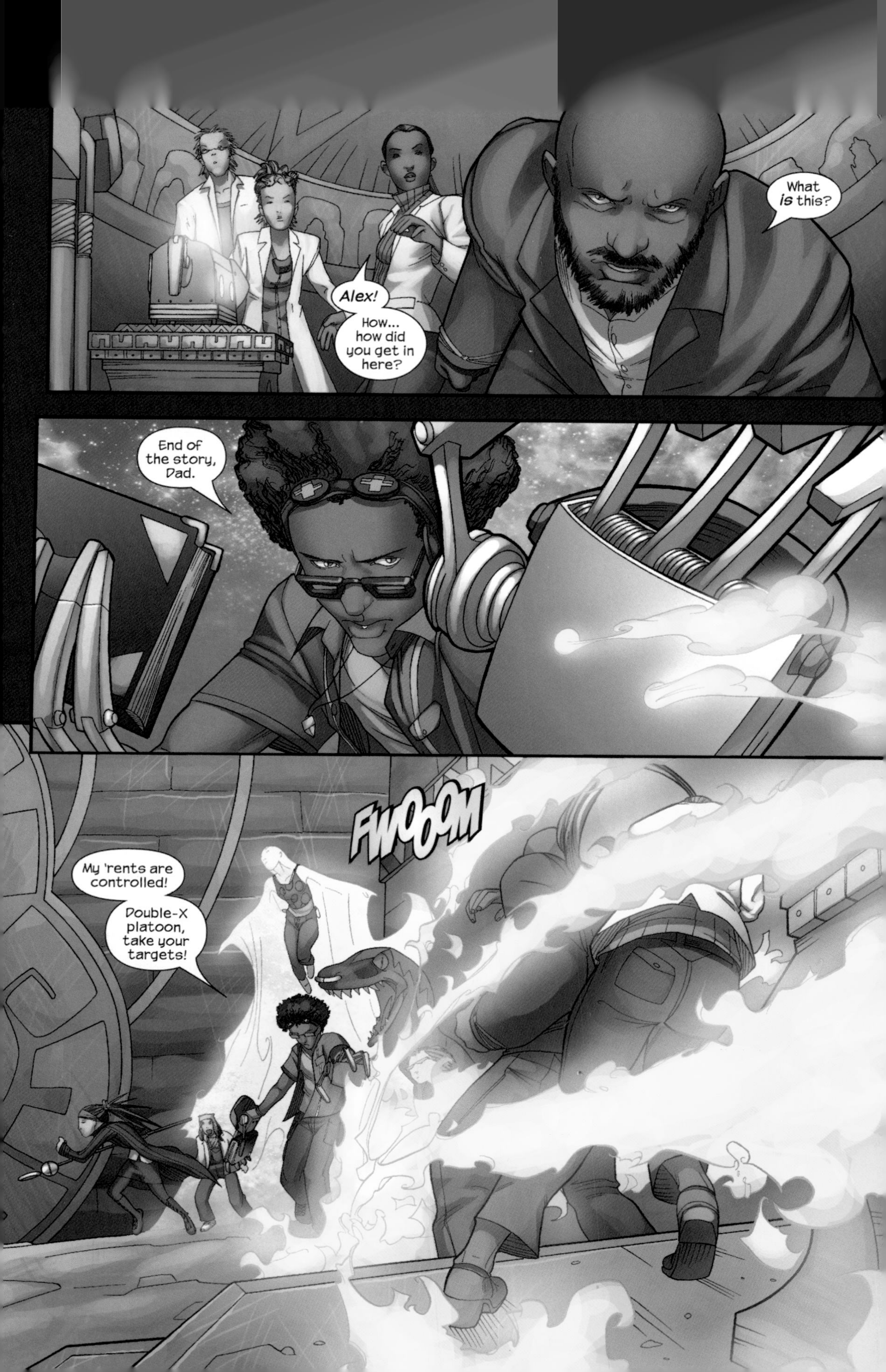
What *is* this?
Alex!
How... how did you get in here?
End of the story, Dad.
FWOOOM
My 'rents are controlled!
Double-X platoon, take your targets!

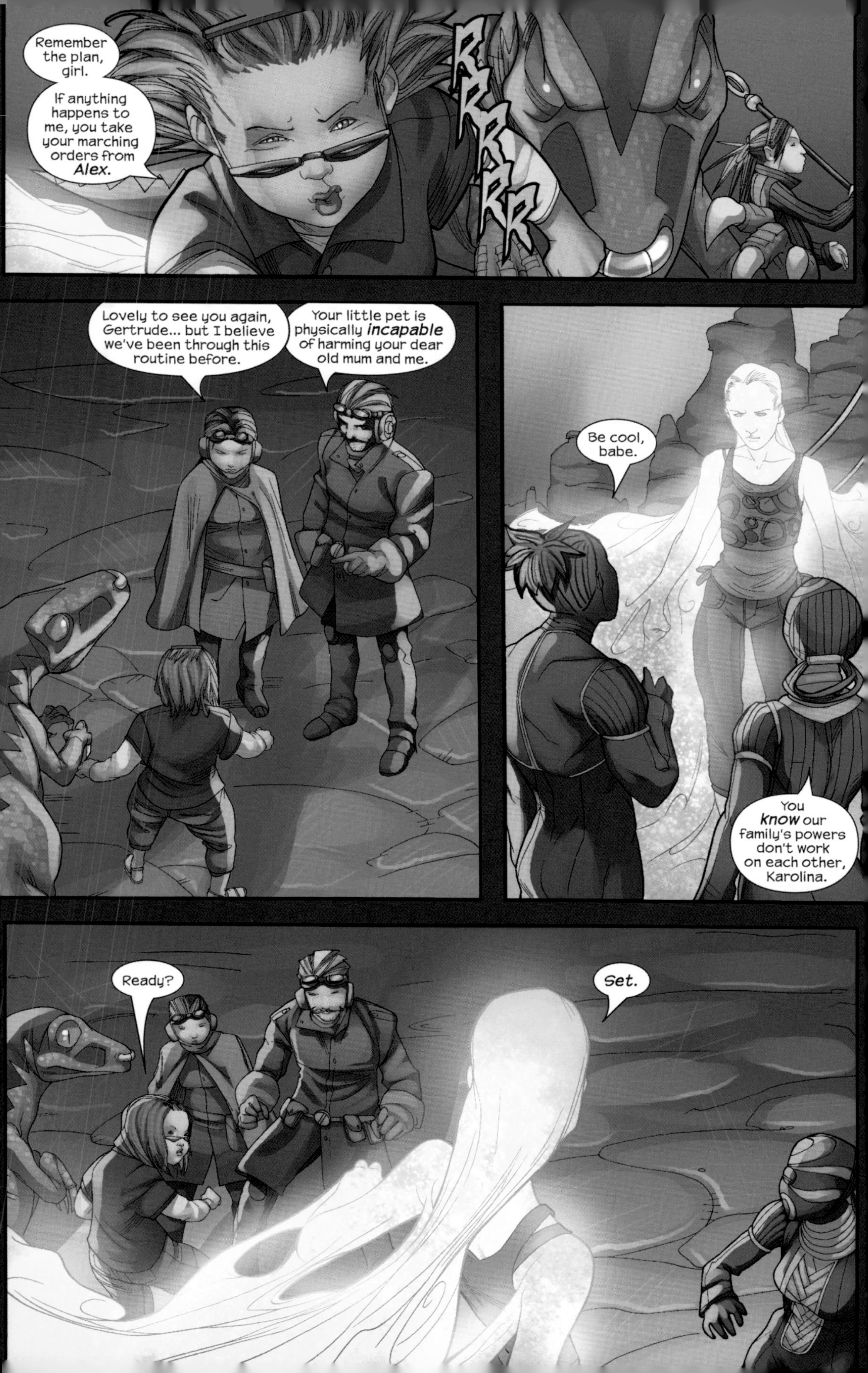
Remember the plan, girl.
If anything happens to me, you take your marching orders from Alex.
RRRRRR
Lovely to see you again, Gertrude... but I believe we've been through this routine before.
Your little pet is physically incapable of harming your dear old mum and me.
Be cool, babe.
You know our family's powers don't work on each other, Karolina.
Ready?
Set.

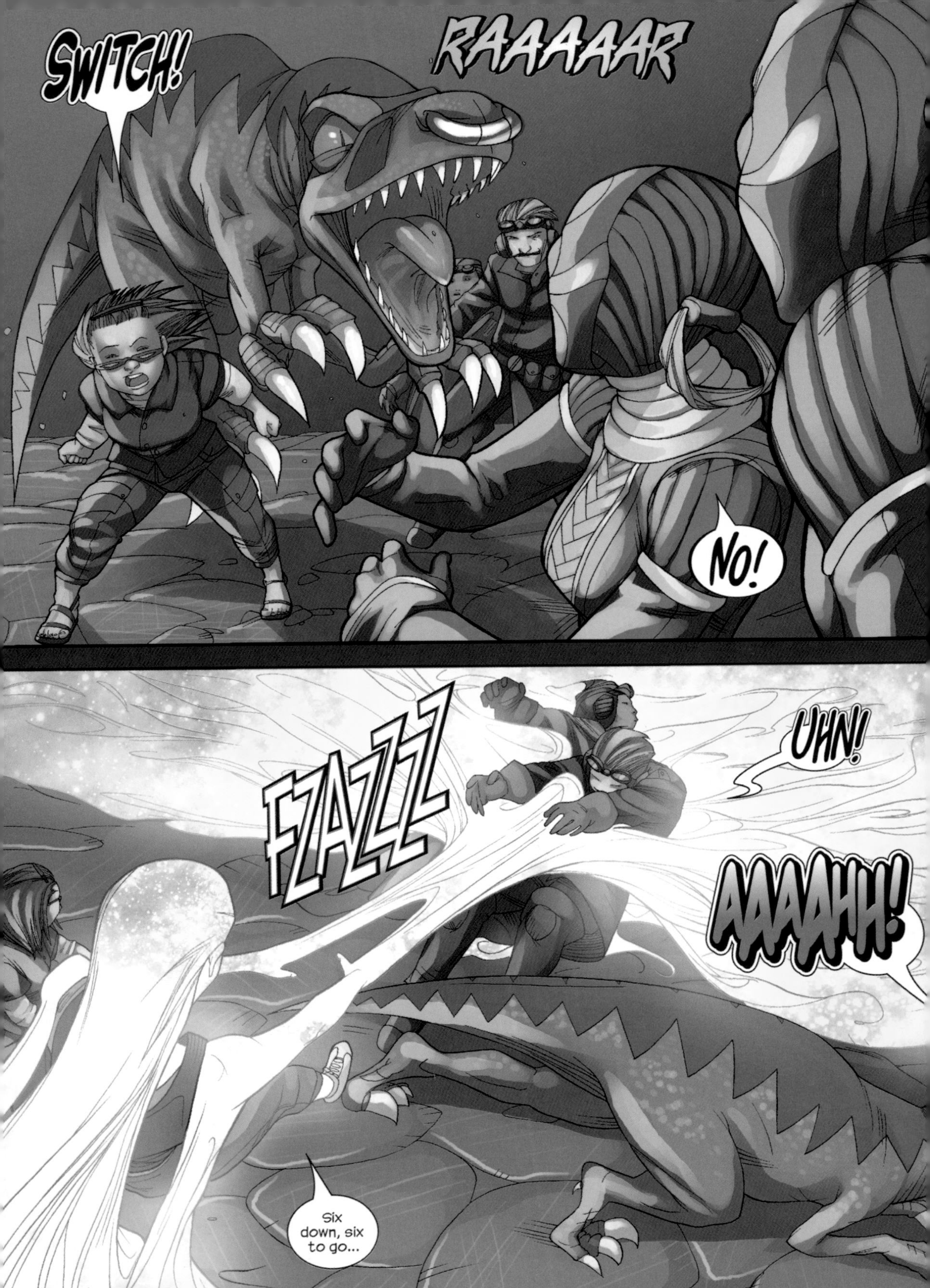
SWITCH!
RAAAAAR
NO!
FZAZZZ
UHN!
AAAAHH!
Six down, six to go...

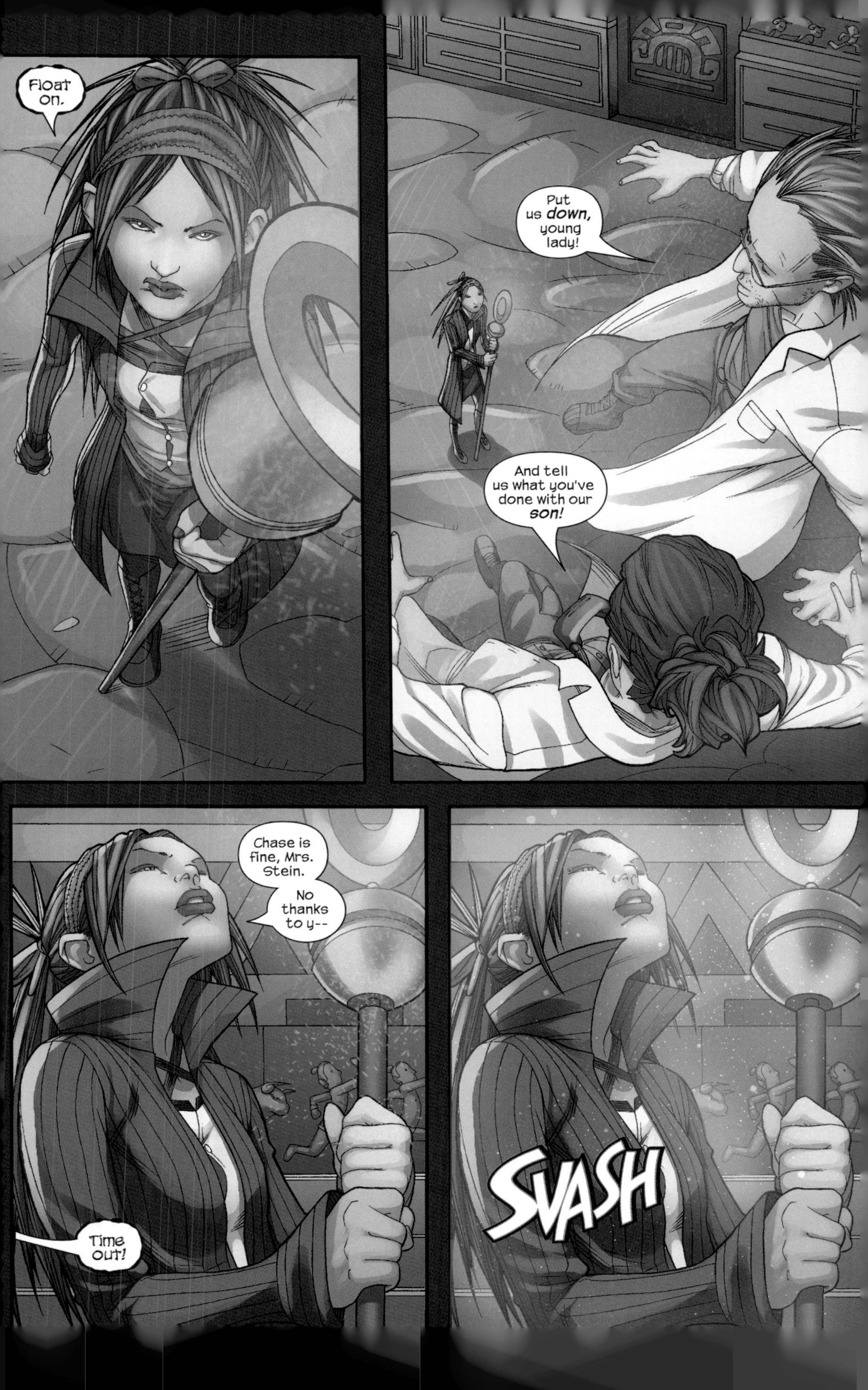
Float on.
Put us down, young lady!
And tell us what you've done with our son!
Chase is fine, Mrs. Stein.
No thanks to y--
Time out!
SVASH

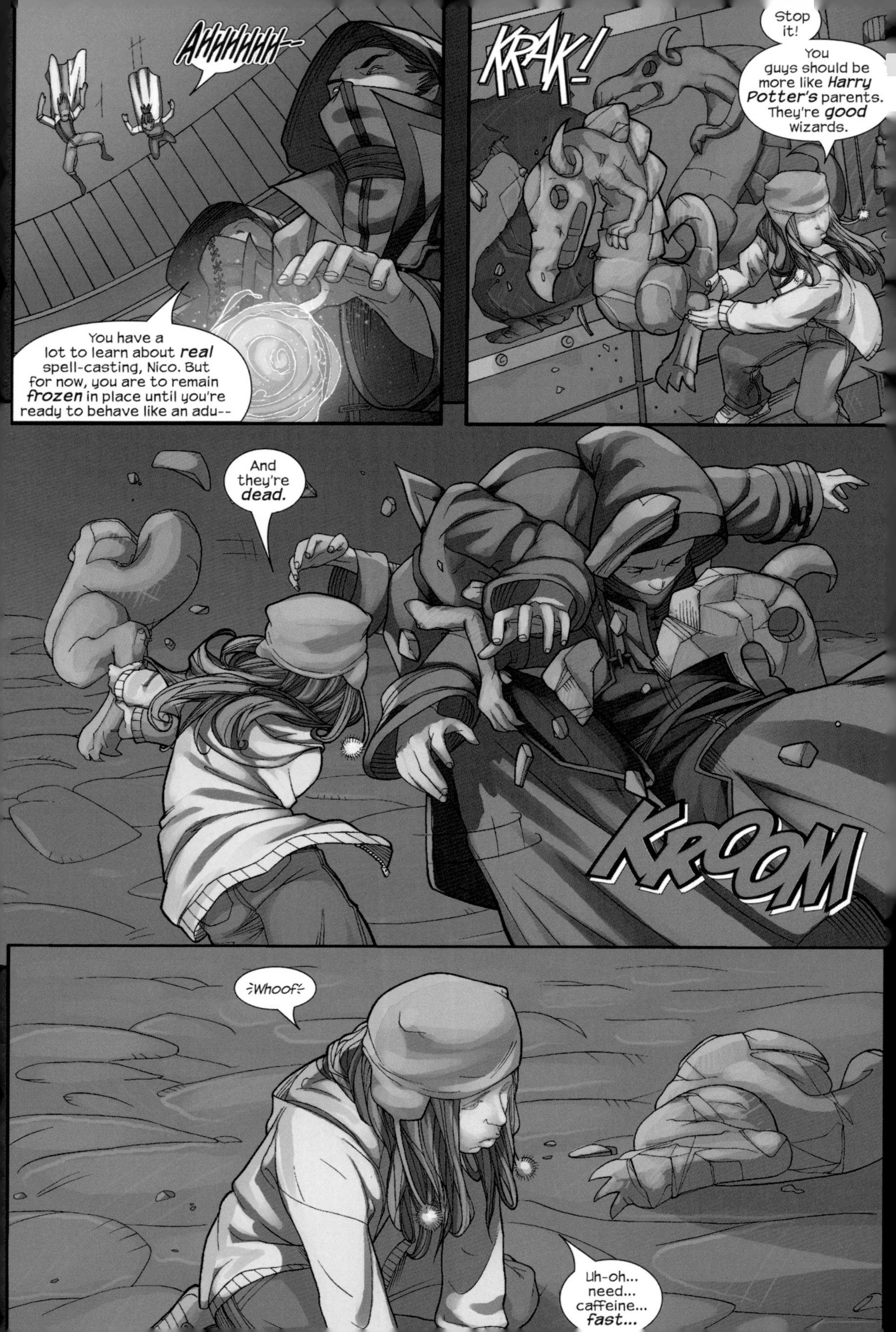
AHHHHHH--
You have a lot to learn about *real* spell-casting, Nico. But for now, you are to remain *frozen* in place until you're ready to behave like an adu--
KRAK!
Stop it!
You guys should be more like *Harry Potter's* parents. They're *good* wizards.
And they're *dead.*
KROOM
Whoof
Uh-oh... need... caffeine... *fast...*

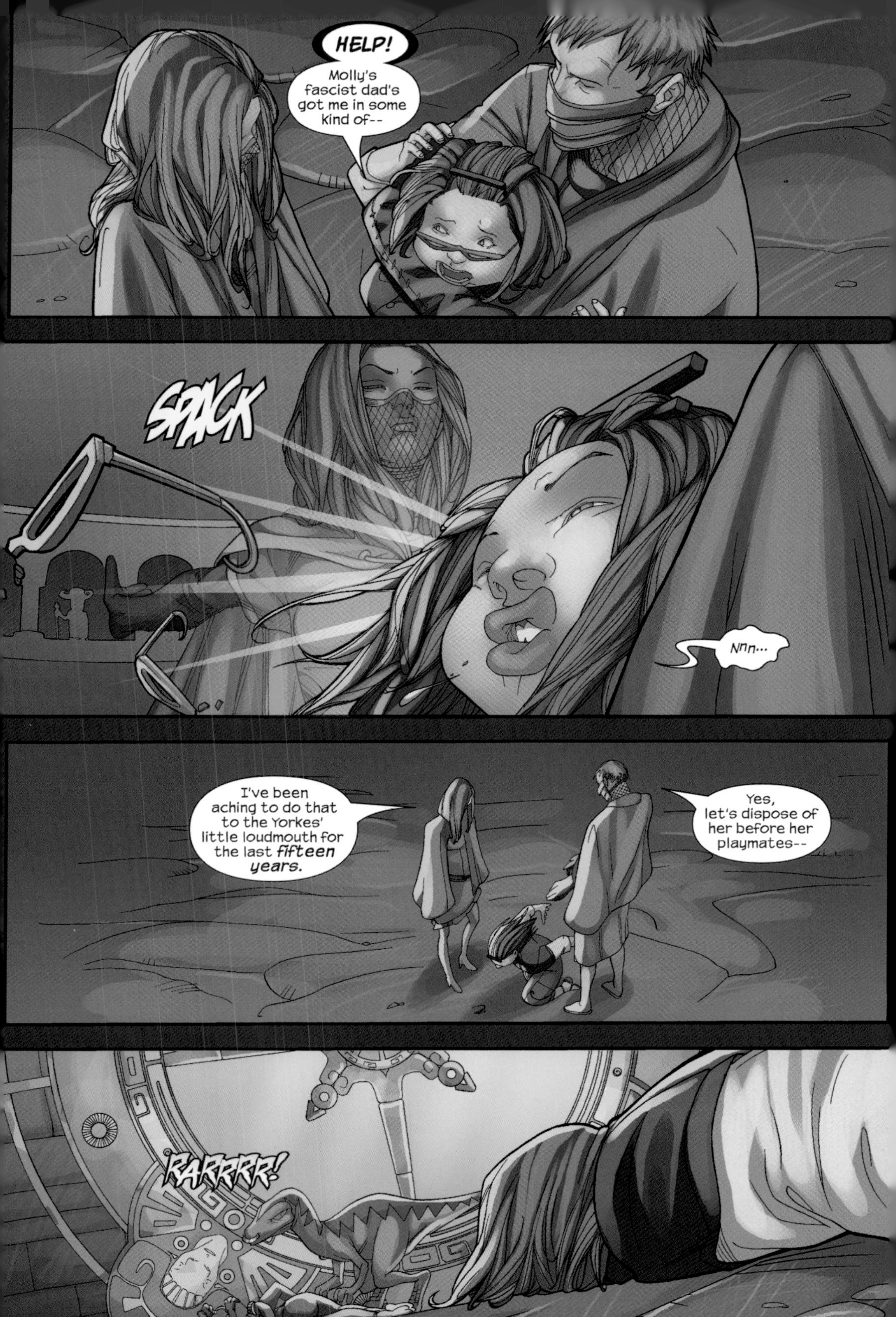
HELP!
Molly's fascist dad's got me in some kind of--
SPACK
Nnn...
I've been aching to do that to the Yorkes' little loudmouth for the last fifteen years.
Yes, let's dispose of her before her playmates--
RARRRR!

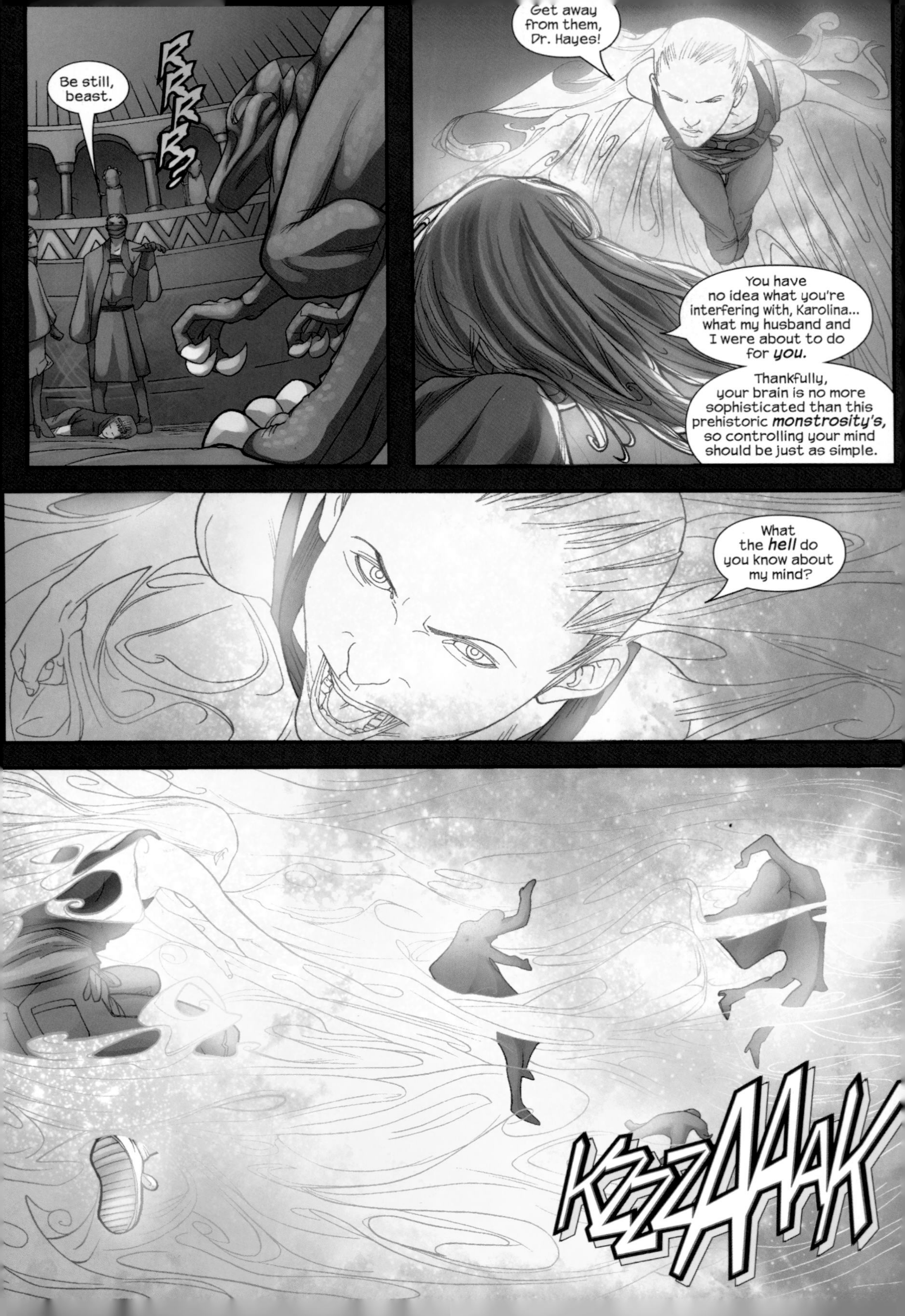

RRRRR
Be still, beast.
Get away from them, Dr. Hayes!
You have no idea what you're interfering with, Karolina... what my husband and I were about to do for *you.*
Thankfully, your brain is no more sophisticated than this prehistoric *monstrosity's,* so controlling your mind should be just as simple.
What the *hell* do you know about my mind?
KSZZAAAK

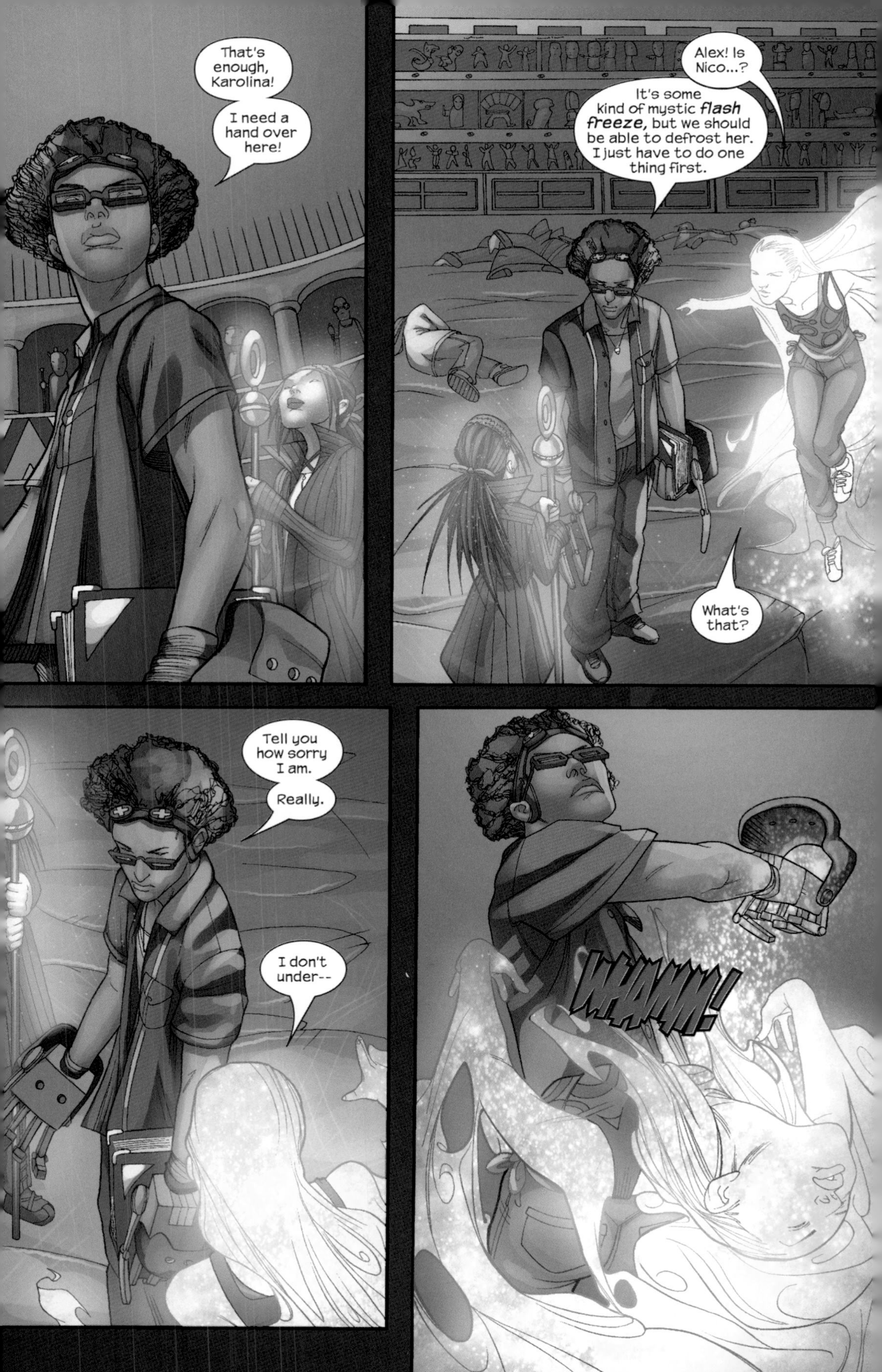

That's enough, Karolina!
I need a hand over here!
Alex! Is Nico...?
It's some kind of mystic *flash freeze,* but we should be able to defrost her. I just have to do one thing first.
What's that?
Tell you how sorry I am.
Really.
I don't under--
WHAMM!

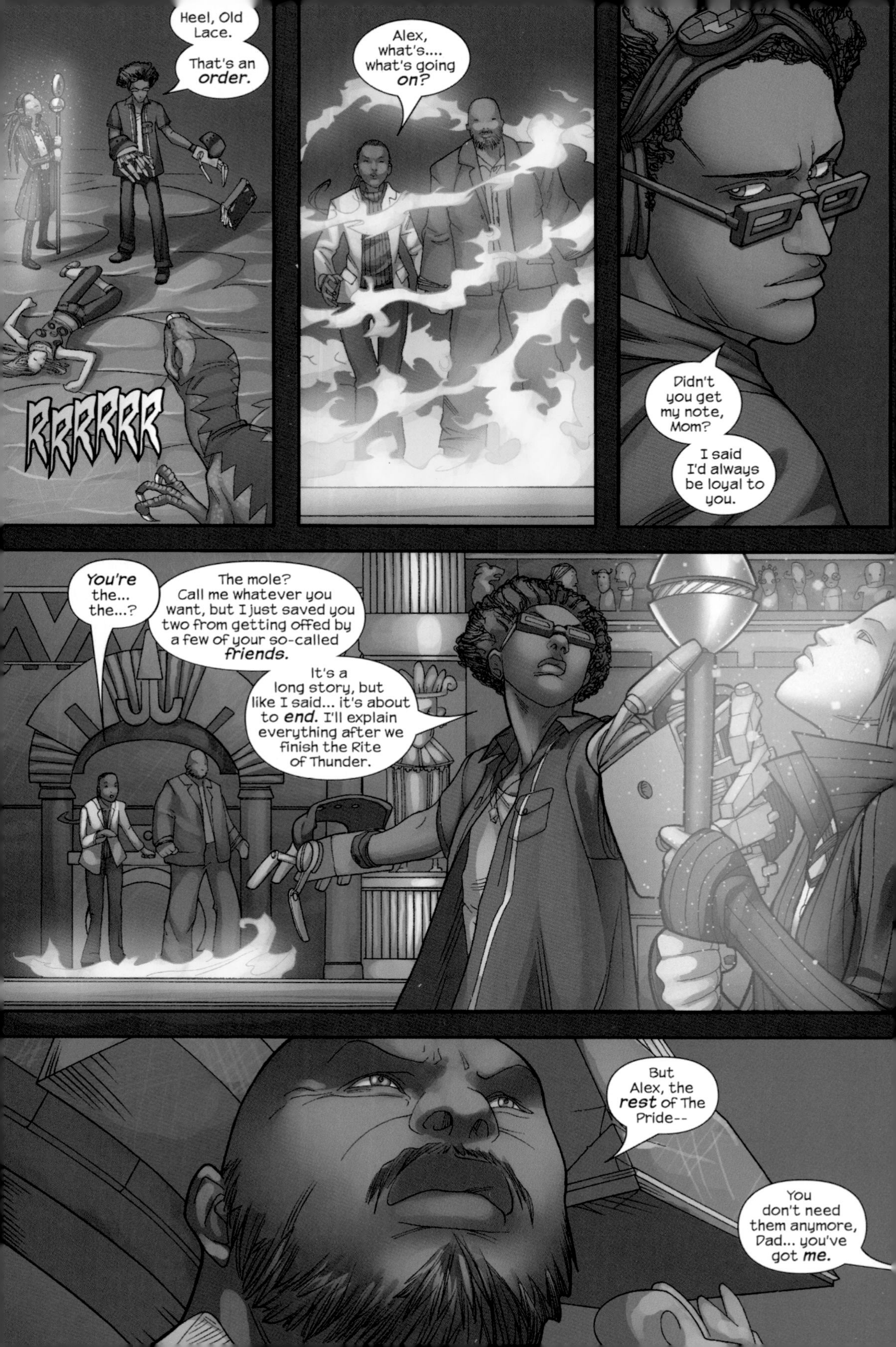
Heel, Old Lace.
That's an order.
RRRRRR
Alex, what's.... what's going on?
Didn't you get my note, Mom?
I said I'd always be loyal to you.
You're the... the...?
The mole? Call me whatever you want, but I just saved you two from getting offed by a few of your so-called friends.
It's a long story, but like I said... it's about to end. I'll explain everything after we finish the Rite of Thunder.
But Alex, the rest of The Pride--
You don't need them anymore, Dad... you've got me.

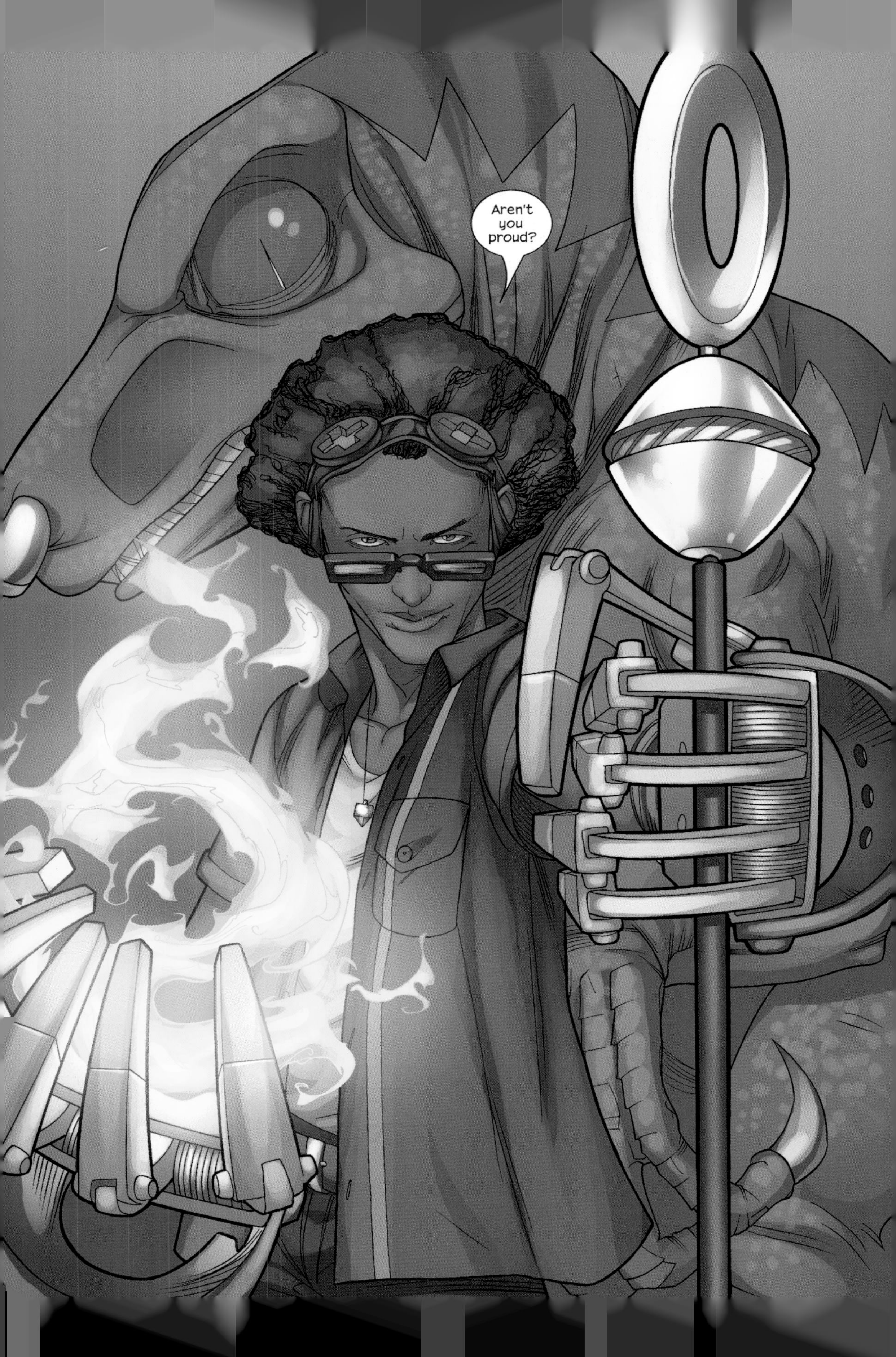
Aren't you proud?

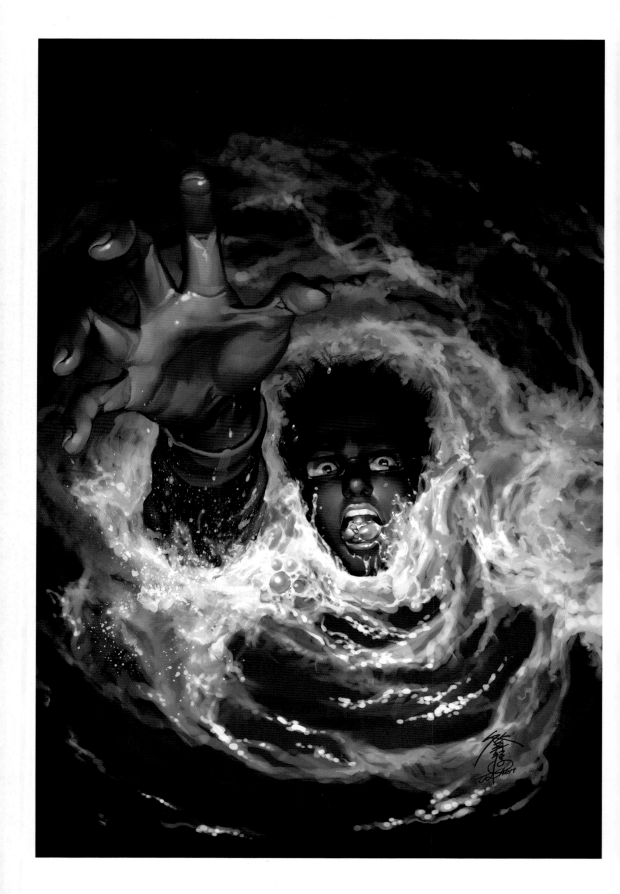

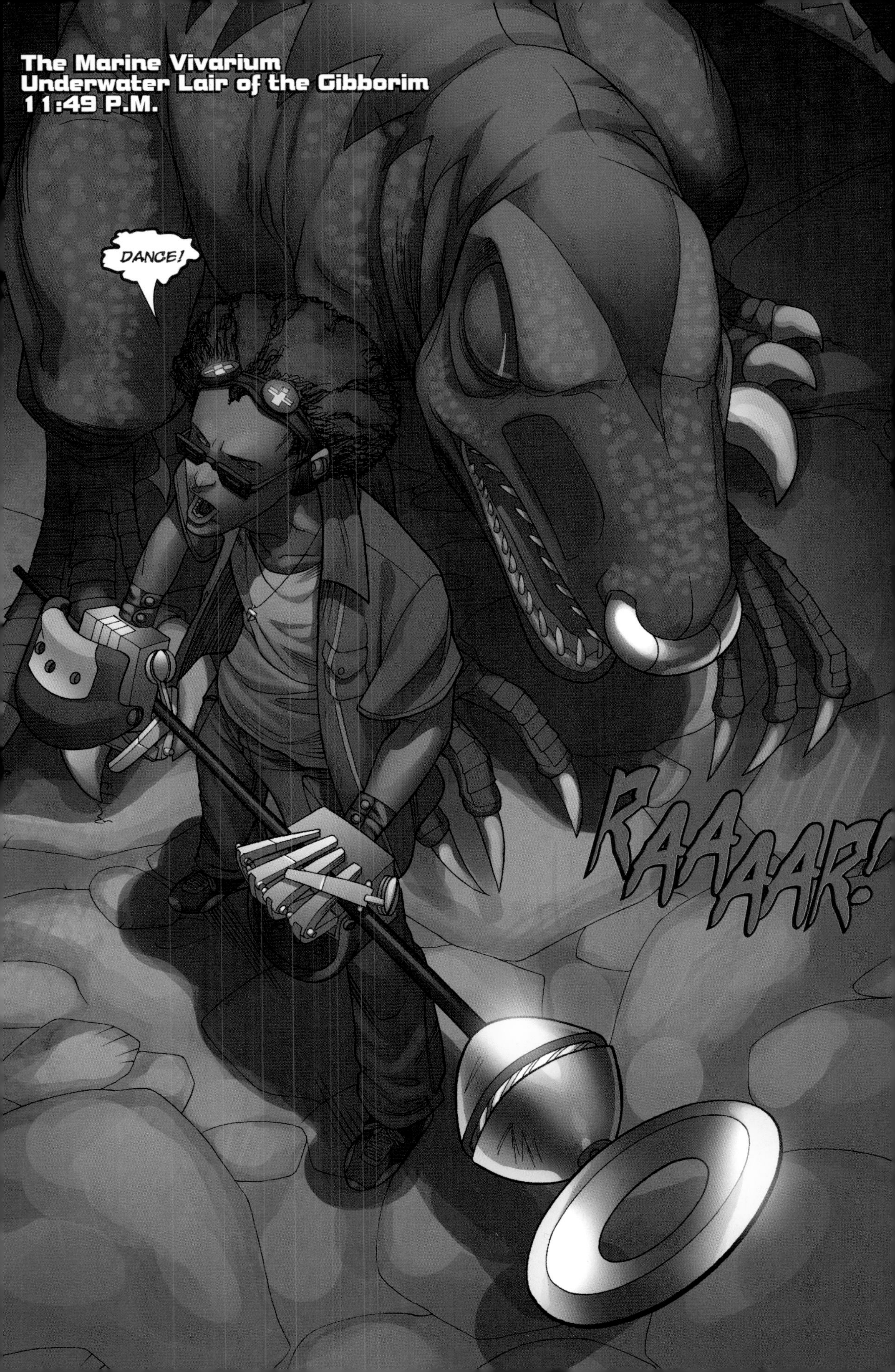
The Marine Vivarium
Underwater Lair of the Gibborim
11:49 P.M.
DANCE!
RAAAAAR!

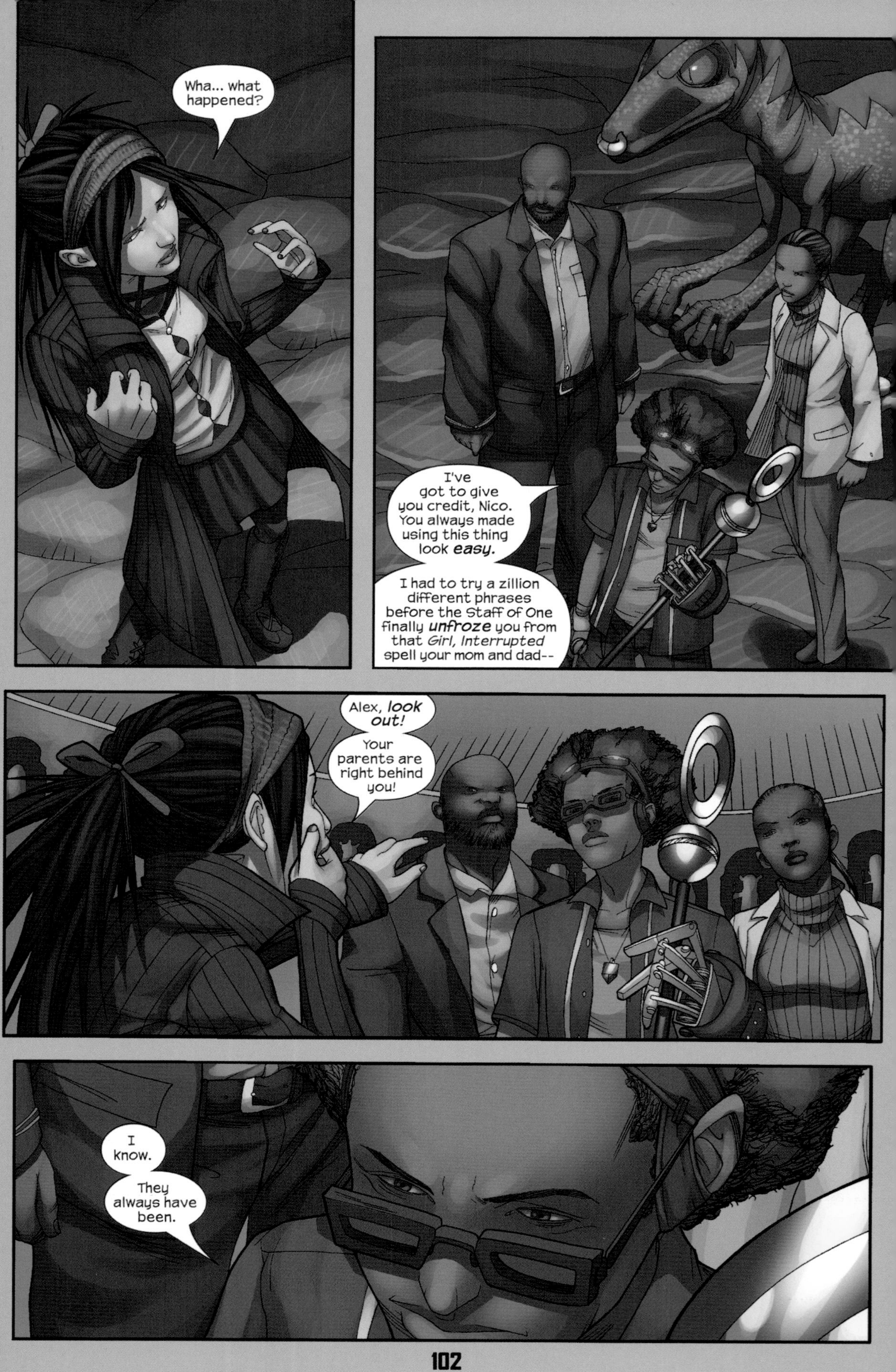
Wha... what happened?
I've got to give you credit, Nico. You always made using this thing look *easy*.
I had to try a zillion different phrases before the Staff of One finally *unfroze* you from that *Girl, Interrupted* spell your mom and dad--
Alex, *look out!*
Your parents are right behind you!
I know.
They always have been.

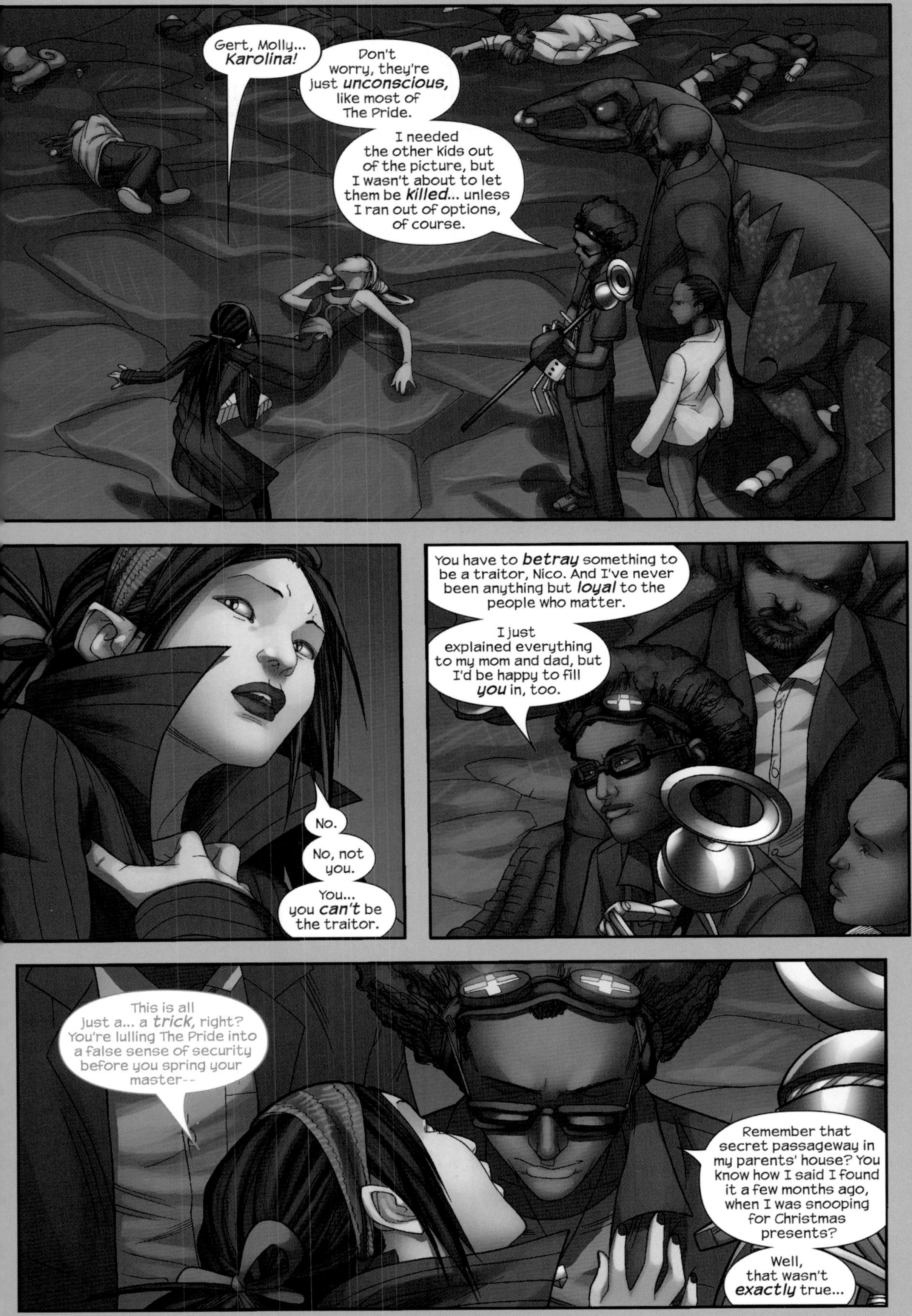
Gert, Molly... Karolina!
Don't worry, they're just unconscious, like most of The Pride.
I needed the other kids out of the picture, but I wasn't about to let them be killed... unless I ran out of options, of course.
No.
No, not you.
You... you can't be the traitor.
You have to betray something to be a traitor, Nico. And I've never been anything but loyal to the people who matter.
I just explained everything to my mom and dad, but I'd be happy to fill you in, too.
This is all just a... a trick, right? You're lulling The Pride into a false sense of security before you spring your master--
Remember that secret passageway in my parents' house? You know how I said I found it a few months ago, when I was snooping for Christmas presents?
Well, that wasn't exactly true...

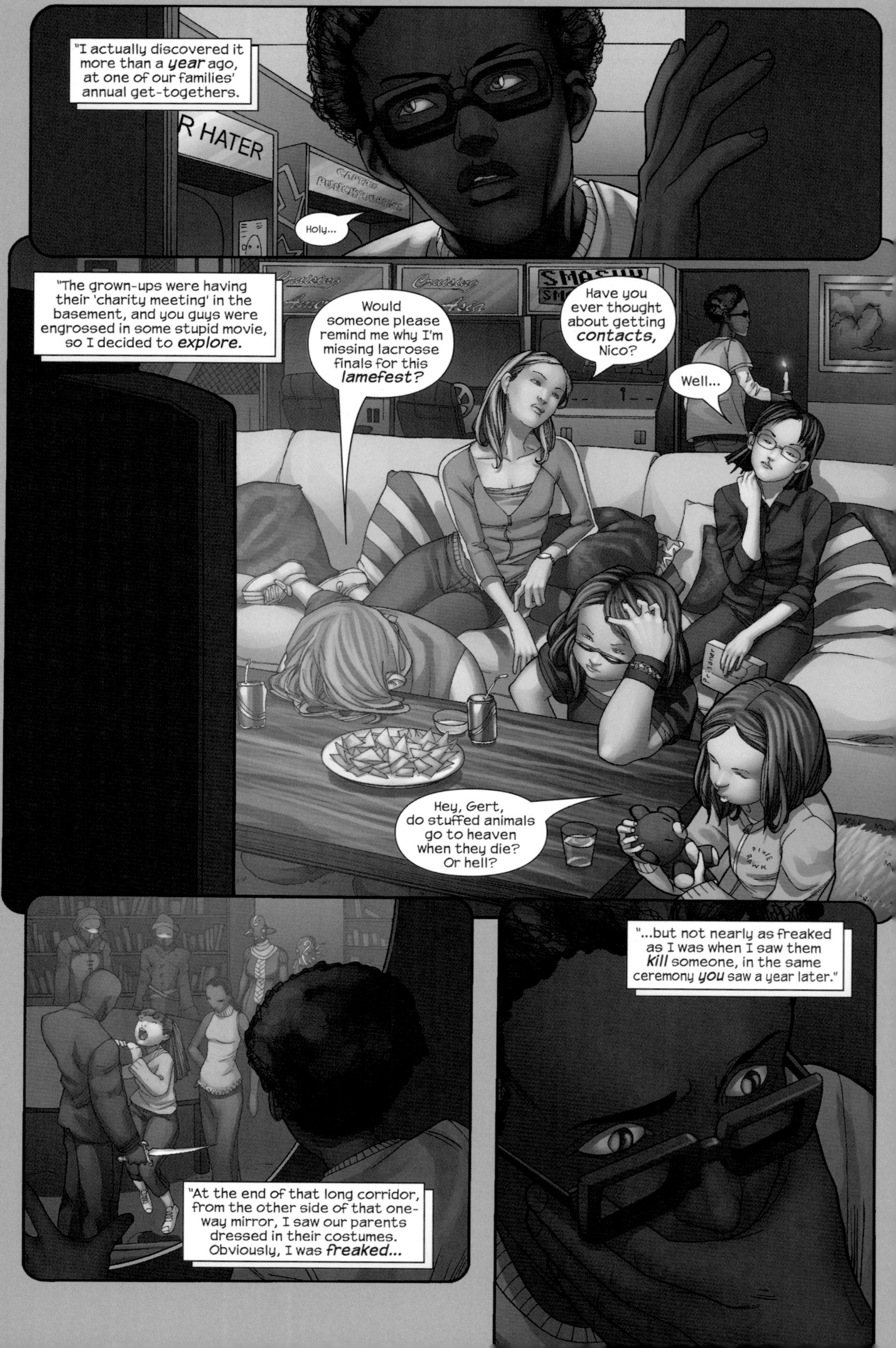
"I actually discovered it more than a year ago, at one of our families' annual get-togethers.
R HATER
Holy...
"The grown-ups were having their 'charity meeting' in the basement, and you guys were engrossed in some stupid movie, so I decided to explore.
Would someone please remind me why I'm missing lacrosse finals for this lamefest?
Have you ever thought about getting contacts, Nico?
Well...
Hey, Gert, do stuffed animals go to heaven when they die? Or hell?
"At the end of that long corridor, from the other side of that one-way mirror, I saw our parents dressed in their costumes. Obviously, I was freaked...
"...but not nearly as freaked as I was when I saw them kill someone, in the same ceremony you saw a year later."

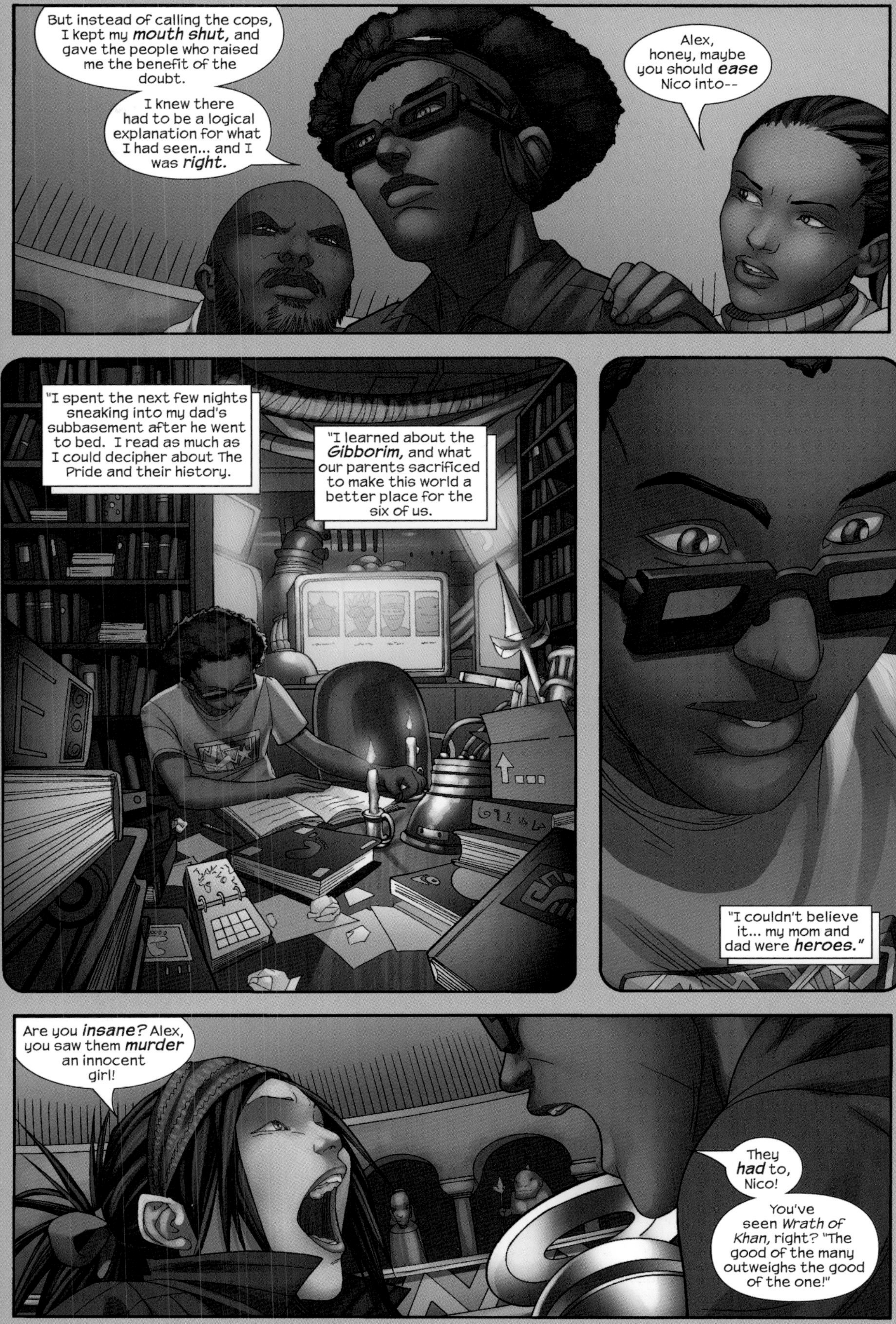
But instead of calling the cops, I kept my ***mouth shut,*** and gave the people who raised me the benefit of the doubt.
I knew there had to be a logical explanation for what I had seen... and I was ***right.***
Alex, honey, maybe you should ***ease*** Nico into--
"I spent the next few nights sneaking into my dad's subbasement after he went to bed. I read as much as I could decipher about The Pride and their history.
"I learned about the ***Gibborim,*** and what our parents sacrificed to make this world a better place for the six of us.
"I couldn't believe it... my mom and dad were ***heroes."***
Are you ***insane?*** Alex, you saw them ***murder*** an innocent girl!
They ***had*** to, Nico!
You've seen *Wrath of Khan,* right? "The good of the many outweighs the good of the one!"

"Anyway, I discovered pretty quickly that not *everyone* in The Pride was as noble as *my* parents..."

You're *certain* the Wilders are asleep?

They won't be if you keep *yammering*, woman.

I'm still not sure I completely understand what we're--

Dr. Hayes, for the last time, the copy of the Abstract that the Gibborim gave each of us details the past *and* future of The Pride.

The mere act of *thinking* the plan we just conceived means that it will now be in the book. We have to destroy those pages before the others read them.

But Mr. Dean, if the Abstract can chronicle what hasn't even happened yet, wouldn't our future misdeeds have been in there from the very *beginning*?

It's magic, mutant.

If you think about it too hard, your *brain* will explode.

Hurry up with that *decoder ring*. We still have to find and alter three more tomes before the night is through.

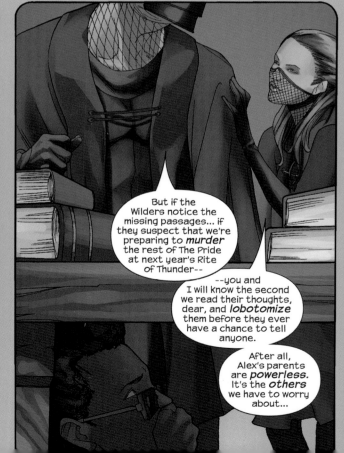

But if the Wilders notice the missing passages... if they suspect that we're preparing to *murder* the rest of The Pride at next year's Rite of Thunder--

--you and I will know the second we read their thoughts, dear, and *lobotomize* them before they ever have a chance to tell anyone.

After all, Alex's parents are *powerless*. It's the *others* we have to worry about...

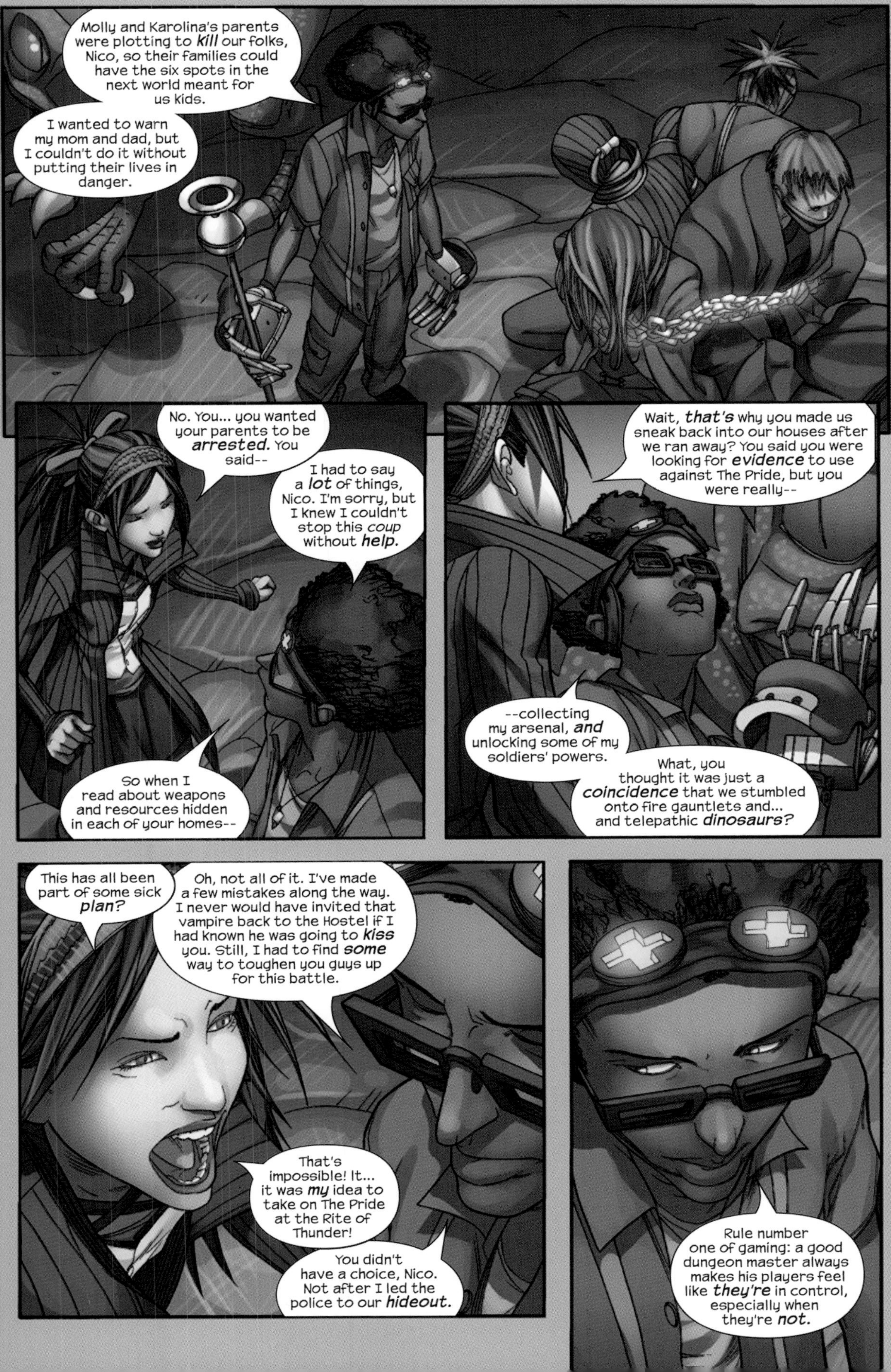
Molly and Karolina's parents were plotting to *kill* our folks, Nico, so their families could have the six spots in the next world meant for us kids.
I wanted to warn my mom and dad, but I couldn't do it without putting their lives in danger.
No. You... you wanted your parents to be *arrested.* You said--
I had to say a *lot* of things, Nico. I'm sorry, but I knew I couldn't stop this *coup* without *help.*
So when I read about weapons and resources hidden in each of your homes--
Wait, *that's* why you made us sneak back into our houses after we ran away? You said you were looking for *evidence* to use against The Pride, but you were really--
--collecting my arsenal, *and* unlocking some of my soldiers' powers.
What, you thought it was just a *coincidence* that we stumbled onto fire gauntlets and... and telepathic *dinosaurs?*
This has all been part of some sick *plan?*
Oh, not all of it. I've made a few mistakes along the way. I never would have invited that vampire back to the Hostel if I had known he was going to *kiss* you. Still, I had to find *some* way to toughen you guys up for this battle.
That's impossible! It... it was *my* idea to take on The Pride at the Rite of Thunder!
You didn't have a choice, Nico. Not after I led the police to our *hideout.*
Rule number one of gaming: a good dungeon master always makes his players feel like *they're* in control, especially when they're *not.*

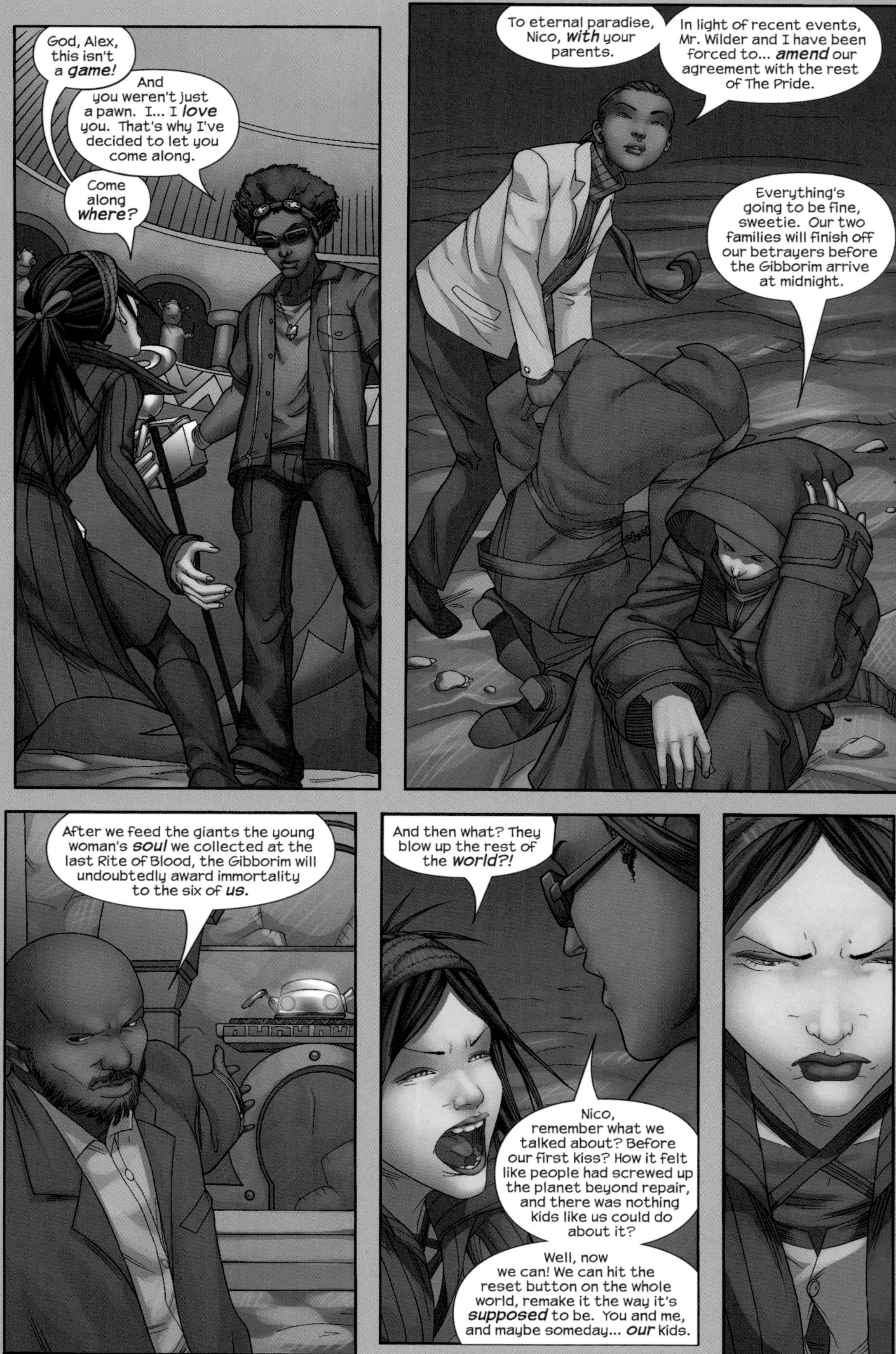
God, Alex, this isn't a *game!*
And you weren't just a pawn. I... I *love* you. That's why I've decided to let you come along.
Come along *where?*
To eternal paradise, Nico, *with* your parents.
In light of recent events, Mr. Wilder and I have been forced to... *amend* our agreement with the rest of The Pride.
Everything's going to be fine, sweetie. Our two families will finish off our betrayers before the Gibborim arrive at midnight.
After we feed the giants the young woman's *soul* we collected at the last Rite of Blood, the Gibborim will undoubtedly award immortality to the six of *us.*
And then what? They blow up the rest of the *world?!*
Nico, remember what we talked about? Before our first kiss? How it felt like people had screwed up the planet beyond repair, and there was nothing kids like us could do about it?
Well, now we can! We can hit the reset button on the whole world, remake it the way it's *supposed* to be. You and me, and maybe someday... *our* kids.

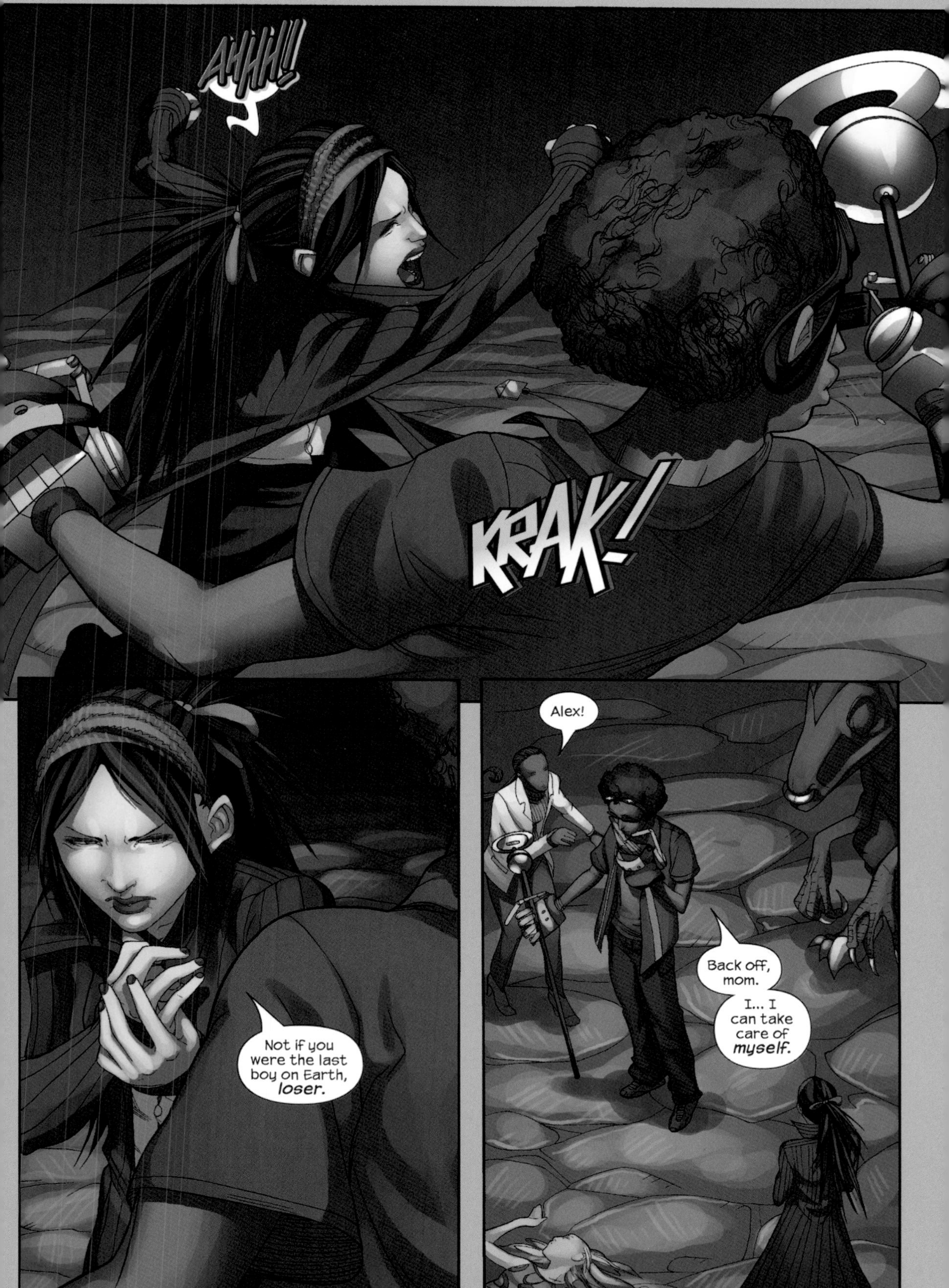
AHHH!!
KRAK!
Not if you were the last boy on Earth, *loser*.
Alex!
Back off, mom.
I... I can take care of *myself*.

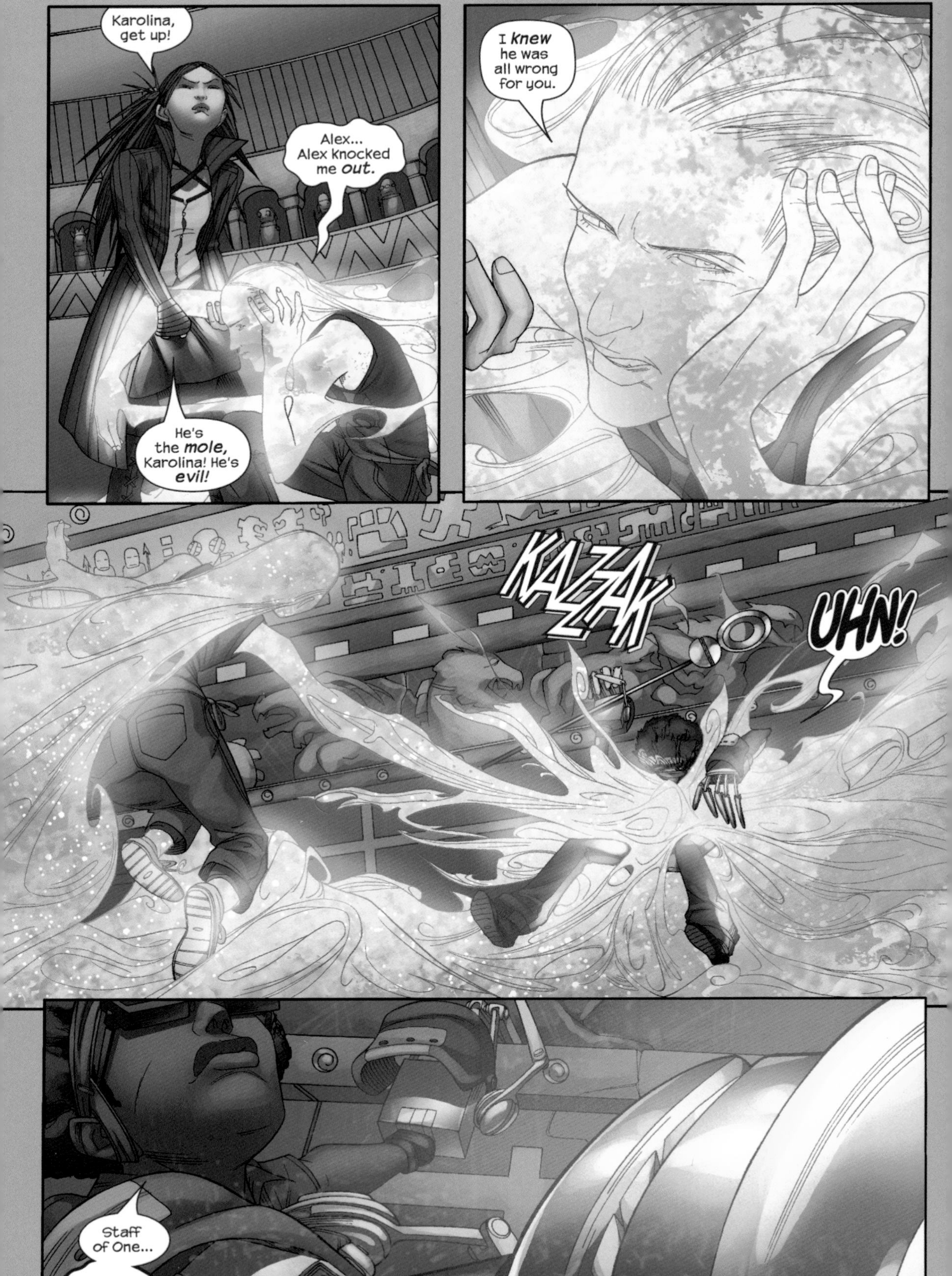
Karolina, get up!
Alex... Alex knocked me *out.*
He's the *mole,* Karolina! He's *evil!*
I *knew* he was all wrong for you.
KAZZAK
UHN!
Staff of One...
BONDAGE.

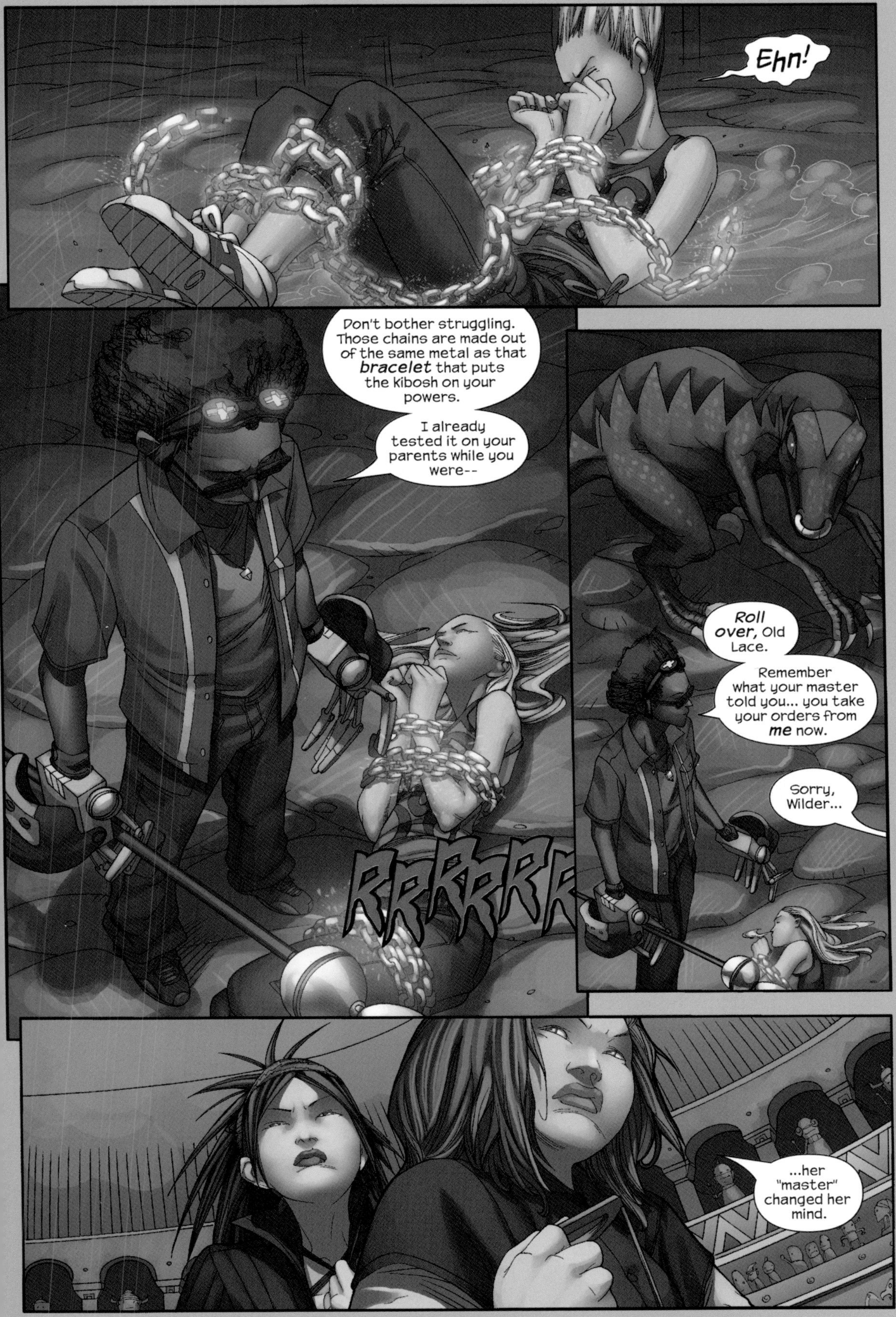
Ehn!
Don't bother struggling. Those chains are made out of the same metal as that bracelet that puts the kibosh on your powers.
I already tested it on your parents while you were--
RRRRRR
Roll over, Old Lace.
Remember what your master told you... you take your orders from me now.
Sorry, Wilder...
...her "master" changed her mind.

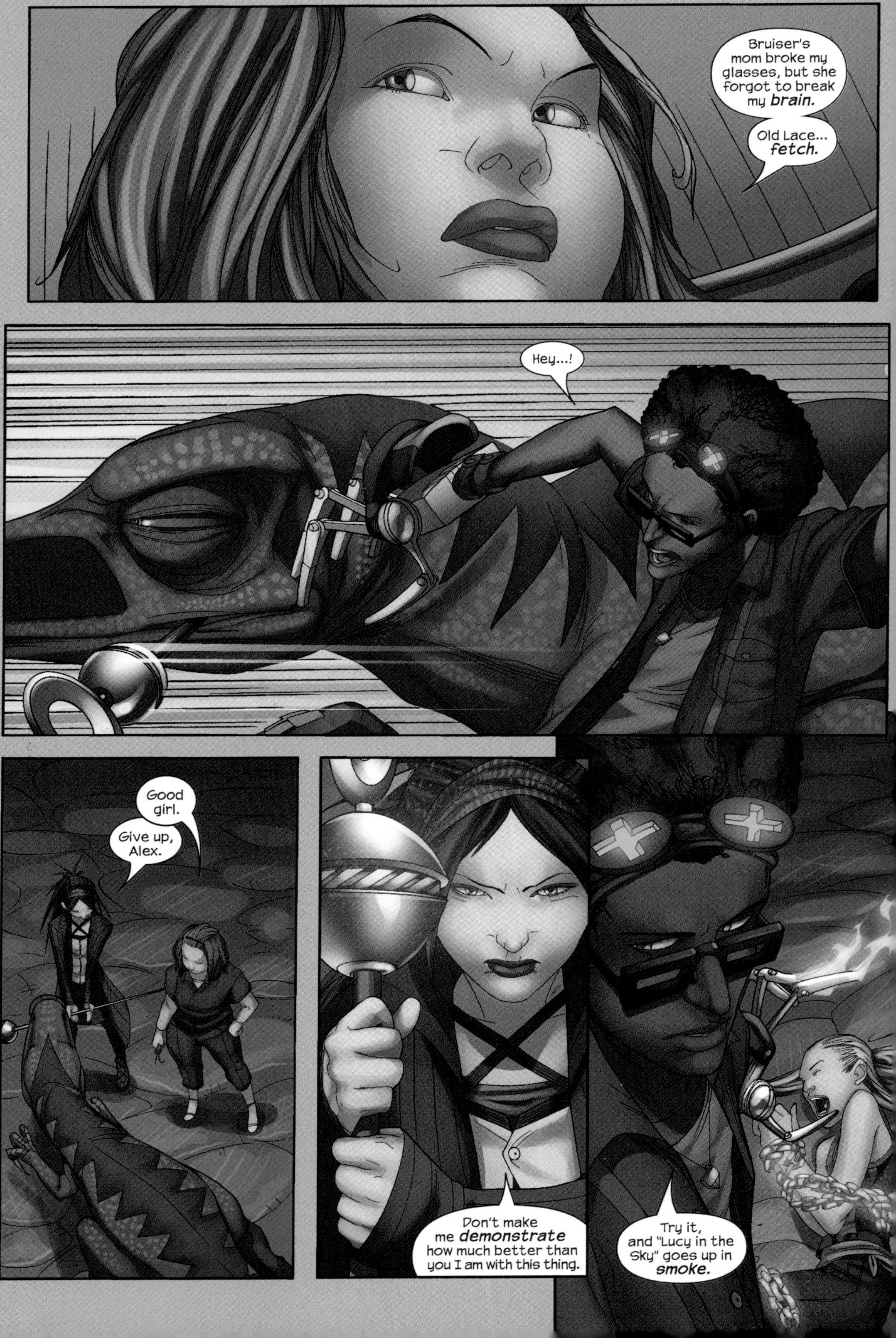
Bruiser's mom broke my glasses, but she forgot to break my *brain.*
Old Lace... *fetch.*
Hey...!
Good girl.
Give up, Alex.
Don't make me *demonstrate* how much better than you I am with this thing.
Try it, and "Lucy in the Sky" goes up in *smoke.*

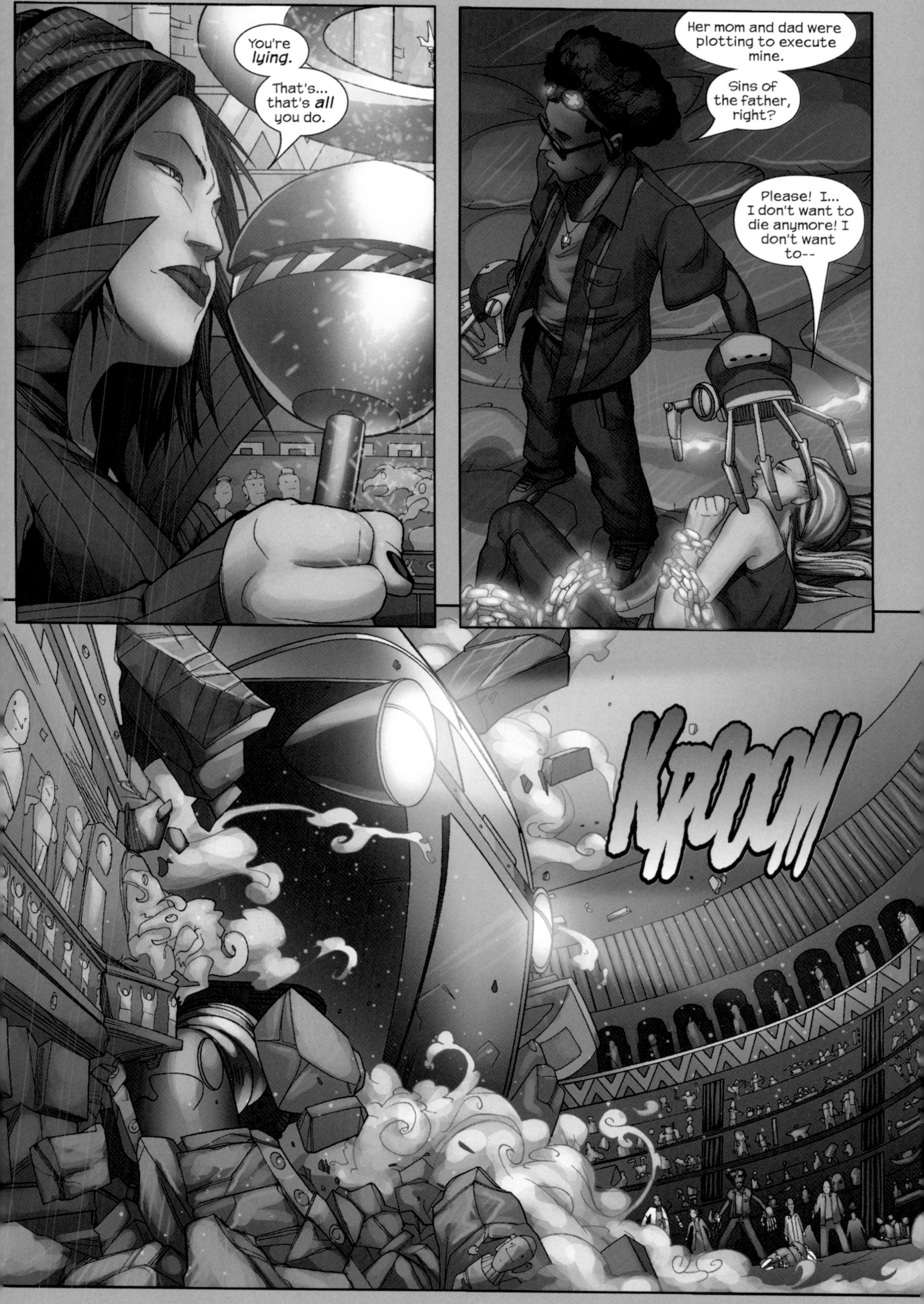
You're *lying.*
That's... that's *all* you do.
Her mom and dad were plotting to execute mine.
Sins of the father, right?
Please! I... I don't want to die anymore! I don't want to--
KROOOM

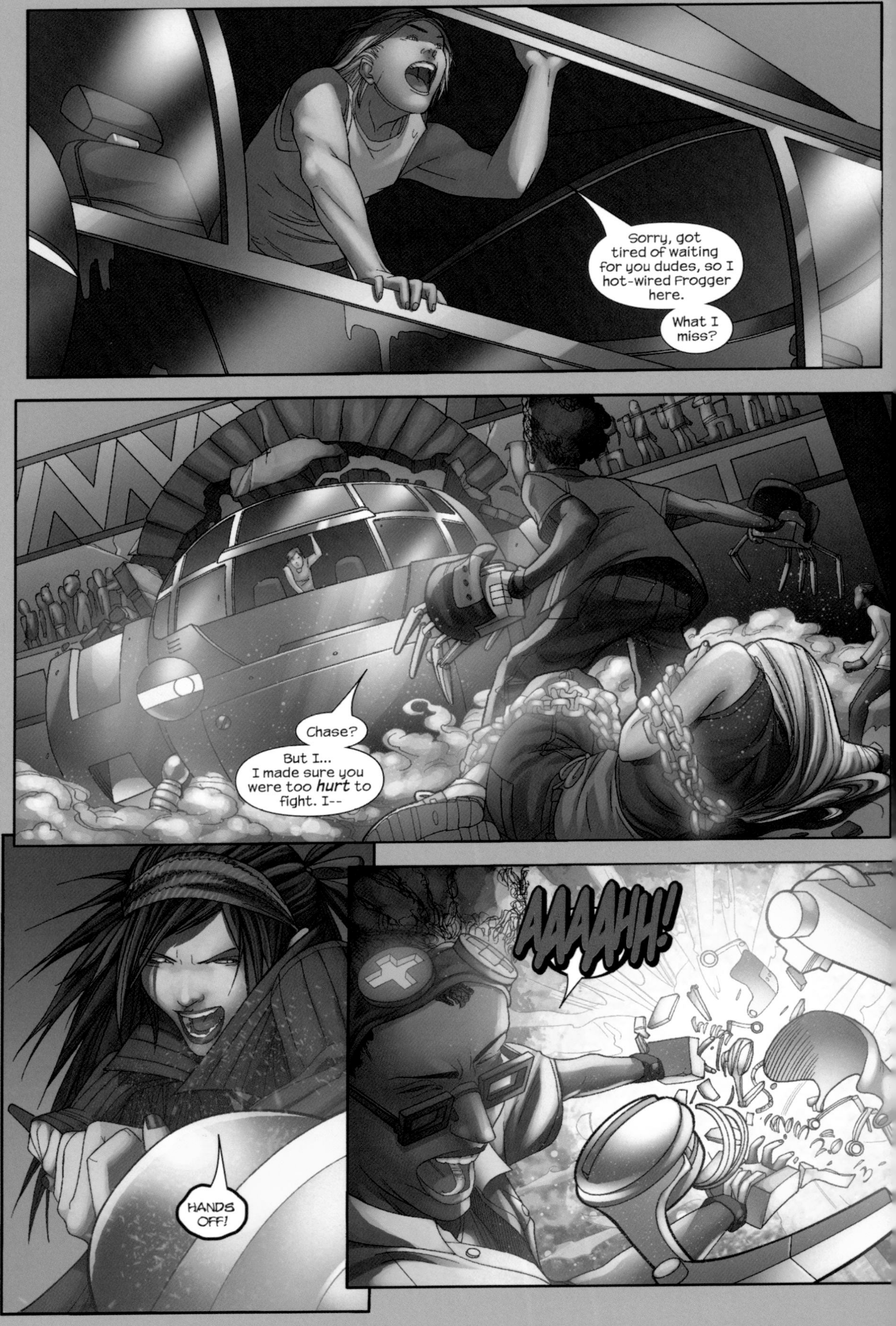
Sorry, got tired of waiting for you dudes, so I hot-wired Frogger here.
What I miss?
Chase?
But I... I made sure you were too *hurt* to fight. I--
HANDS OFF!
AAAAHH!

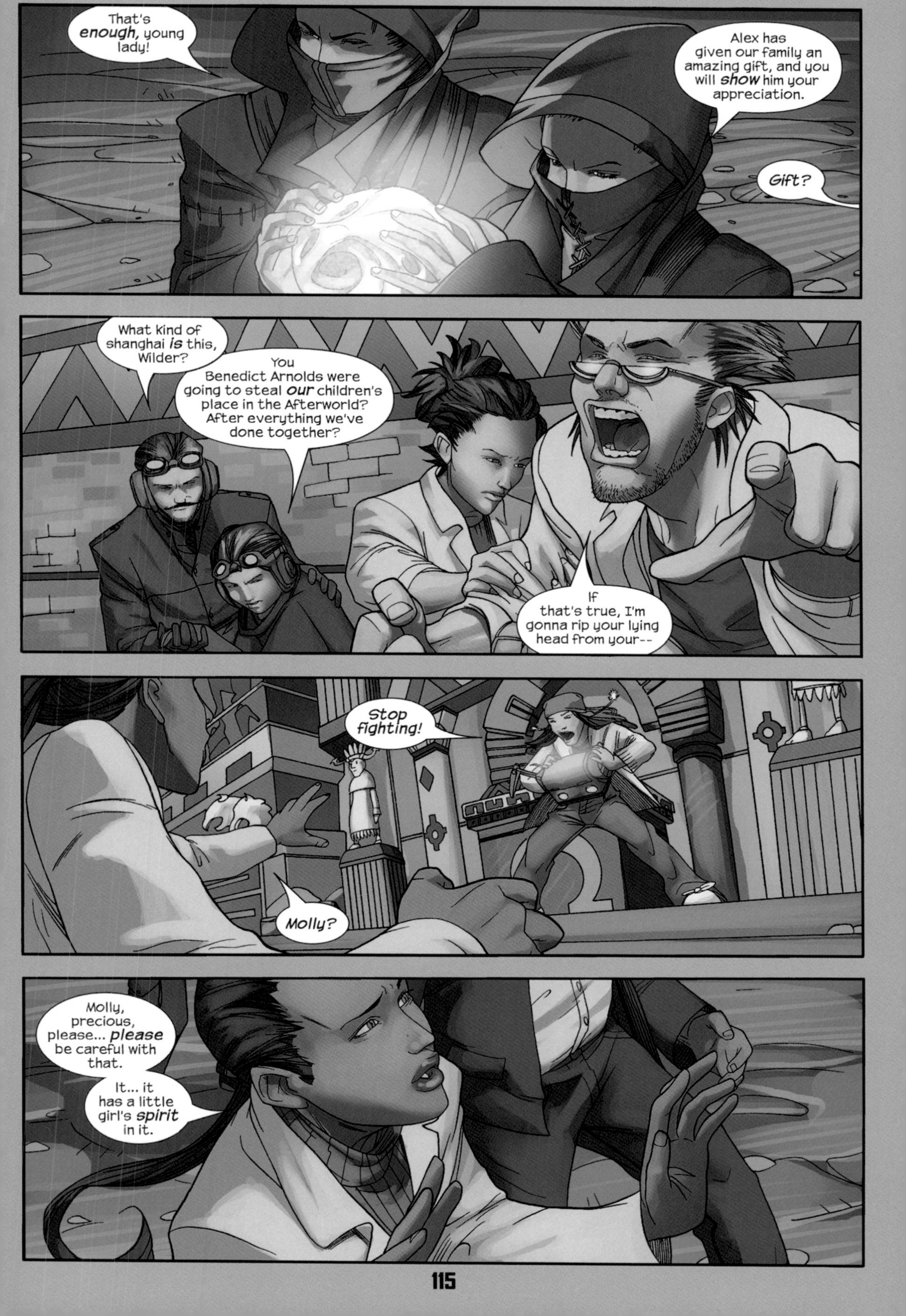

That's *enough*, young lady!
Alex has given our family an amazing gift, and you will *show* him your appreciation.
Gift?
What kind of shanghai *is* this, Wilder?
You Benedict Arnolds were going to steal *our* children's place in the Afterworld? After everything we've done together?
If that's true, I'm gonna rip your lying head from your--
Stop fighting!
Molly?
Molly, precious, please... *please* be careful with that.
It... it has a little girl's *spirit* in it.

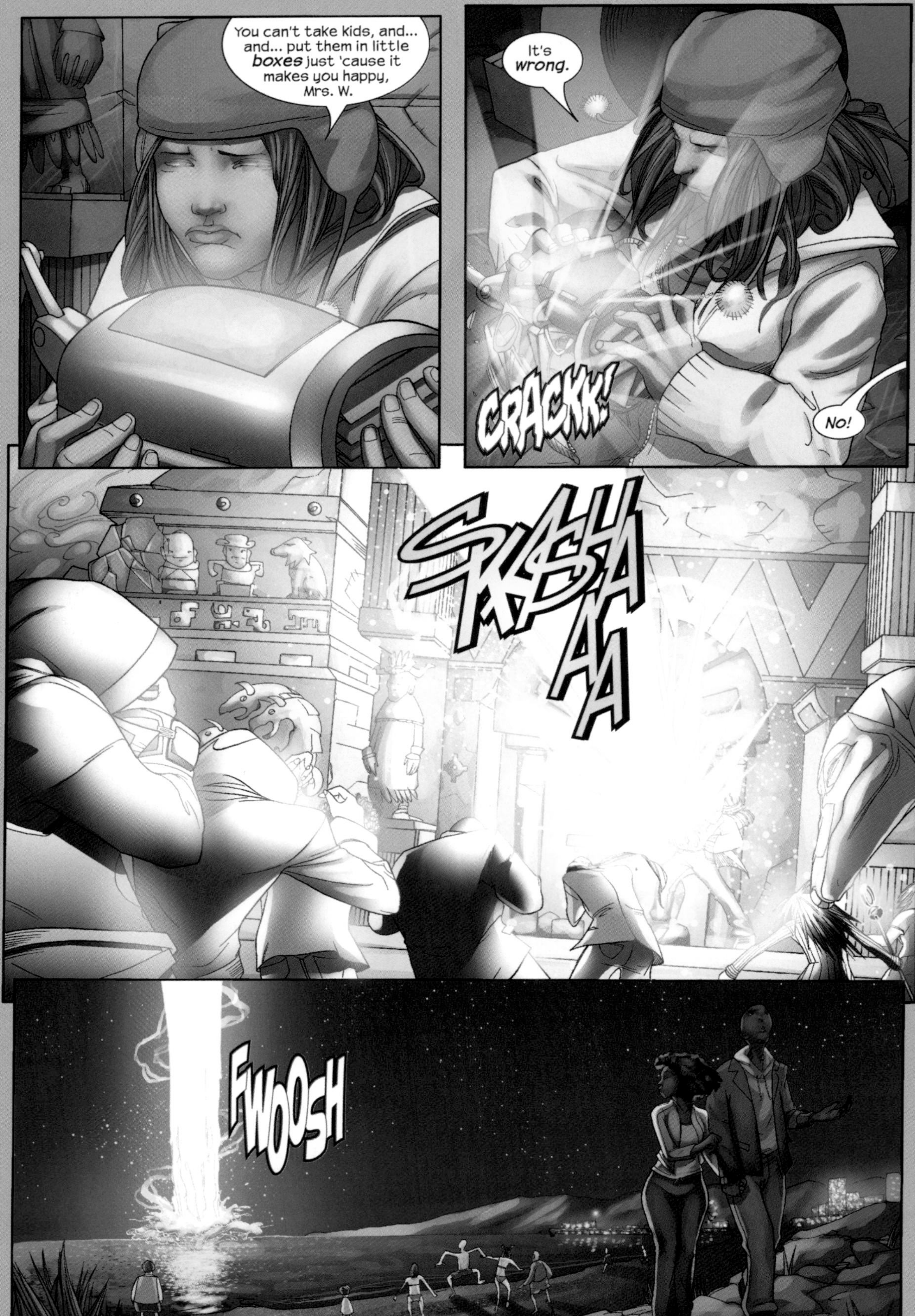
You can't take kids, and... and... put them in little *boxes* just 'cause it makes you happy, Mrs. W.
It's *wrong.*
CRACKK!
No!
SKRASHAAAA
FWOOSH

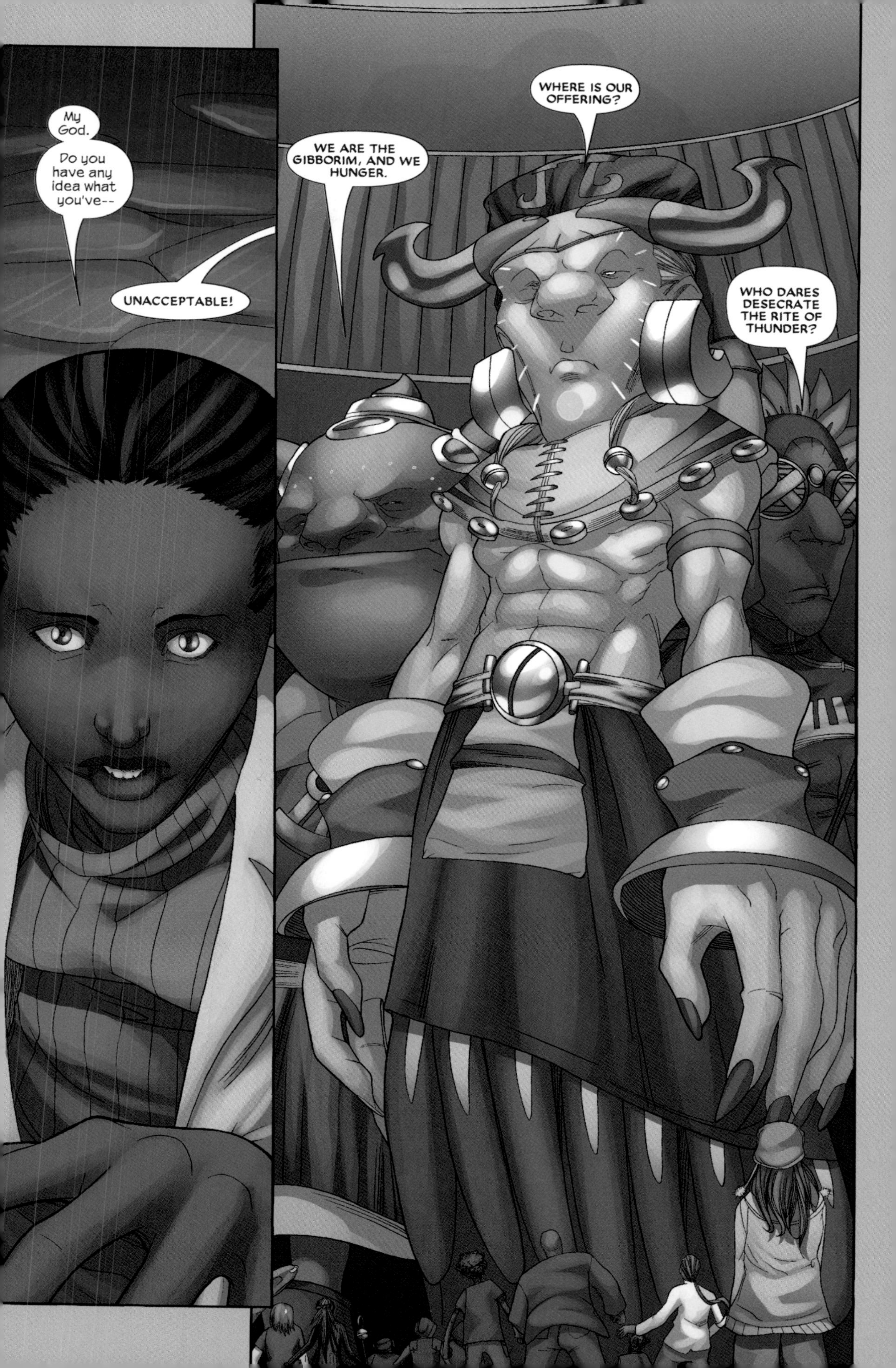

My God.
Do you have any idea what you've--
UNACCEPTABLE!
WE ARE THE GIBBORIM, AND WE HUNGER.
WHERE IS OUR OFFERING?
WHO DARES DESECRATE THE RITE OF THUNDER?

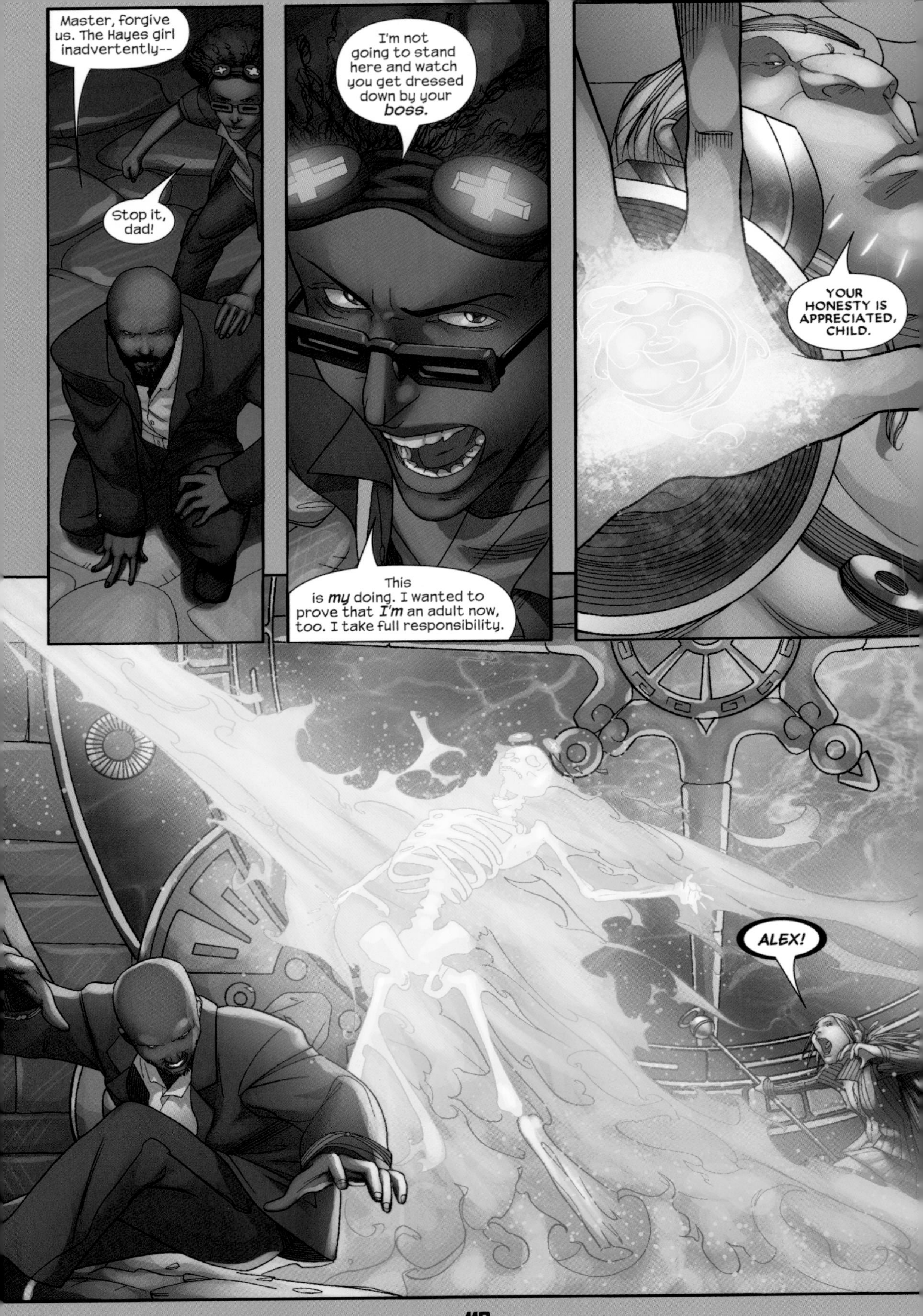
Master, forgive us. The Hayes girl inadvertently--
Stop it, dad!
I'm not going to stand here and watch you get dressed down by your boss.
This is my doing. I wanted to prove that I'm an adult now, too. I take full responsibility.
YOUR HONESTY IS APPRECIATED, CHILD.
ALEX!

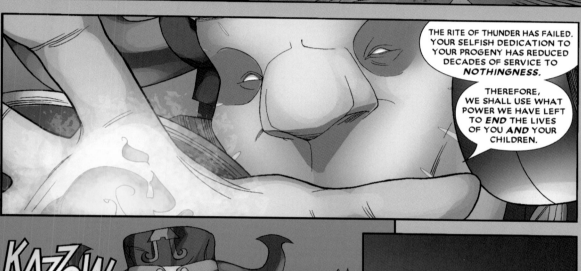

THE RITE OF THUNDER HAS FAILED. YOUR SELFISH DEDICATION TO YOUR PROGENY HAS REDUCED DECADES OF SERVICE TO *NOTHINGNESS*.

THEREFORE, WE SHALL USE WHAT POWER WE HAVE LEFT TO *END* THE LIVES OF YOU *AND* YOUR CHILDREN.

KAZZOW

AHHH!

Nico, get out of here! Your father and I will try to hold them off!

No! I won't let them butcher you! I don't care what you've done, I--

I am still your mother, and you will do as I *say!*

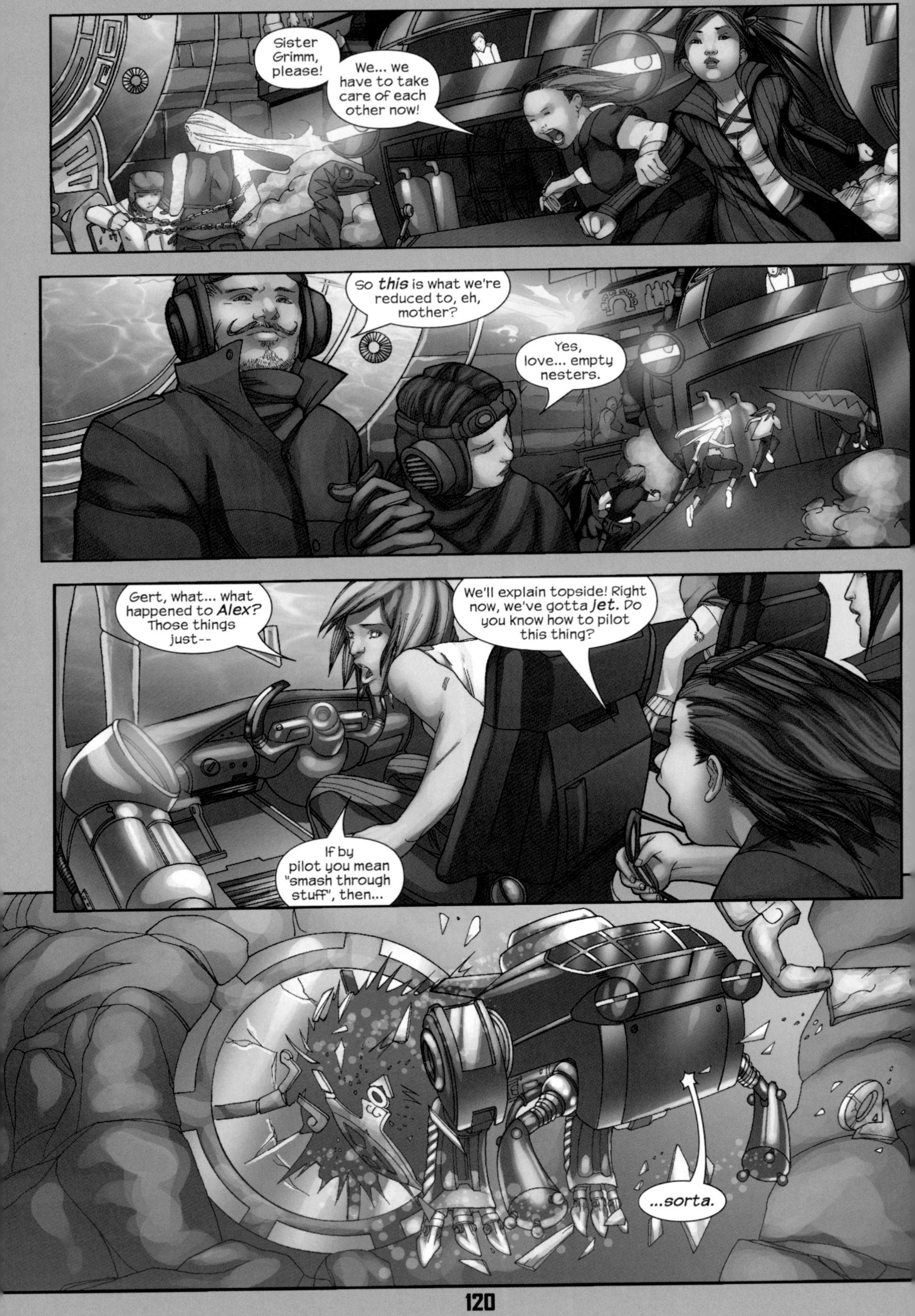
Sister Grimm, please!
We... we have to take care of each other now!
So *this* is what we're reduced to, eh, mother?
Yes, love... empty nesters.
Gert, what... what happened to *Alex?* Those things just--
We'll explain topside! Right now, we've gotta *jet.* Do you know how to pilot this thing?
If by pilot you mean "smash through stuff", then...
...sorta.

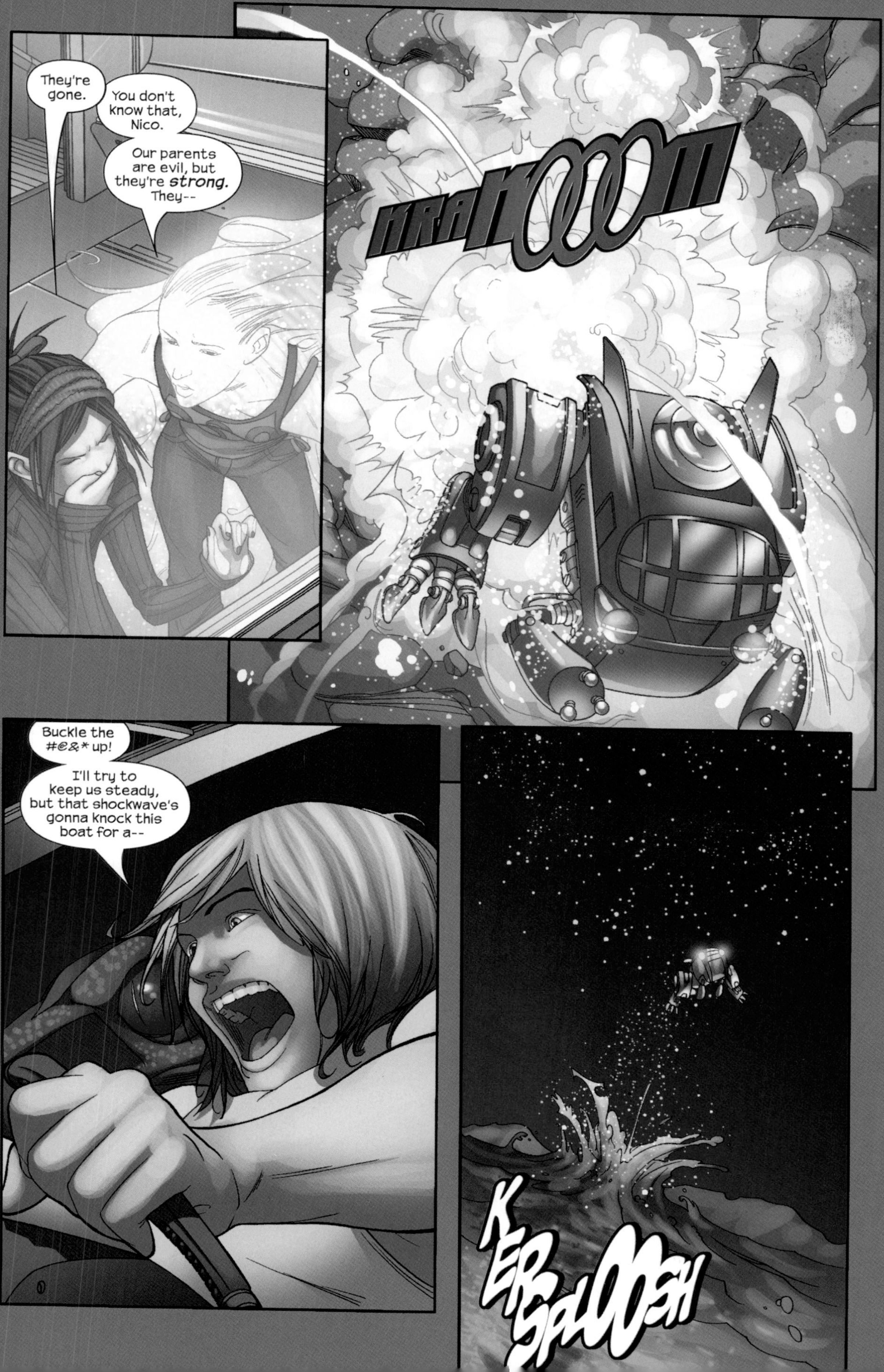
They're gone.
You don't know that, Nico.
Our parents are evil, but they're *strong.* They--
KRAKOOOM
Buckle the #@&* up!
I'll try to keep us steady, but that shockwave's gonna knock this boat for a--
KERSPLOOSH

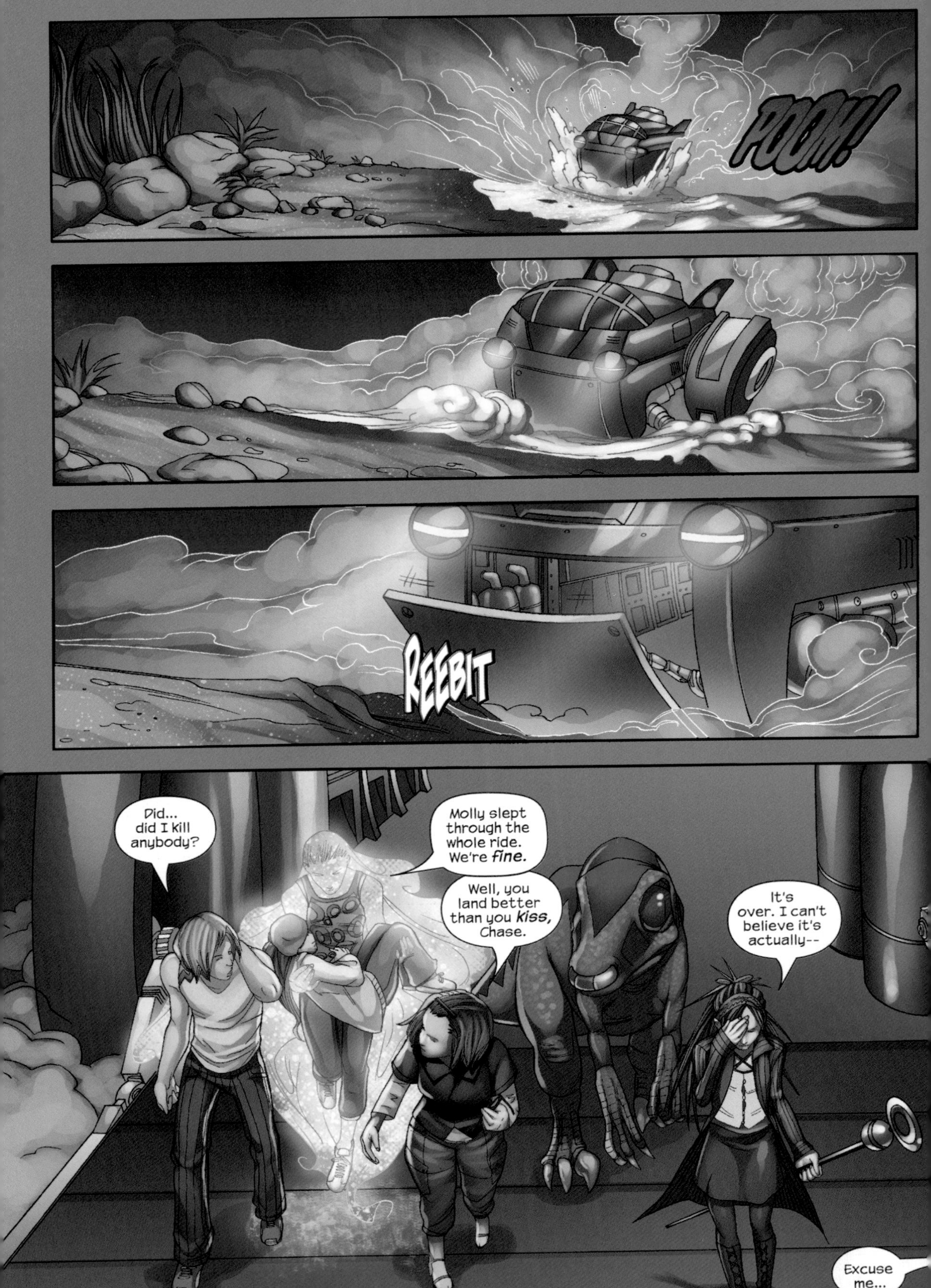
POOM!
REEBIT
Did... did I kill anybody?
Molly slept through the whole ride. We're *fine.*
Well, you land better than you *kiss,* Chase.
It's over. I can't believe it's actually--
Excuse me...

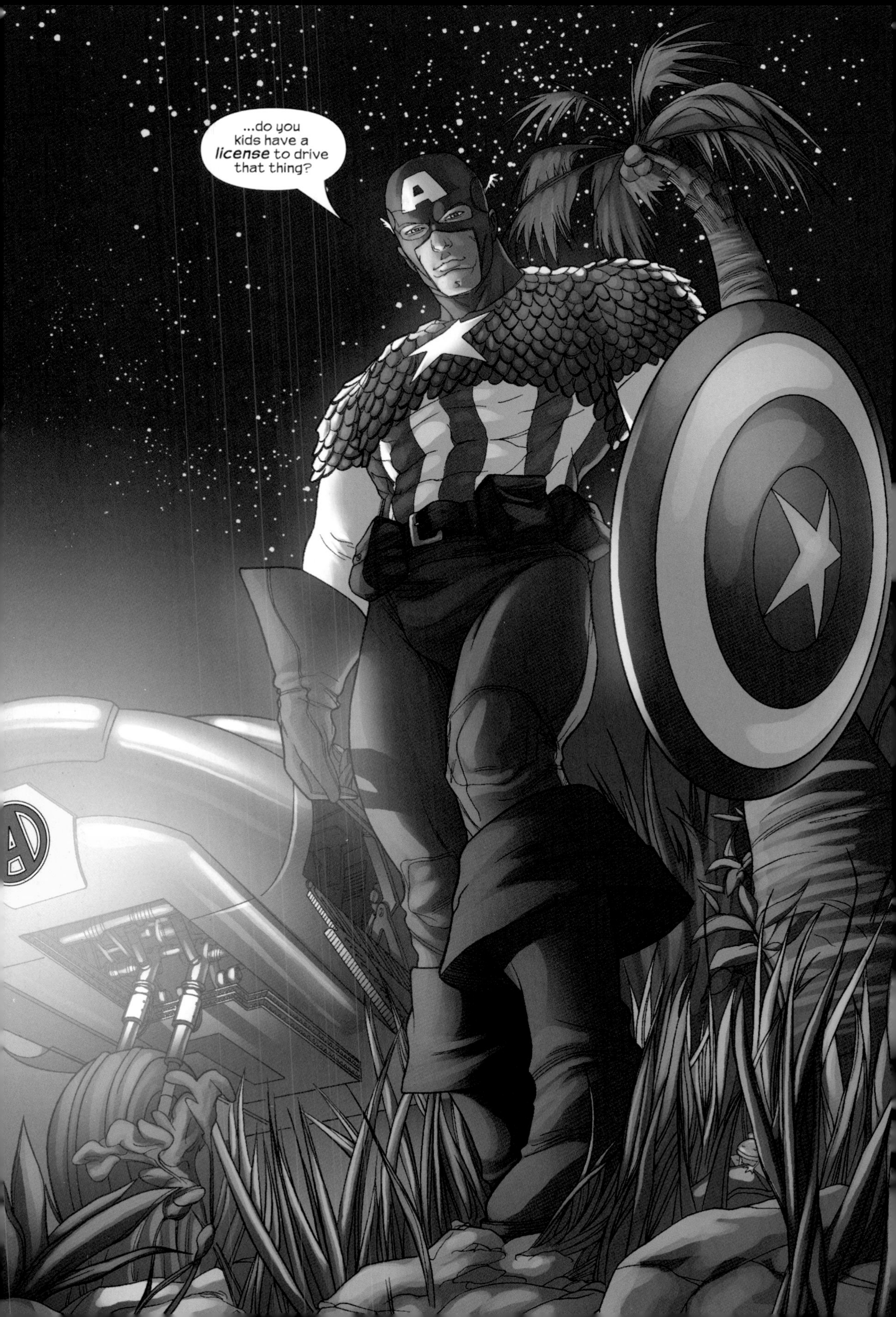
...do you kids have a *license* to drive that thing?

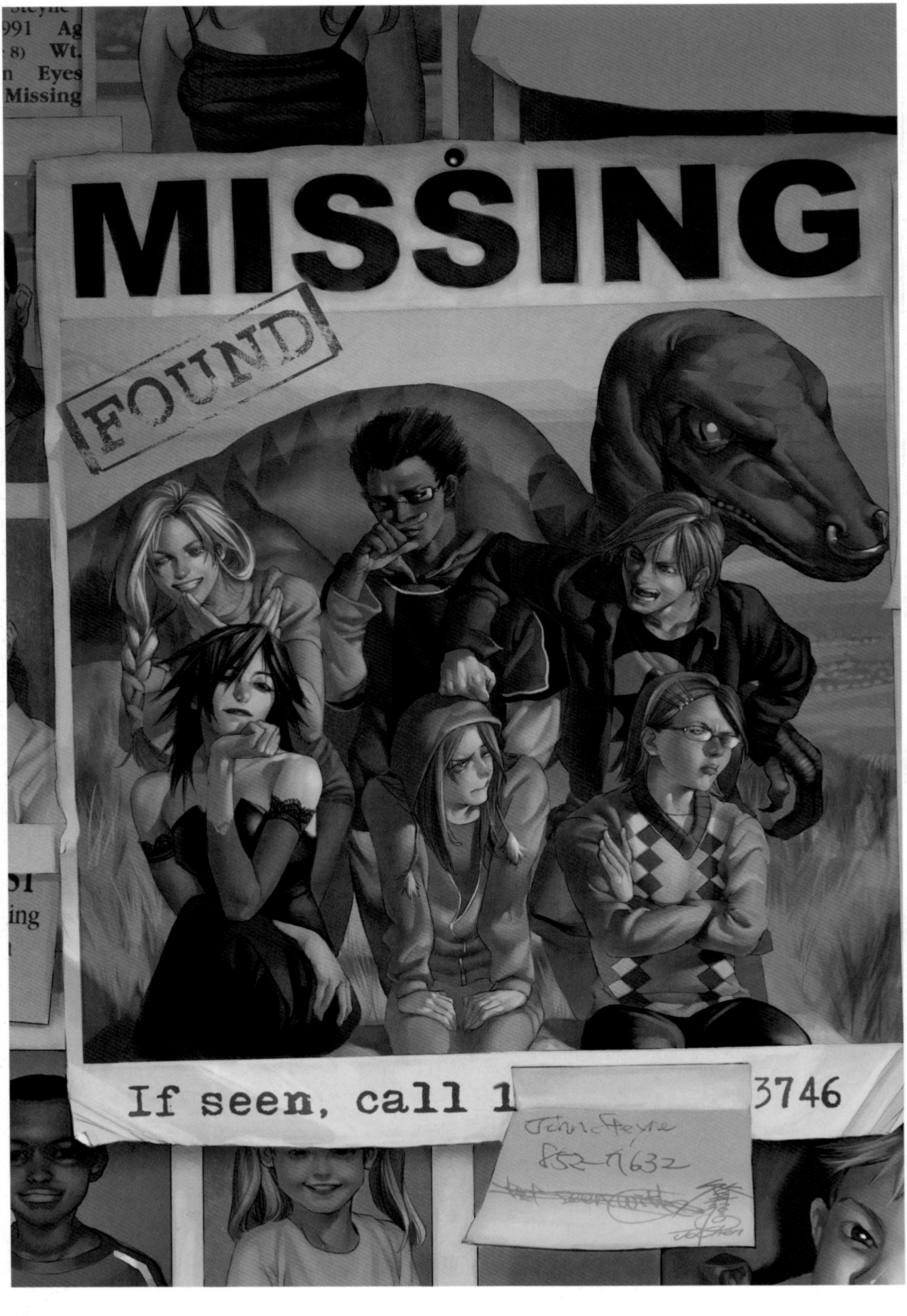
MISSING
FOUND
If seen, call 1
3746

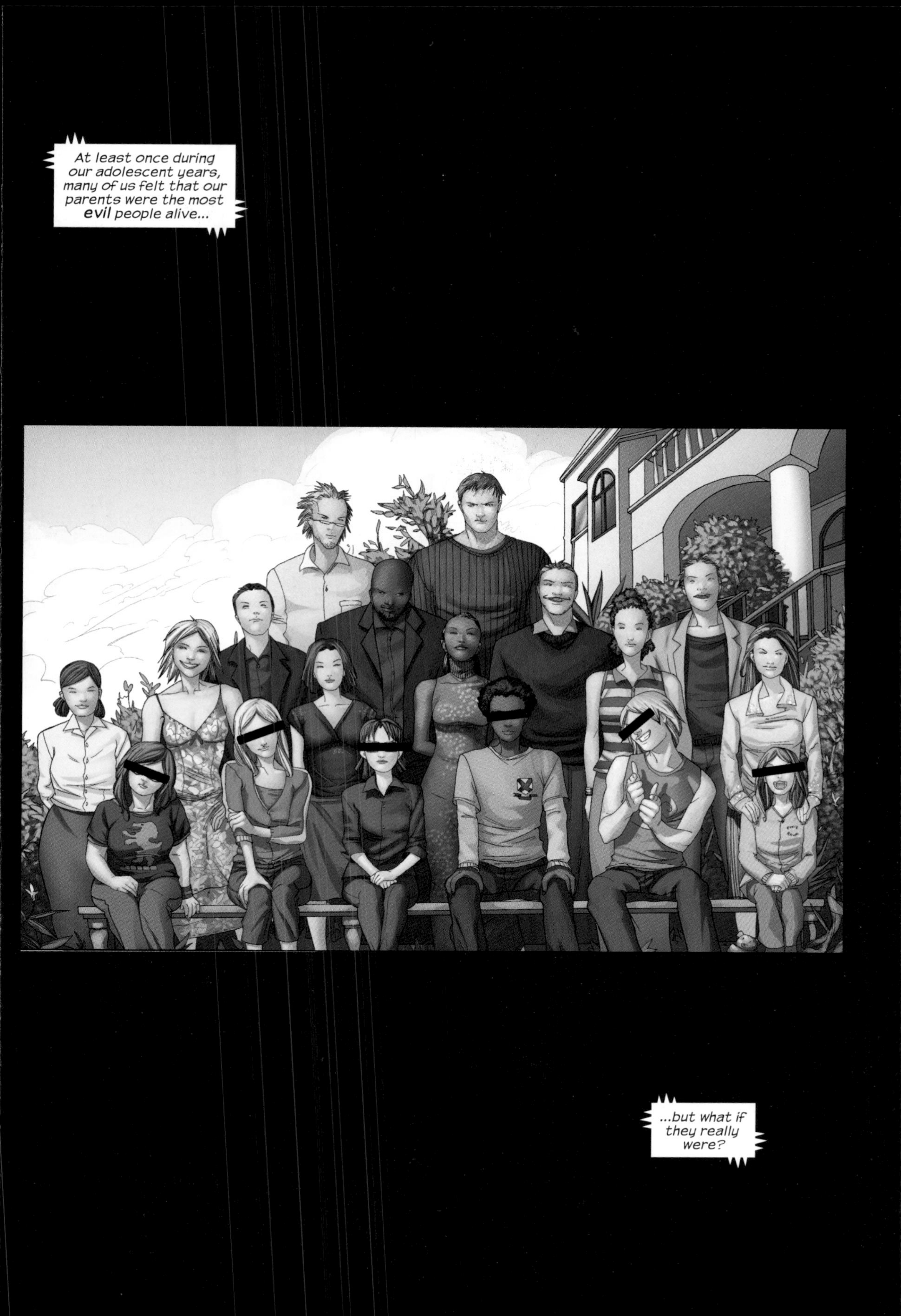
At least once during our adolescent years, many of us felt that our parents were the most **evil** people alive...
...but what if they really were?

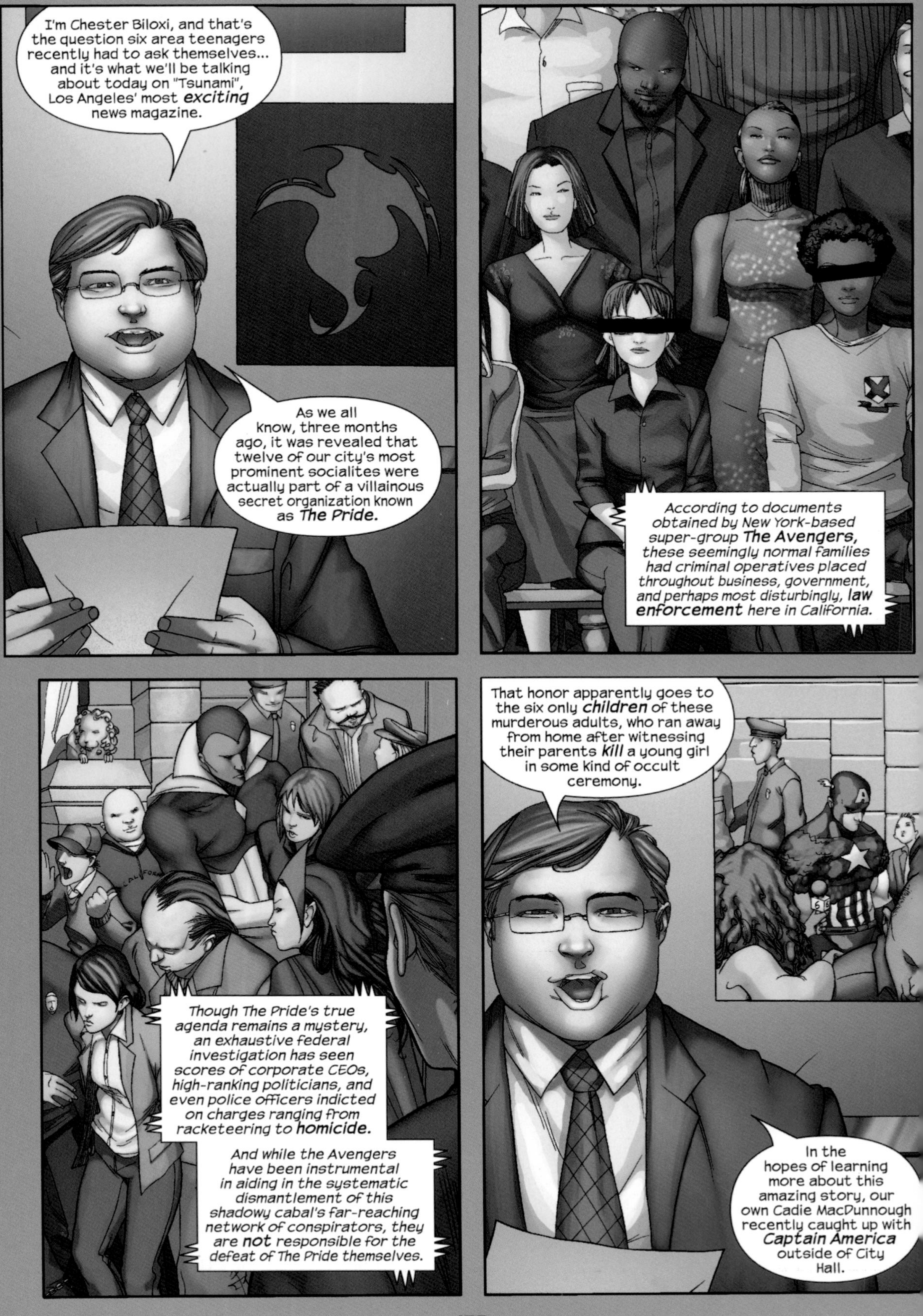
I'm Chester Biloxi, and that's the question six area teenagers recently had to ask themselves... and it's what we'll be talking about today on "Tsunami", Los Angeles' most ***exciting*** news magazine.
As we all know, three months ago, it was revealed that twelve of our city's most prominent socialites were actually part of a villainous secret organization known as ***The Pride.***
According to documents obtained by New York-based super-group ***The Avengers,*** *these seemingly normal families had criminal operatives placed throughout business, government, and perhaps most disturbingly,* ***law enforcement*** *here in California.*
Though The Pride's true agenda remains a mystery, an exhaustive federal investigation has seen scores of corporate CEOs, high-ranking politicians, and even police officers indicted on charges ranging from racketeering to ***homicide.***
And while the Avengers have been instrumental in aiding in the systematic dismantlement of this shadowy cabal's far-reaching network of conspirators, they are ***not*** *responsible for the defeat of The Pride themselves.*
That honor apparently goes to the six only ***children*** of these murderous adults, who ran away from home after witnessing their parents ***kill*** a young girl in some kind of occult ceremony.
In the hopes of learning more about this amazing story, our own Cadie MacDunnough recently caught up with ***Captain America*** outside of City Hall.

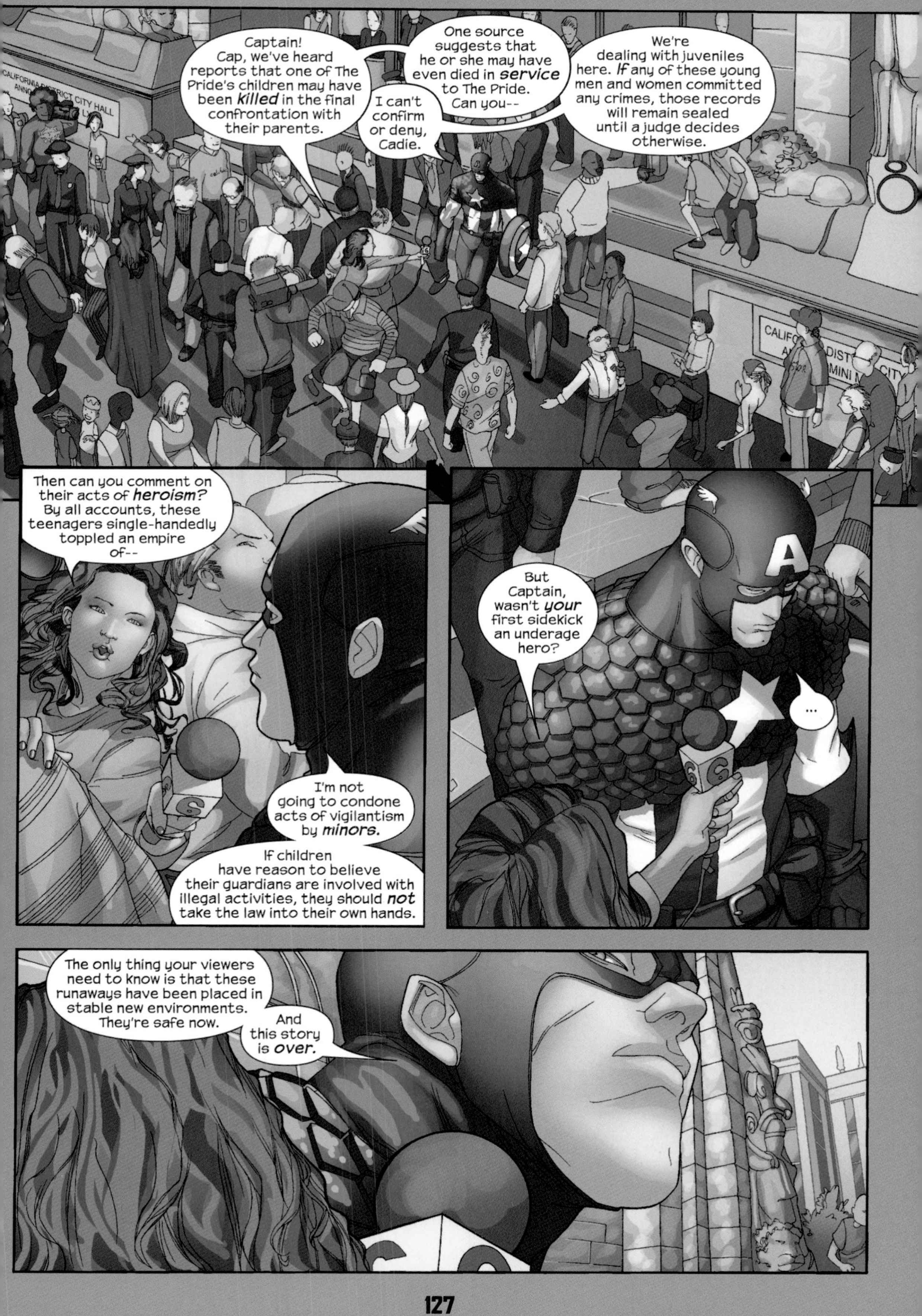
Captain! Cap, we've heard reports that one of The Pride's children may have been killed in the final confrontation with their parents.
One source suggests that he or she may have even died in service to The Pride. Can you--
I can't confirm or deny, Cadie.
We're dealing with juveniles here. If any of these young men and women committed any crimes, those records will remain sealed until a judge decides otherwise.
CALIFORNIA DISTRICT CITY HALL
Then can you comment on their acts of heroism? By all accounts, these teenagers single-handedly toppled an empire of--
I'm not going to condone acts of vigilantism by minors.
If children have reason to believe their guardians are involved with illegal activities, they should not take the law into their own hands.
But Captain, wasn't your first sidekick an underage hero?
...
The only thing your viewers need to know is that these runaways have been placed in stable new environments. They're safe now.
And this story is over.

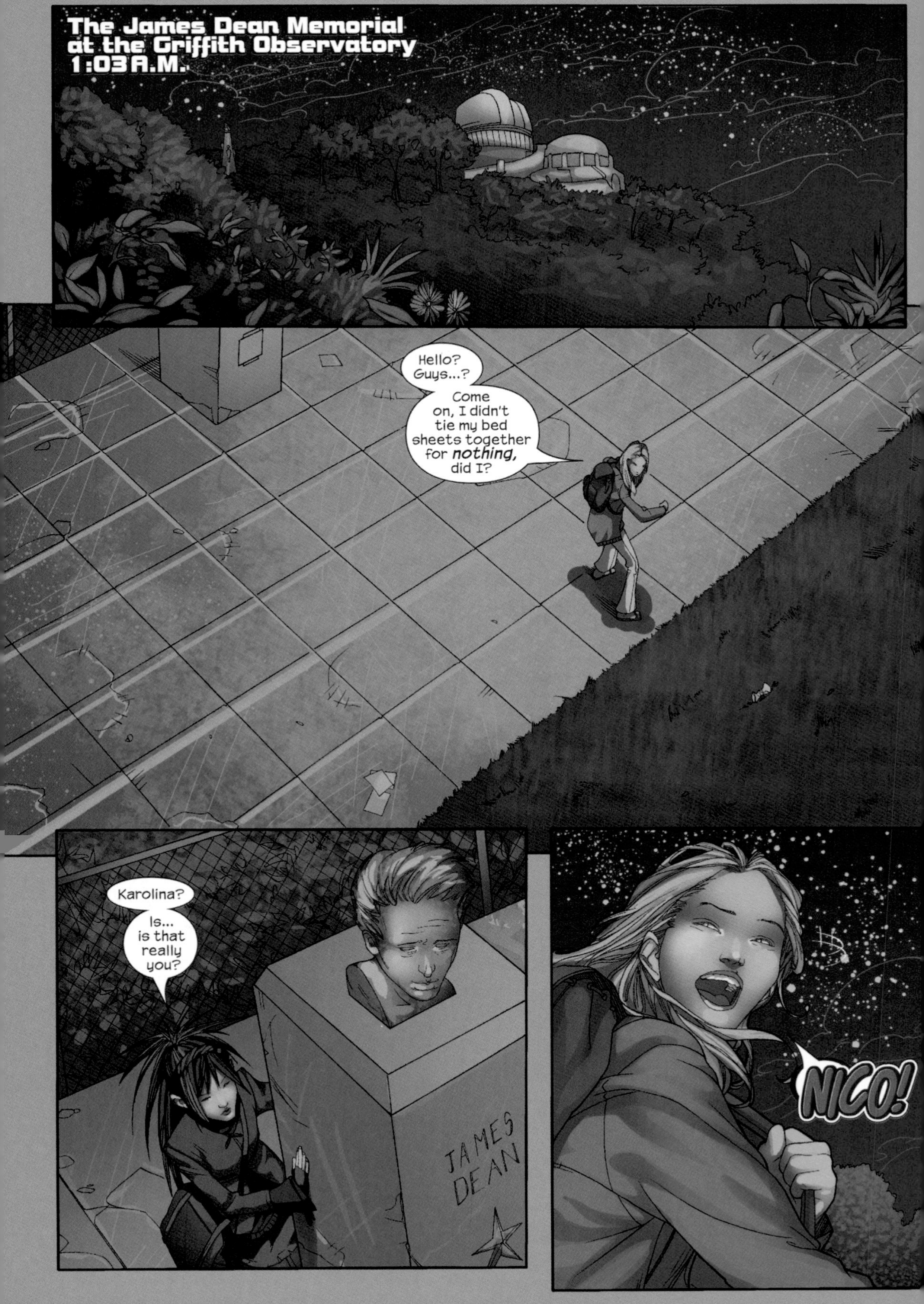

The James Dean Memorial at the Griffith Observatory 1:03 A.M.
Hello? Guys...?
Come on, I didn't tie my bed sheets together for *nothing,* did I?
Karolina?
Is... is that really you?
JAMES DEAN
NICO!

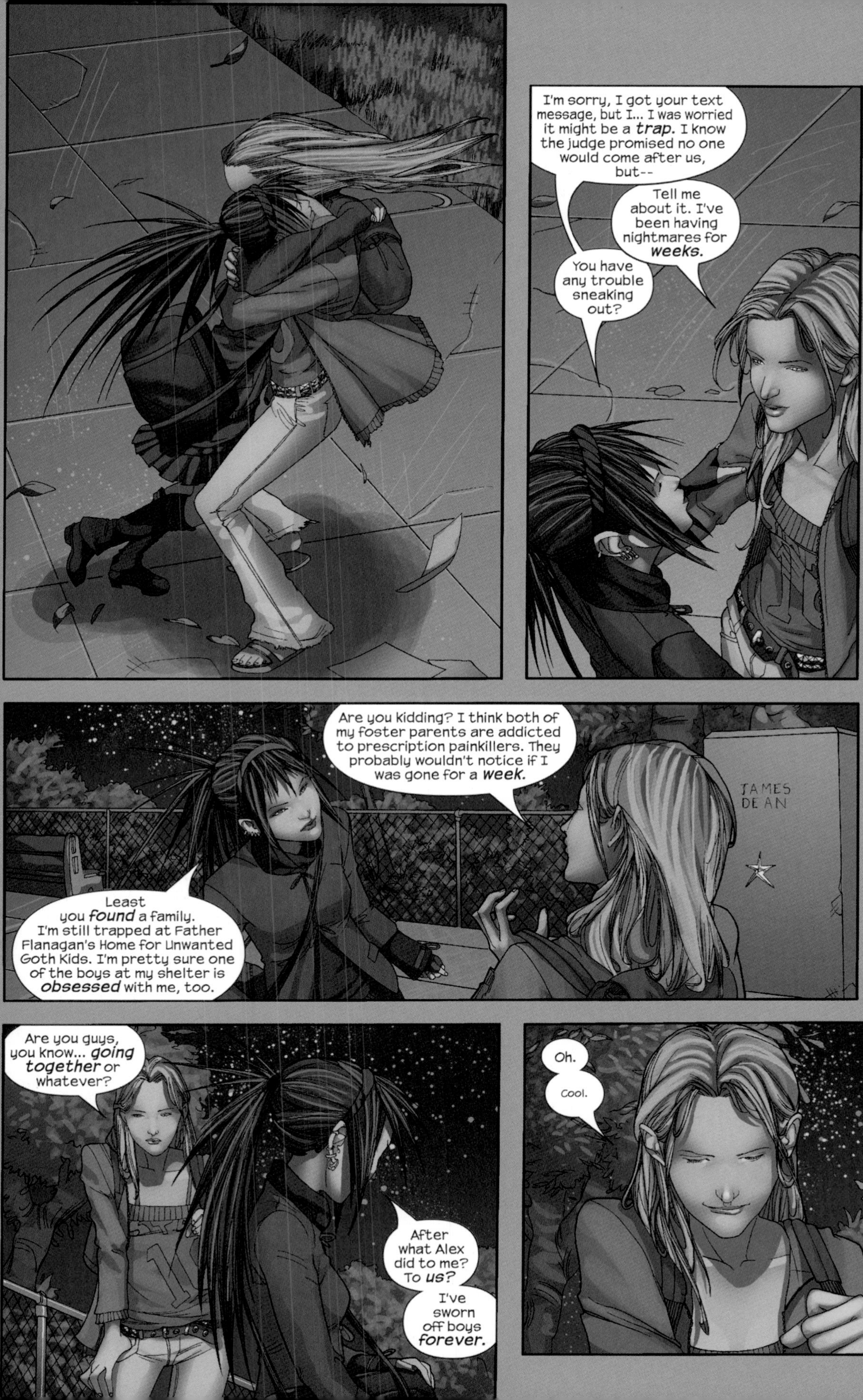
I'm sorry, I got your text message, but I... I was worried it might be a trap. I know the judge promised no one would come after us, but--
Tell me about it. I've been having nightmares for weeks.
You have any trouble sneaking out?
Are you kidding? I think both of my foster parents are addicted to prescription painkillers. They probably wouldn't notice if I was gone for a week.
JAMES DE AN
Least you found a family. I'm still trapped at Father Flanagan's Home for Unwanted Goth Kids. I'm pretty sure one of the boys at my shelter is obsessed with me, too.
Are you guys, you know... going together or whatever?
After what Alex did to me? To us?
I've sworn off boys forever.
Oh.
Cool.

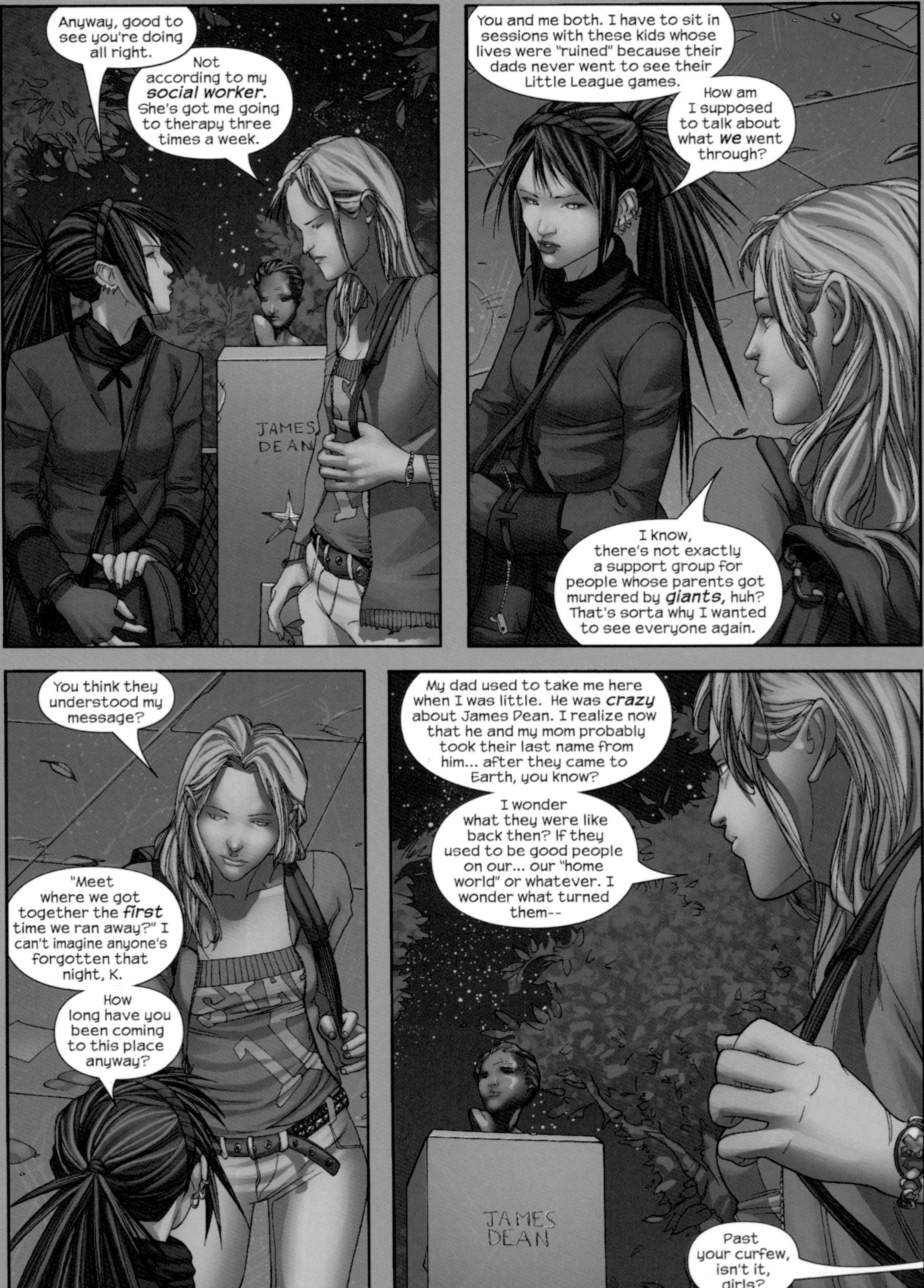
Anyway, good to see you're doing all right.
Not according to my *social worker.* She's got me going to therapy three times a week.
JAMES DEAN
You and me both. I have to sit in sessions with these kids whose lives were "ruined" because their dads never went to see their Little League games.
How am I supposed to talk about what *we* went through?
I know, there's not exactly a support group for people whose parents got murdered by *giants,* huh? That's sorta why I wanted to see everyone again.
You think they understood my message?
"Meet where we got together the *first* time we ran away?" I can't imagine anyone's forgotten that night, K.
How long have you been coming to this place anyway?
My dad used to take me here when I was little. He was *crazy* about James Dean. I realize now that he and my mom probably took their last name from him... after they came to Earth, you know?
I wonder what they were like back then? If they used to be good people on our... our "home world" or whatever. I wonder what turned them--
JAMES DEAN
Past your curfew, isn't it, girls?

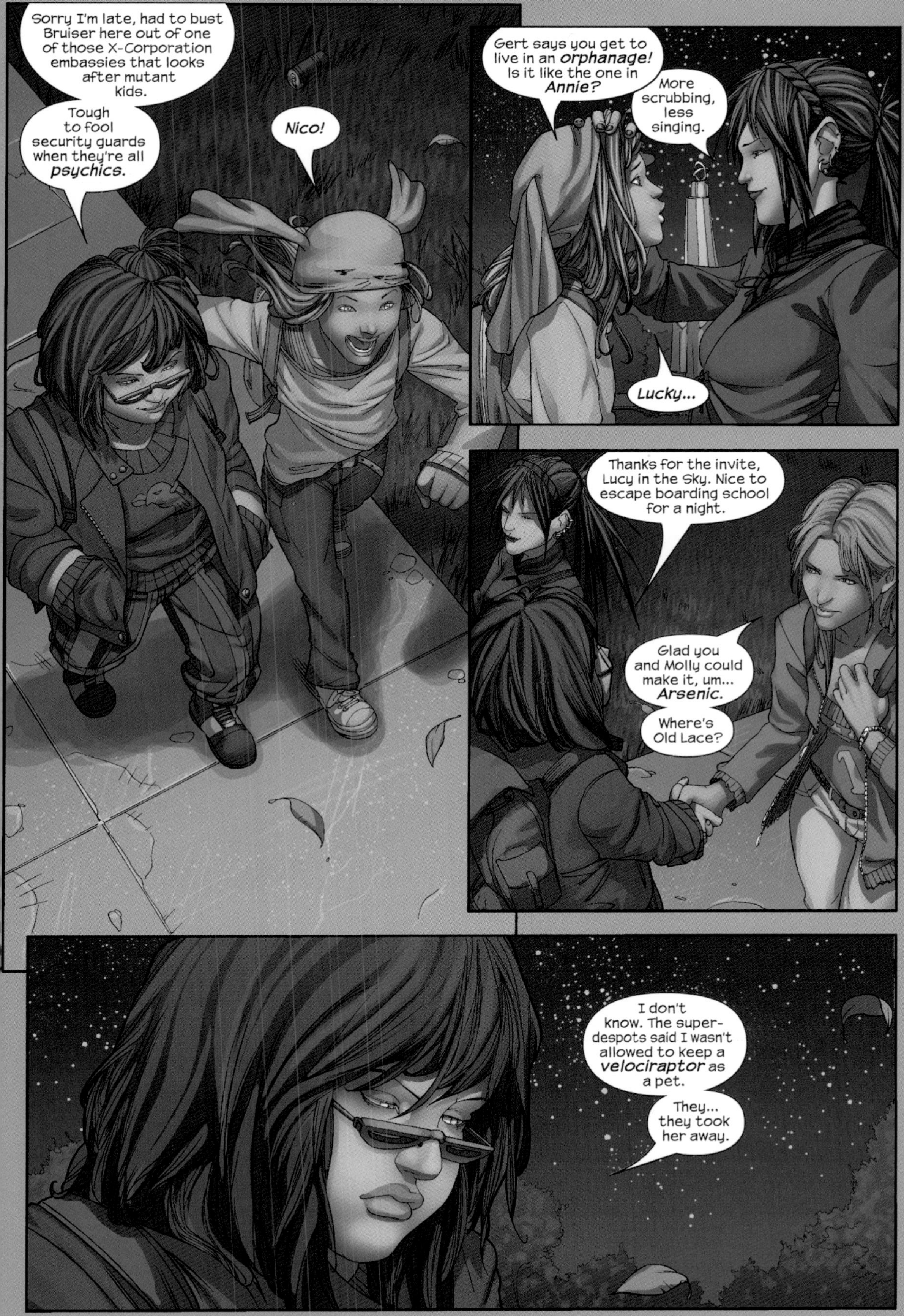

Sorry I'm late, had to bust Bruiser here out of one of those X-Corporation embassies that looks after mutant kids.
Tough to fool security guards when they're all psychics.
Nico!
Gert says you get to live in an orphanage! Is it like the one in Annie?
More scrubbing, less singing.
Lucky...
Thanks for the invite, Lucy in the Sky. Nice to escape boarding school for a night.
Glad you and Molly could make it, um... Arsenic.
Where's Old Lace?
I don't know. The super-despots said I wasn't allowed to keep a velociraptor as a pet.
They... they took her away.

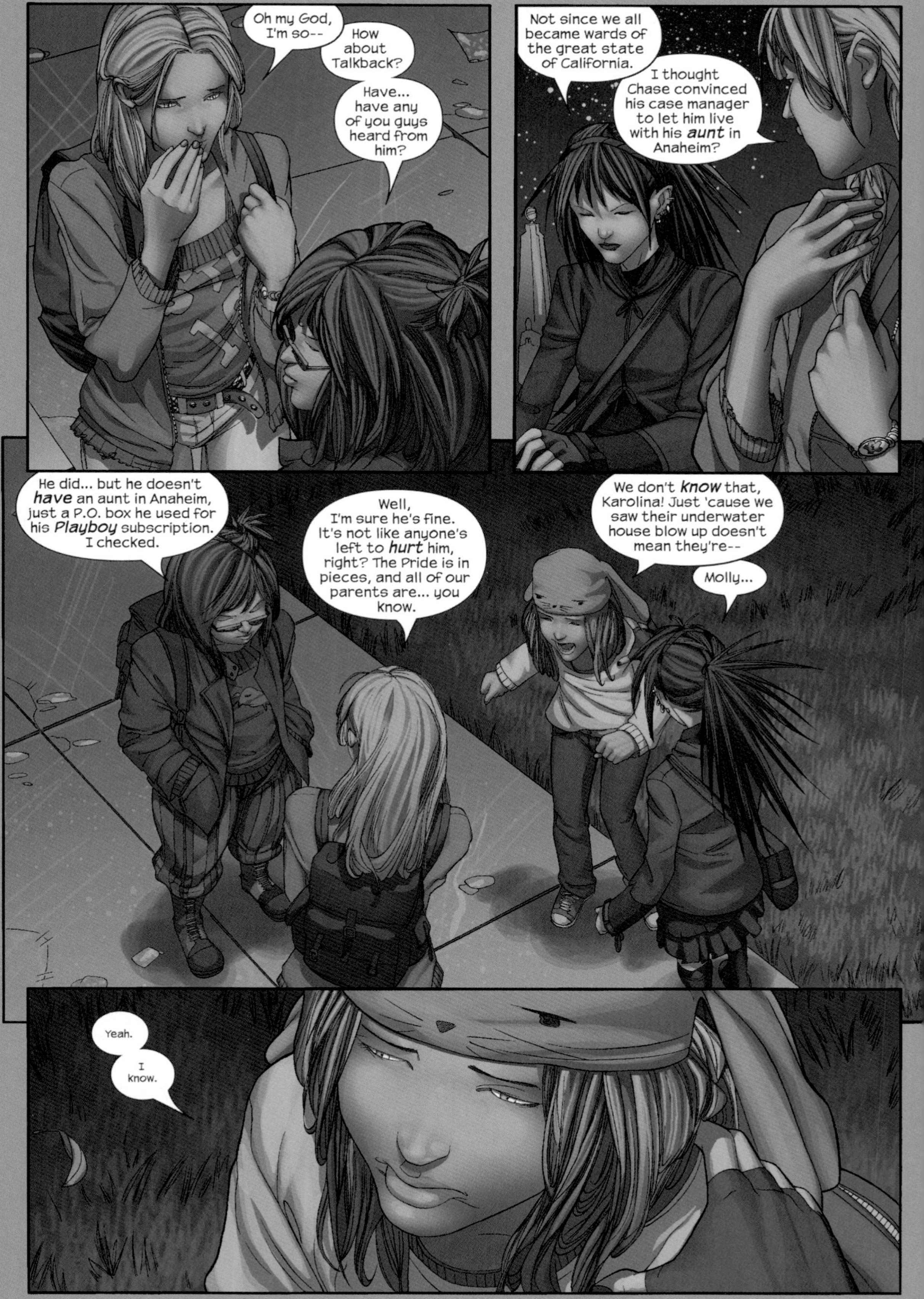
Oh my God, I'm so--
How about Talkback?
Have... have any of you guys heard from him?
Not since we all became wards of the great state of California.
I thought Chase convinced his case manager to let him live with his *aunt* in Anaheim?
He did... but he doesn't *have* an aunt in Anaheim, just a P.O. box he used for his *Playboy* subscription. I checked.
Well, I'm sure he's fine. It's not like anyone's left to *hurt* him, right? The Pride is in pieces, and all of our parents are... you know.
We don't *know* that, Karolina! Just 'cause we saw their underwater house blow up doesn't mean they're--
Molly...
Yeah.
I know.

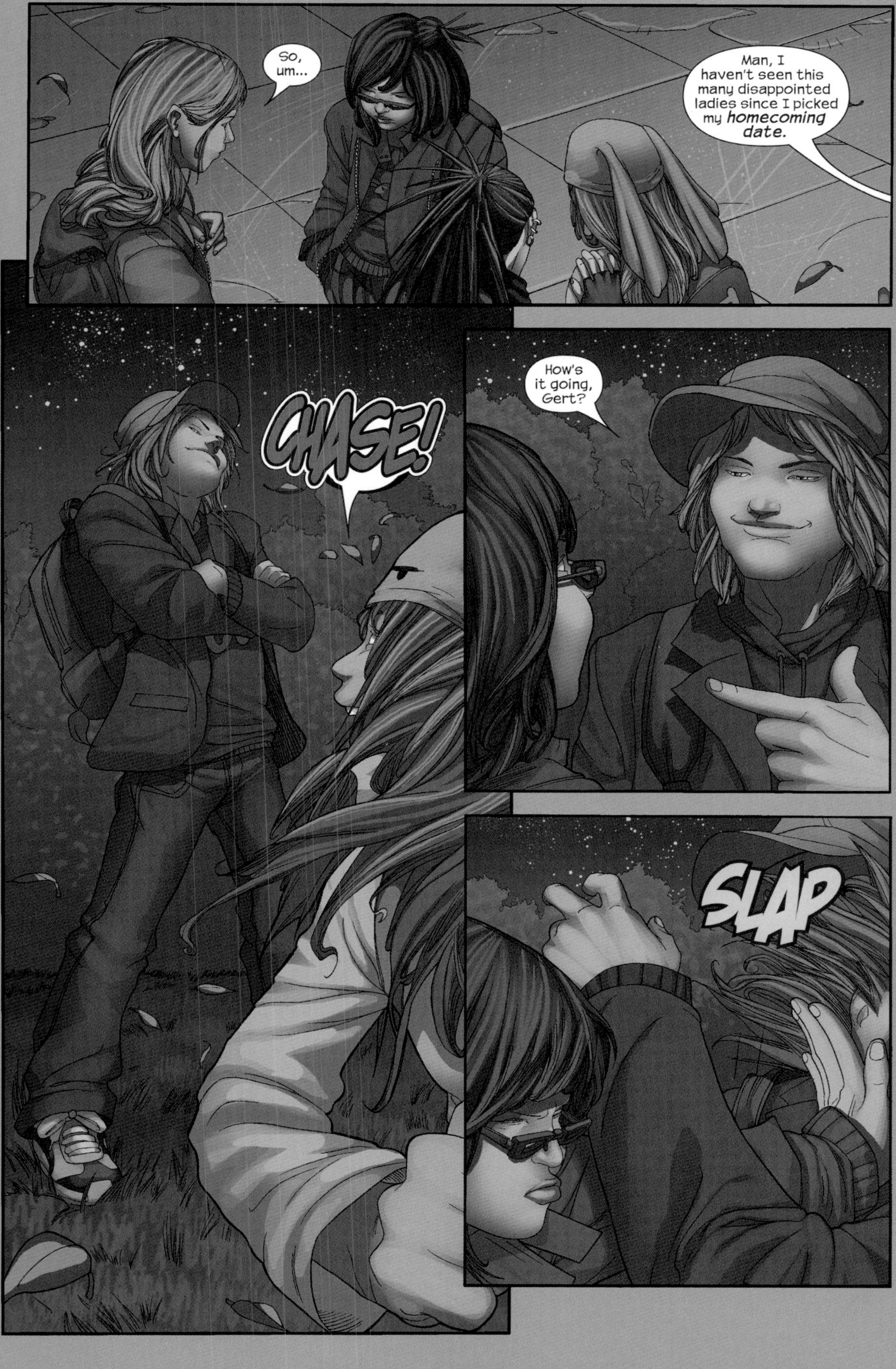
So, um...
Man, I haven't seen this many disappointed ladies since I picked my *homecoming date.*
CHASE!
How's it going, Gert?
SLAP

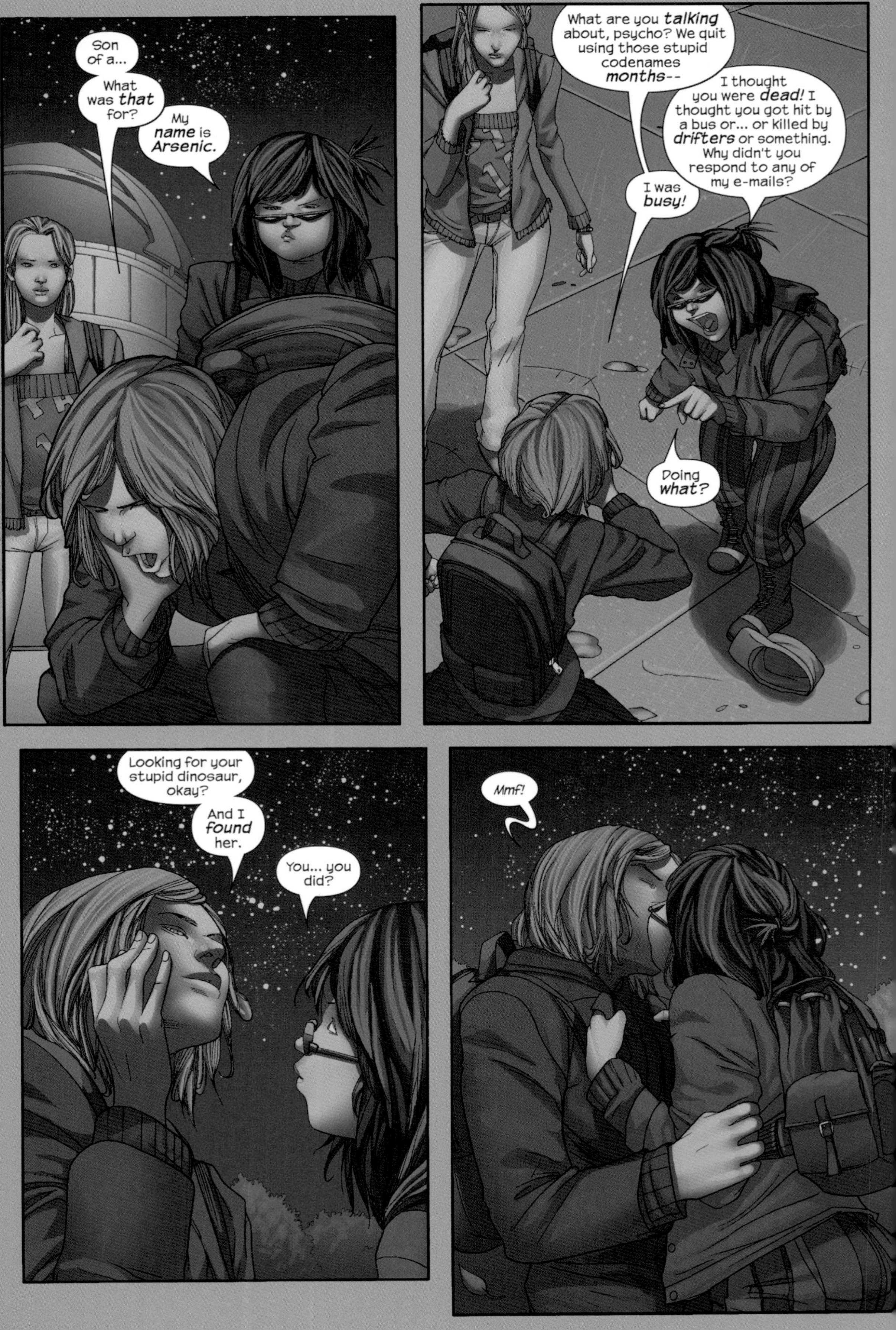
Son of a...
What was *that* for?
My *name* is Arsenic.
What are you *talking* about, psycho? We quit using those stupid codenames *months*--
I thought you were *dead!* I thought you got hit by a bus or... or killed by *drifters* or something. Why didn't you respond to any of my e-mails?
I was *busy!*
Doing *what?*
Looking for your stupid dinosaur, okay?
And I *found* her.
You... you did?
Mmf!

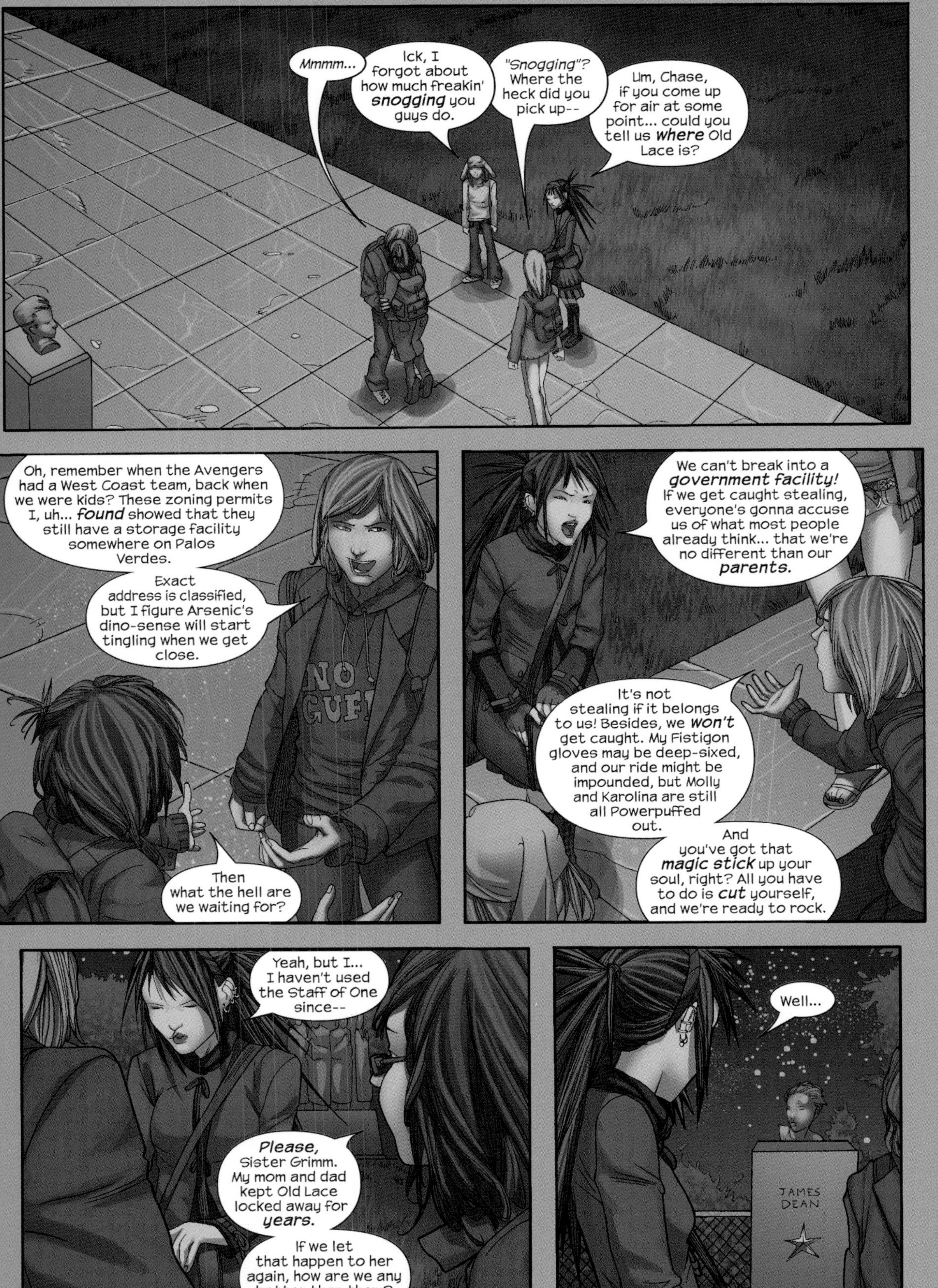
Mmmm...
Ick, I forgot about how much freakin' *snogging* you guys do.
"Snogging"? Where the heck did you pick up--
Um, Chase, if you come up for air at some point... could you tell us *where* Old Lace is?
Oh, remember when the Avengers had a West Coast team, back when we were kids? These zoning permits I, uh... *found* showed that they still have a storage facility somewhere on Palos Verdes.
Exact address is classified, but I figure Arsenic's dino-sense will start tingling when we get close.
NO GUFF
Then what the hell are we waiting for?
We can't break into a *government facility!* If we get caught stealing, everyone's gonna accuse us of what most people already think... that we're no different than our *parents.*
It's not stealing if it belongs to us! Besides, we *won't* get caught. My Fistigon gloves may be deep-sixed, and our ride might be impounded, but Molly and Karolina are still all Powerpuffed out.
And you've got that *magic stick* up your soul, right? All you have to do is *cut* yourself, and we're ready to rock.
Yeah, but I... I haven't used the Staff of One since--
Please, Sister Grimm. My mom and dad kept Old Lace locked away for *years.*
If we let that happen to her again, how are we any better than them?
Well...
JAMES DEAN

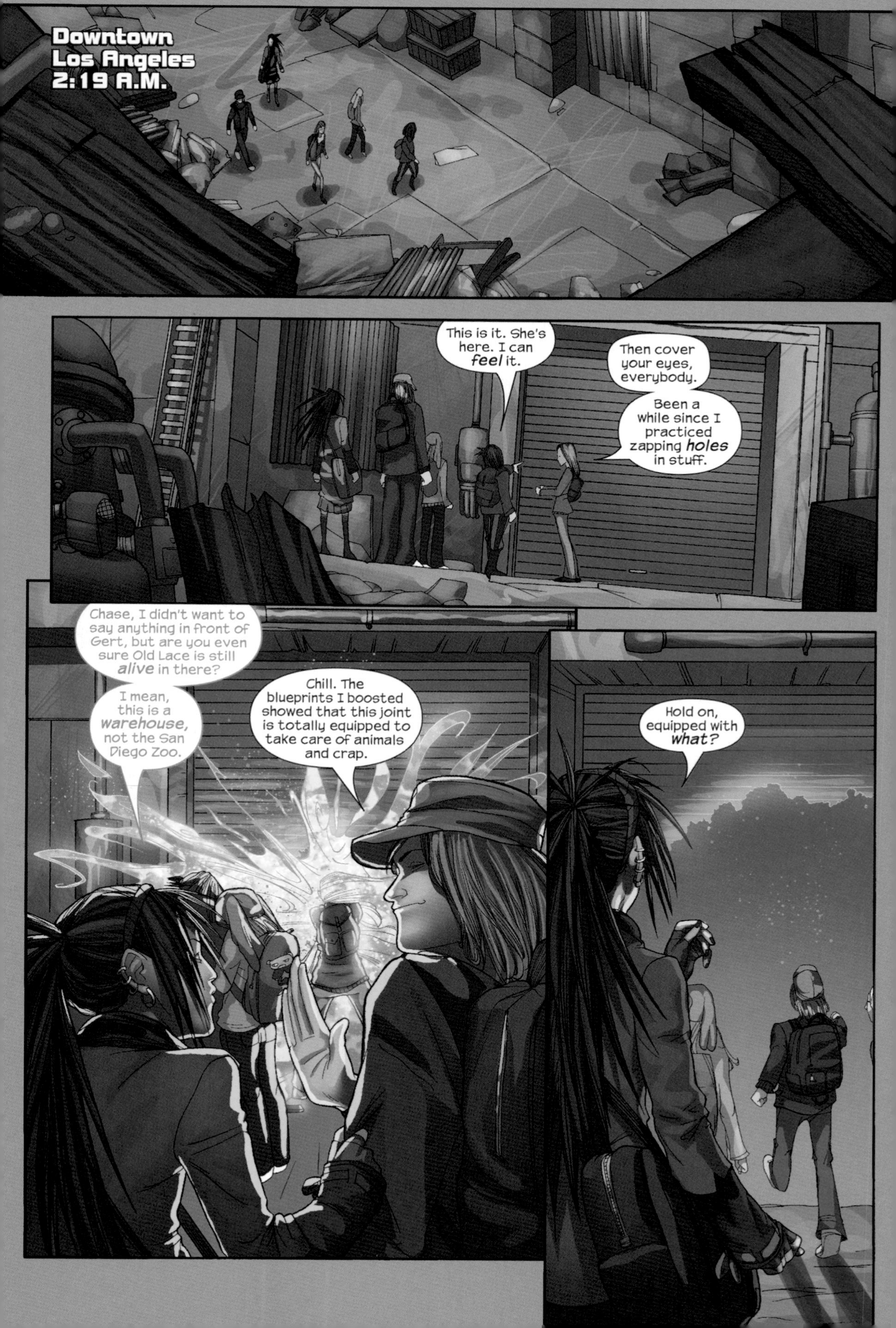
Downtown Los Angeles 2:19 A.M.
This is it. She's here. I can feel it.
Then cover your eyes, everybody.
Been a while since I practiced zapping holes in stuff.
Chase, I didn't want to say anything in front of Gert, but are you even sure Old Lace is still alive in there?
I mean, this is a warehouse, not the San Diego Zoo.
Chill. The blueprints I boosted showed that this joint is totally equipped to take care of animals and crap.
Hold on, equipped with what?

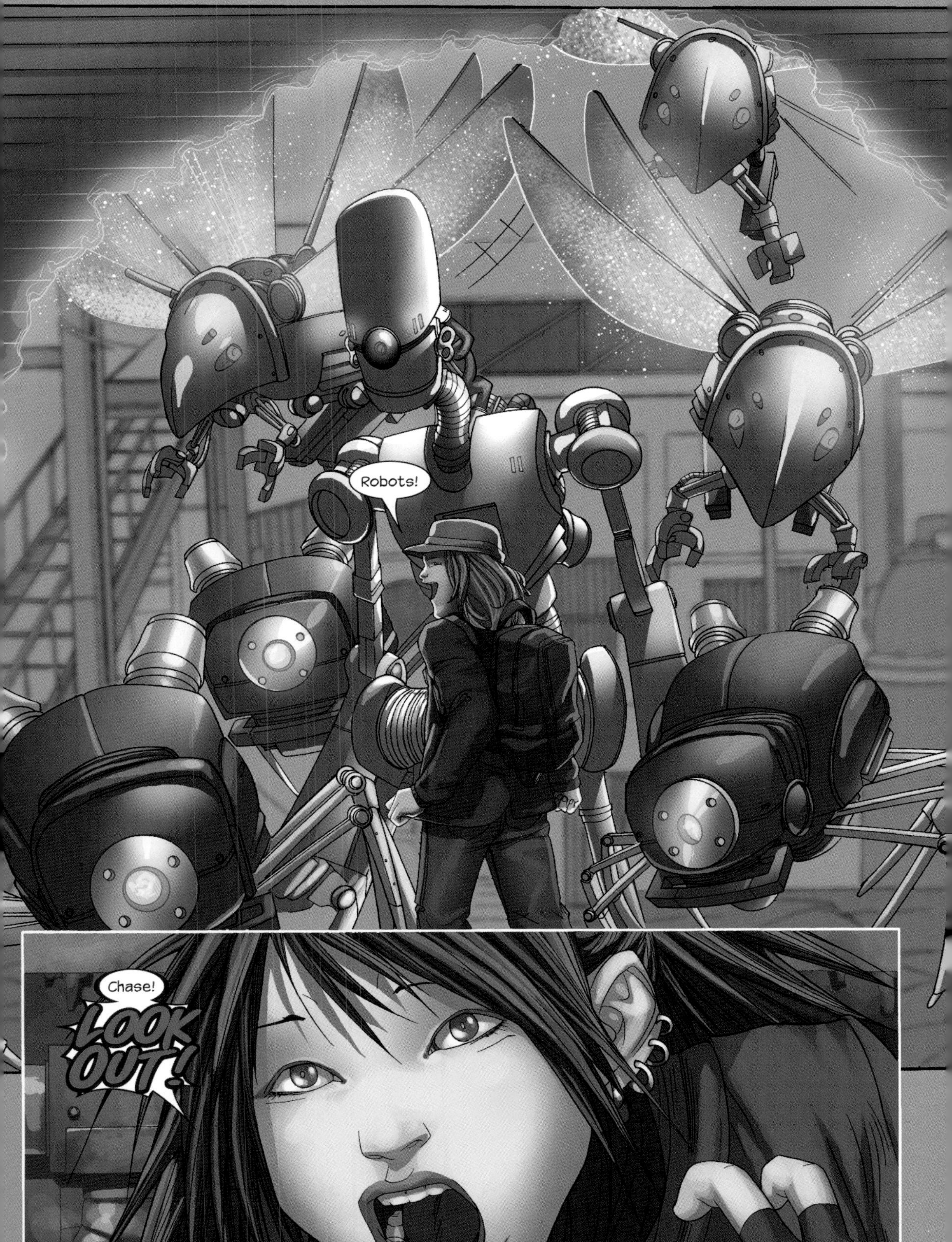
Robots!
Chase!
LOOK OUT!

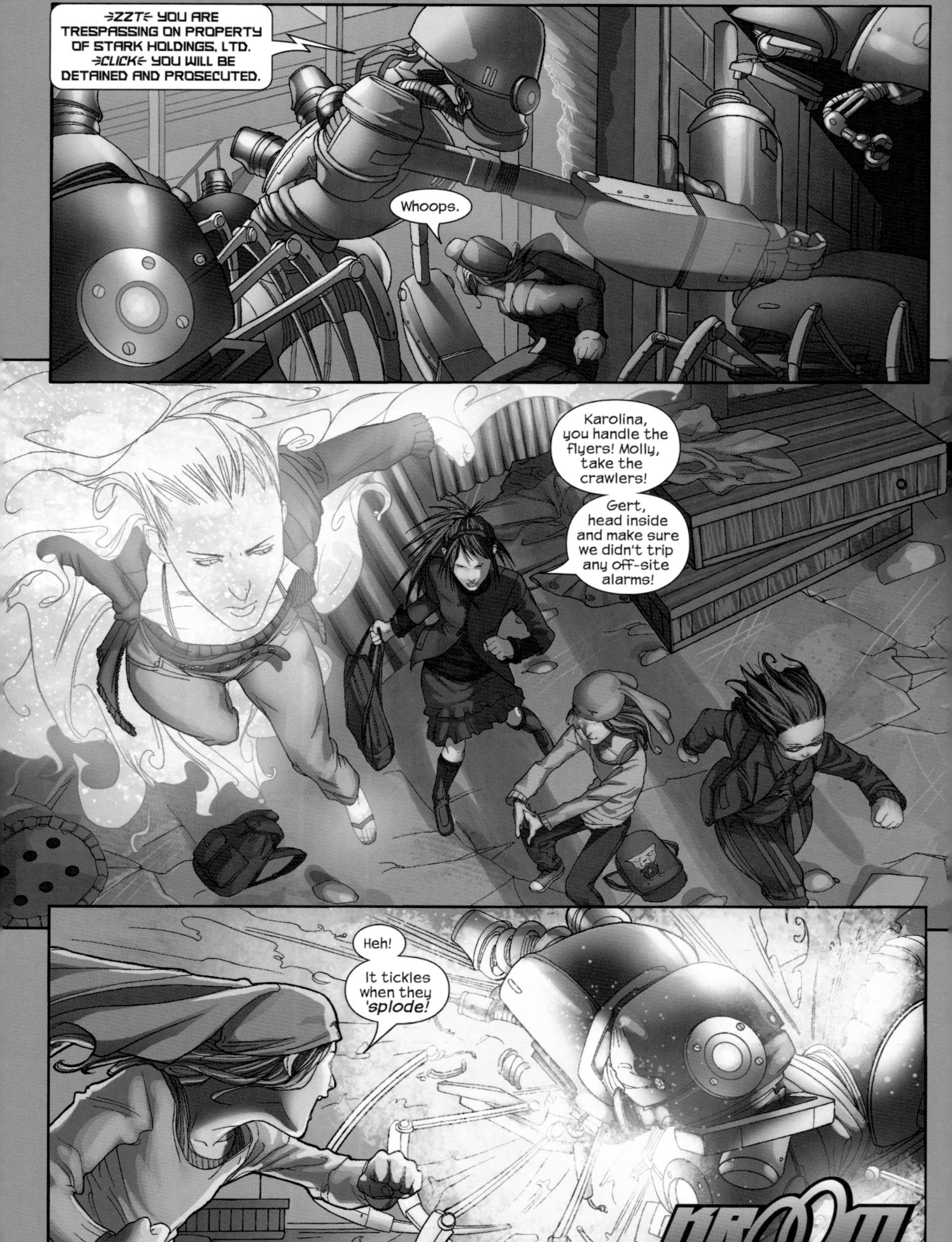
⇒ZZT⇐ YOU ARE TRESPASSING ON PROPERTY OF STARK HOLDINGS, LTD. ⇒CLICK⇐ YOU WILL BE DETAINED AND PROSECUTED.
Whoops.
Karolina, you handle the flyers! Molly, take the crawlers!
Gert, head inside and make sure we didn't trip any off-site alarms!
Heh!
It tickles when they *'splode!*
KROOM

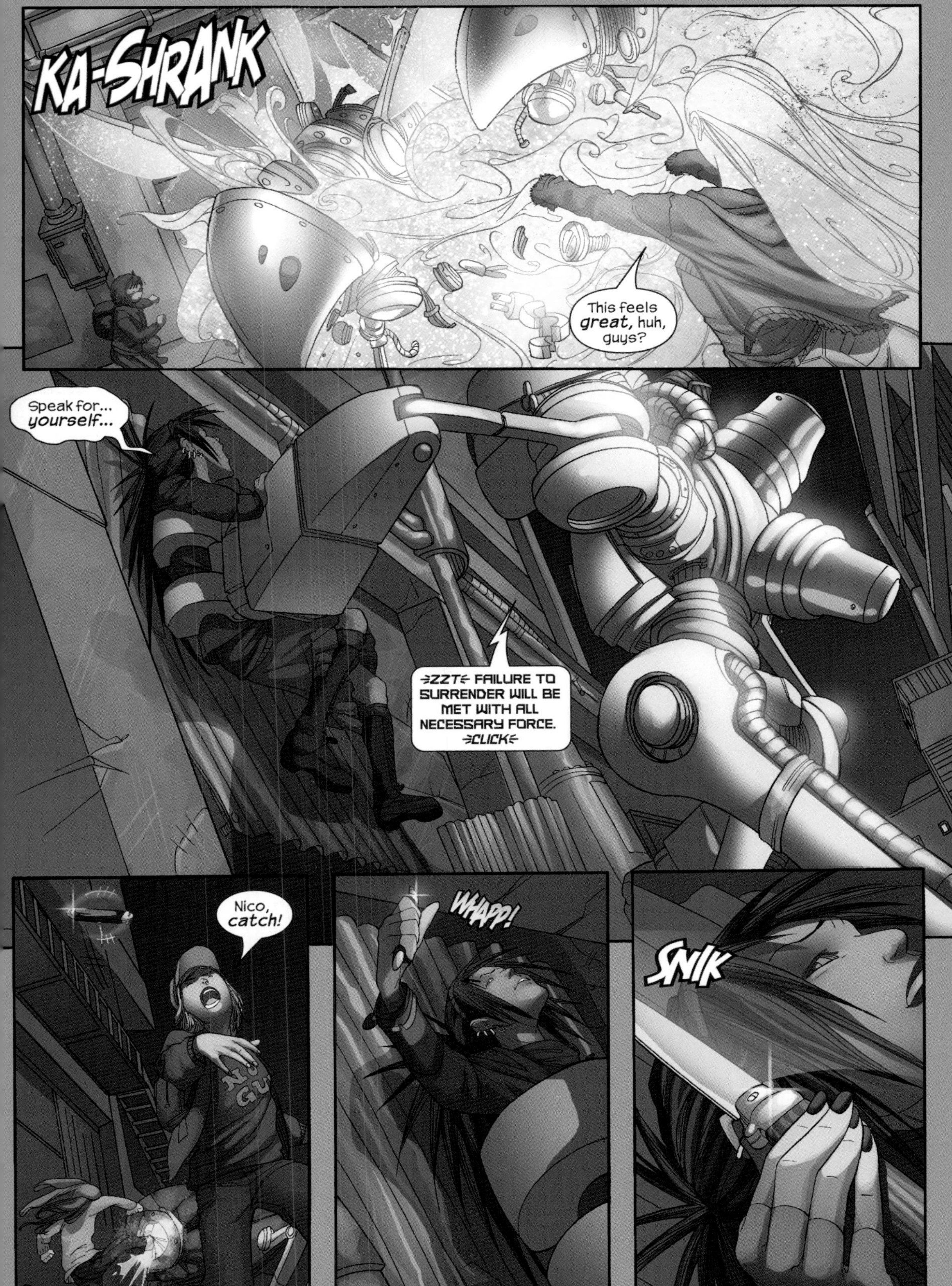
KA-SHRANK
This feels great, huh, guys?
Speak for... yourself...
ZZT FAILURE TO SURRENDER WILL BE MET WITH ALL NECESSARY FORCE. CLICK
Nico, catch!
WHAPP!
SNIK

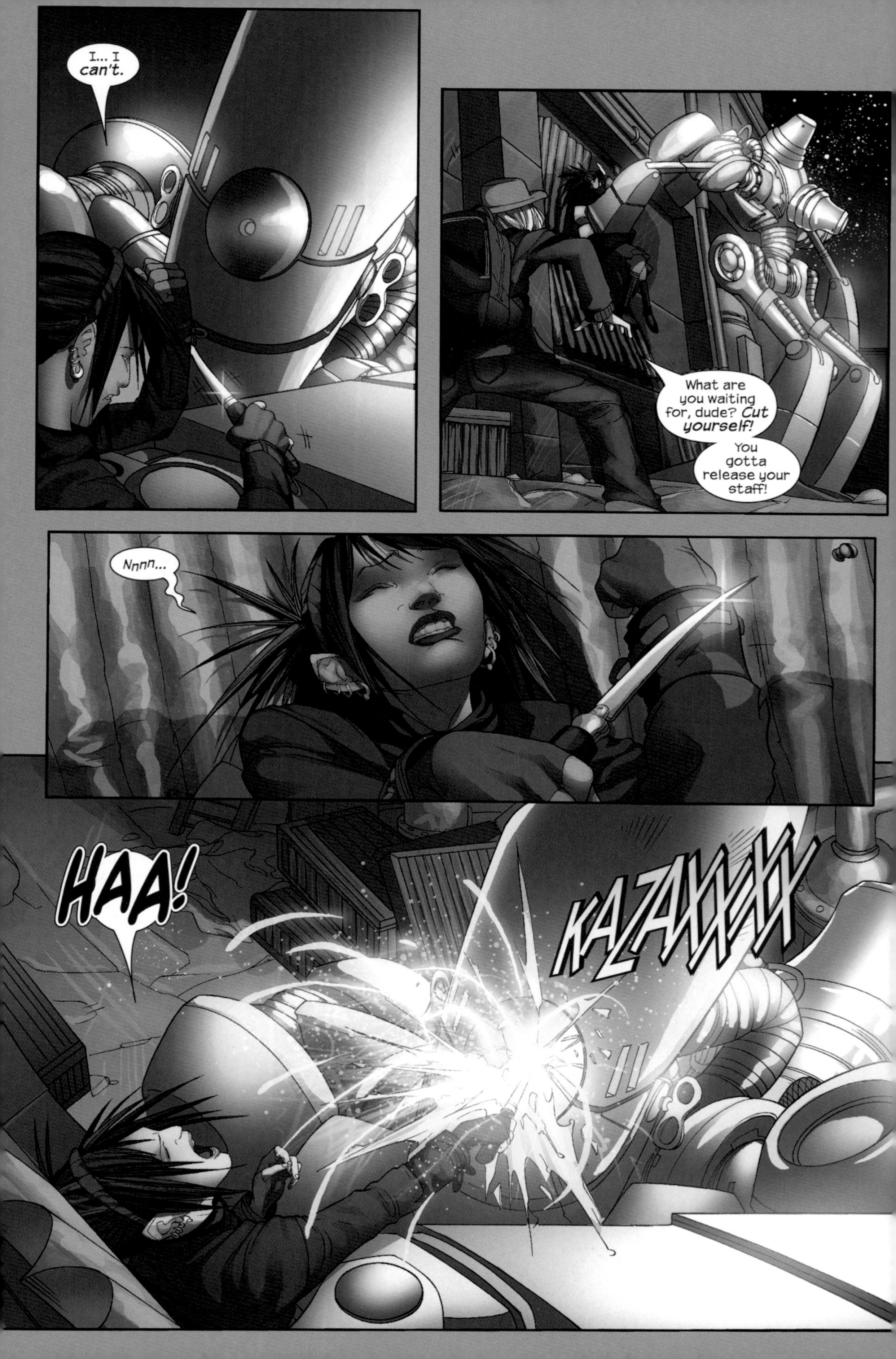
I... I *can't.*
What are you waiting for, dude? ***Cut yourself!***
You gotta release your staff!
Nnnn...
HAA!
KA-ZAAKKKK

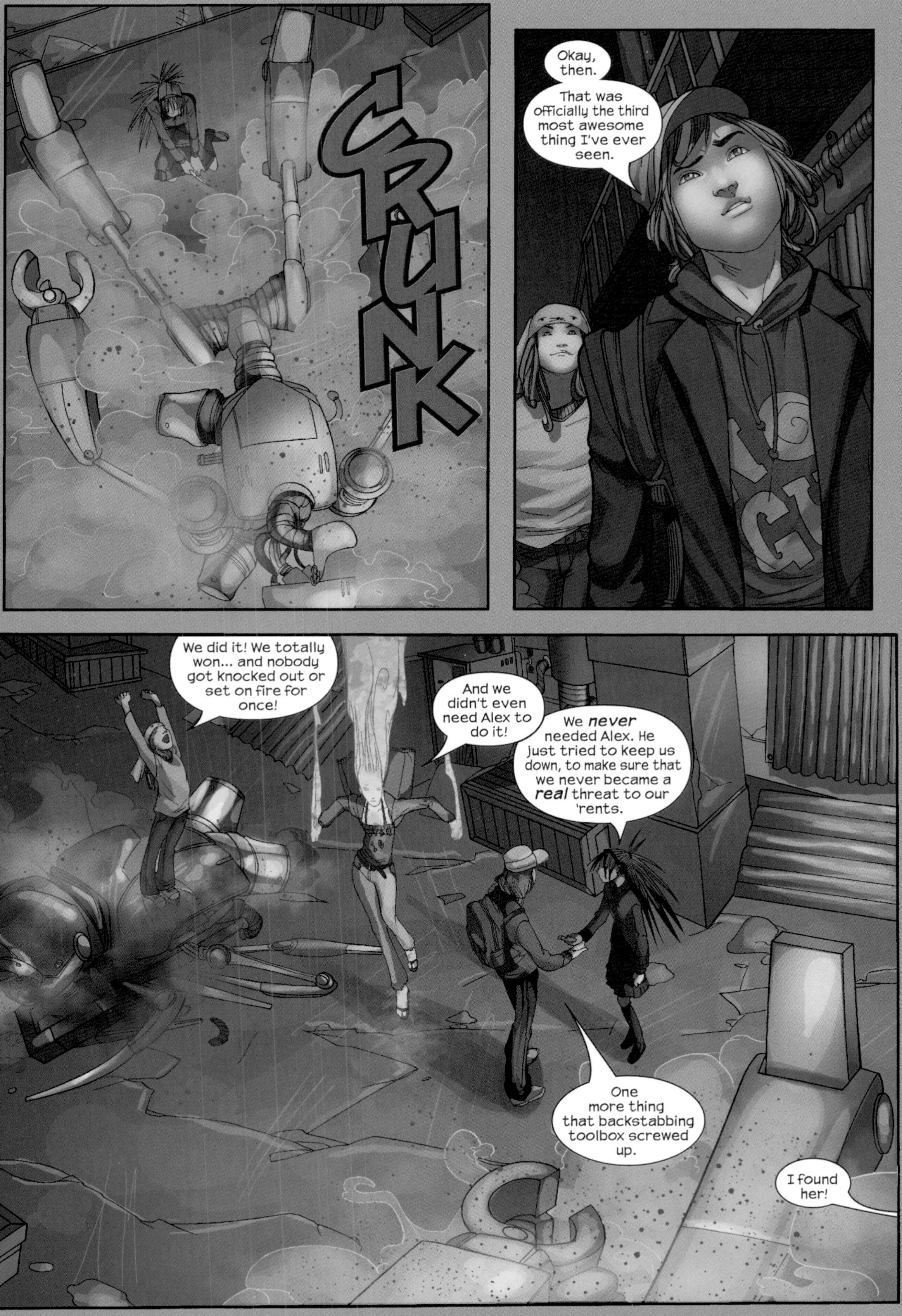
CRUNK
Okay, then.
That was officially the third most awesome thing I've ever seen.
We did it! We totally won... and nobody got knocked out or set on fire for once!
And we didn't even need Alex to do it!
We *never* needed Alex. He just tried to keep us down, to make sure that we never became a *real* threat to our 'rents.
One more thing that backstabbing toolbox screwed up.
I found her!

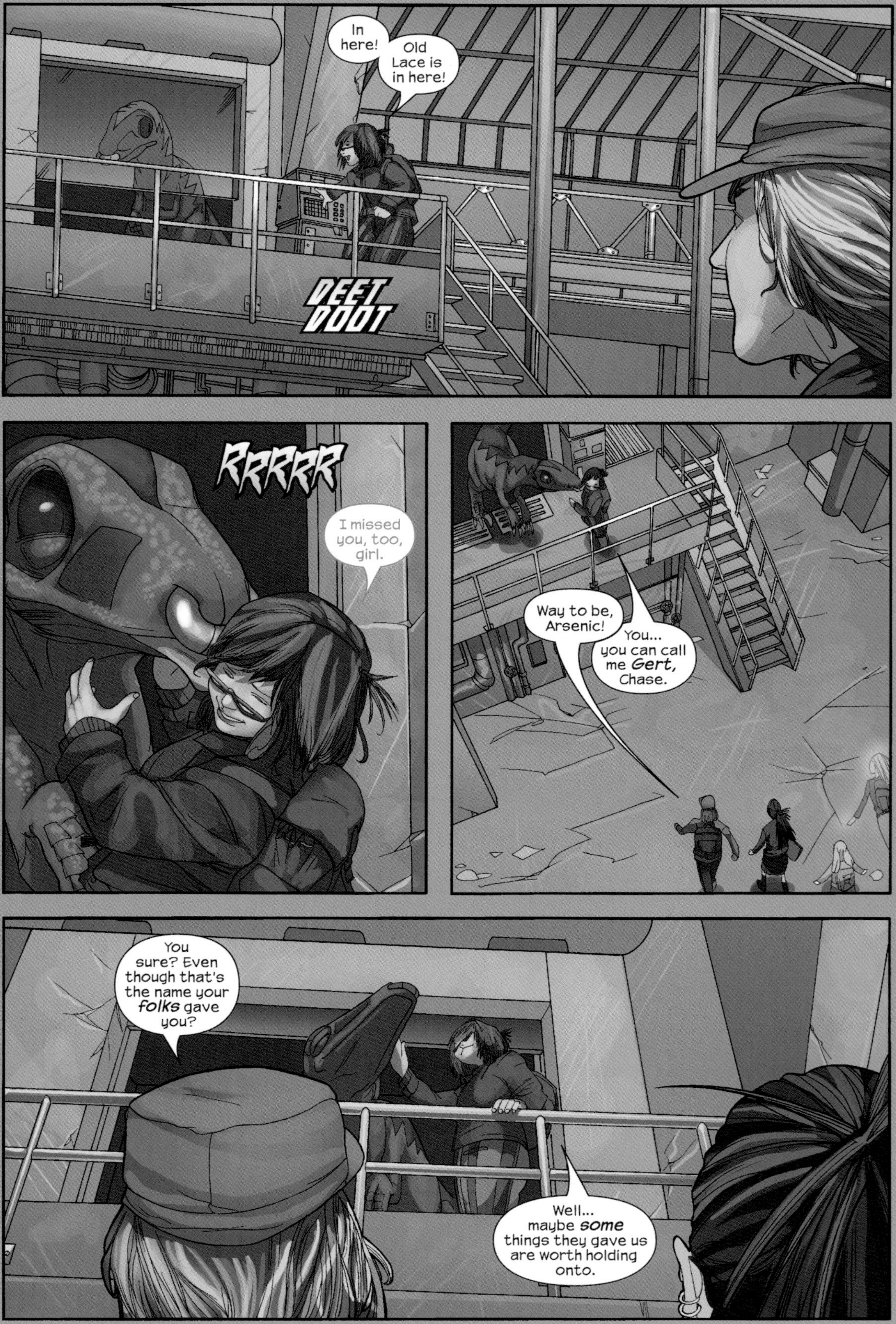
In here!
Old Lace is in here!
DEET DOOT
RRRRR
I missed you, too, girl.
Way to be, Arsenic!
You... you can call me *Gert,* Chase.
You sure? Even though that's the name your *folks* gave you?
Well... maybe *some* things they gave us are worth holding onto.

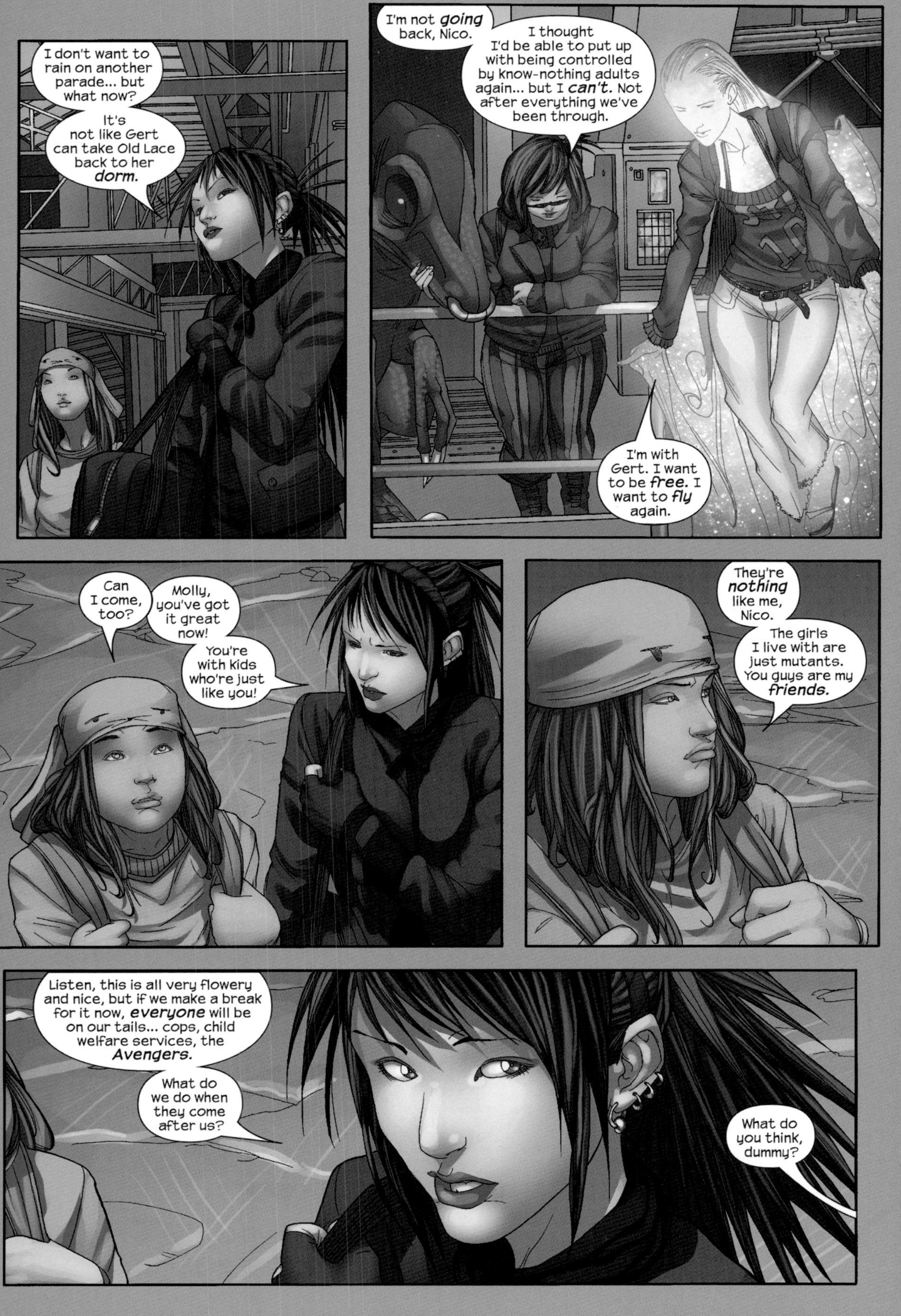
I don't want to rain on another parade... but what now?
It's not like Gert can take Old Lace back to her dorm.
I'm not going back, Nico.
I thought I'd be able to put up with being controlled by know-nothing adults again... but I can't. Not after everything we've been through.
I'm with Gert. I want to be free. I want to fly again.
Can I come, too?
Molly, you've got it great now!
You're with kids who're just like you!
They're nothing like me, Nico.
The girls I live with are just mutants. You guys are my friends.
Listen, this is all very flowery and nice, but if we make a break for it now, everyone will be on our tails... cops, child welfare services, the Avengers.
What do we do when they come after us?
What do you think, dummy?

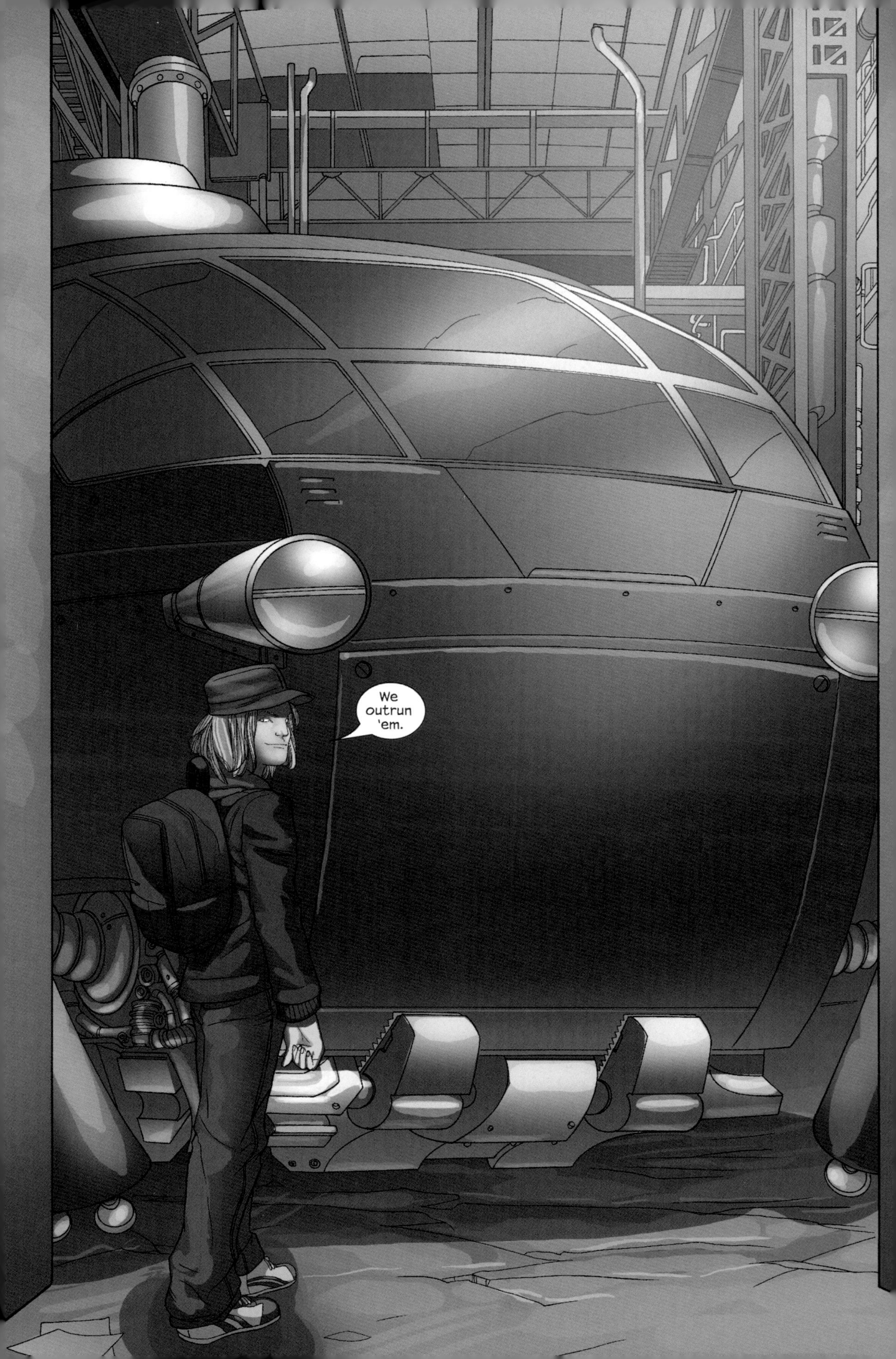
We outrun 'em.

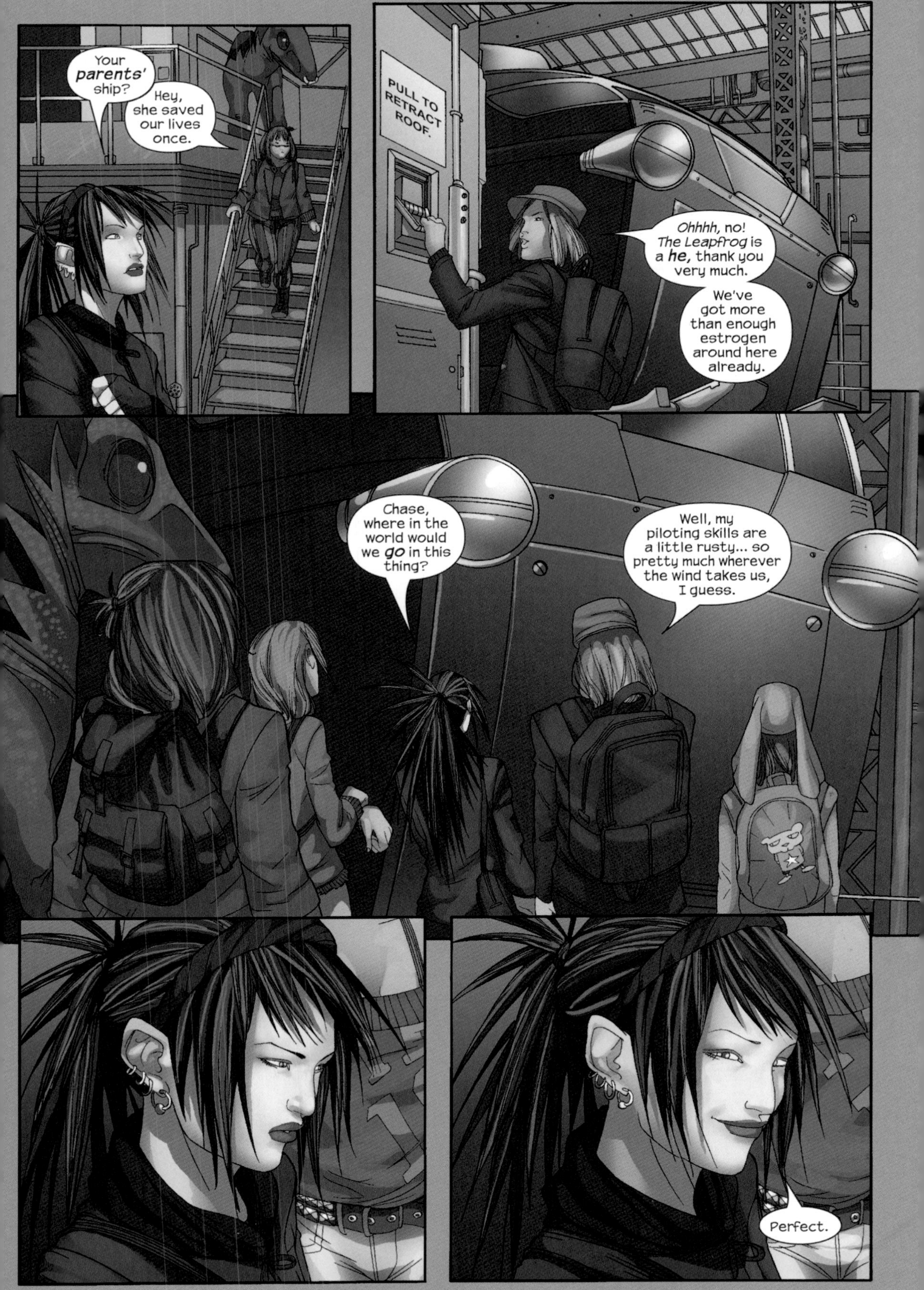
Your *parents'* ship?
Hey, she saved our lives once.
PULL TO RETRACT ROOF.
Ohhhh, no! *The Leapfrog* is a ***he,*** thank you very much.
We've got more than enough estrogen around here already.
Chase, where in the world would we ***go*** in this thing?
Well, my piloting skills are a little rusty... so pretty much wherever the wind takes us, I guess.
Perfect.

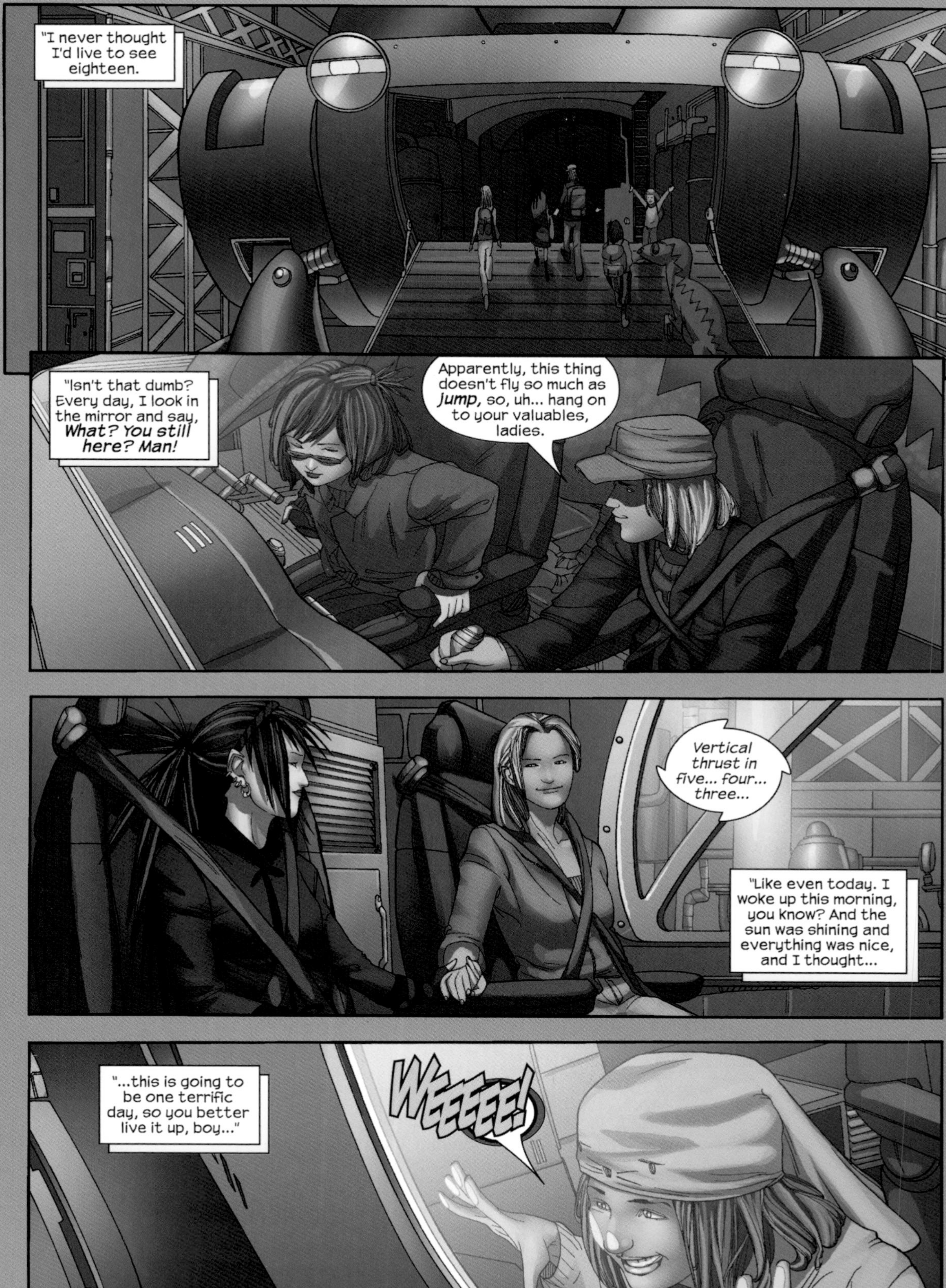
"I never thought I'd live to see eighteen.
"Isn't that dumb? Every day, I look in the mirror and say, *What? You still here? Man!*
Apparently, this thing doesn't fly so much as *jump,* so, uh... hang on to your valuables, ladies.
Vertical thrust in five... four... three...
"Like even today. I woke up this morning, you know? And the sun was shining and everything was nice, and I thought...
"...this is going to be one terrific day, so you better live it up, boy..."
WEEEEE!

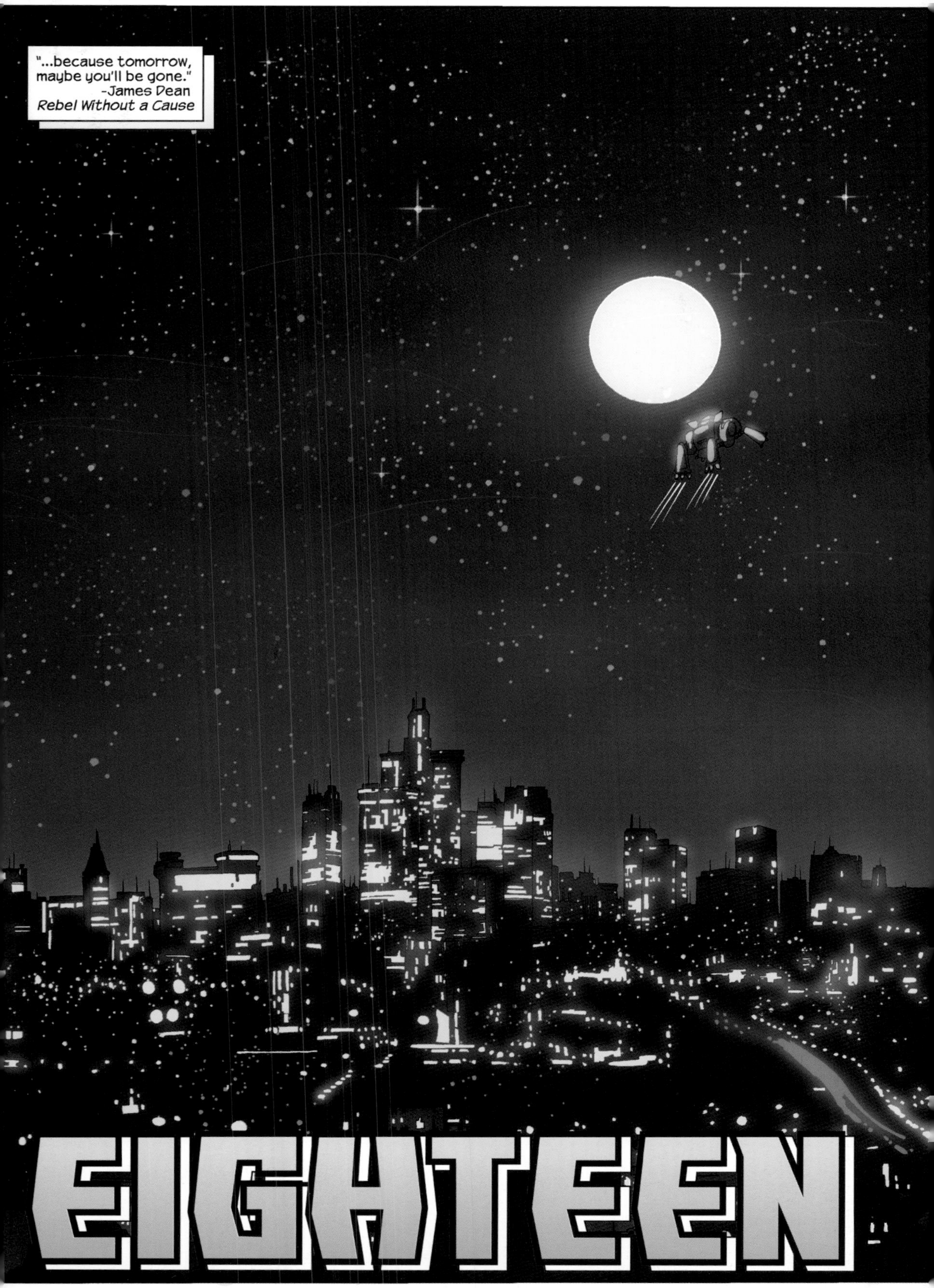
"...because tomorrow, maybe you'll be gone."
-James Dean
Rebel Without a Cause
EIGHTEEN

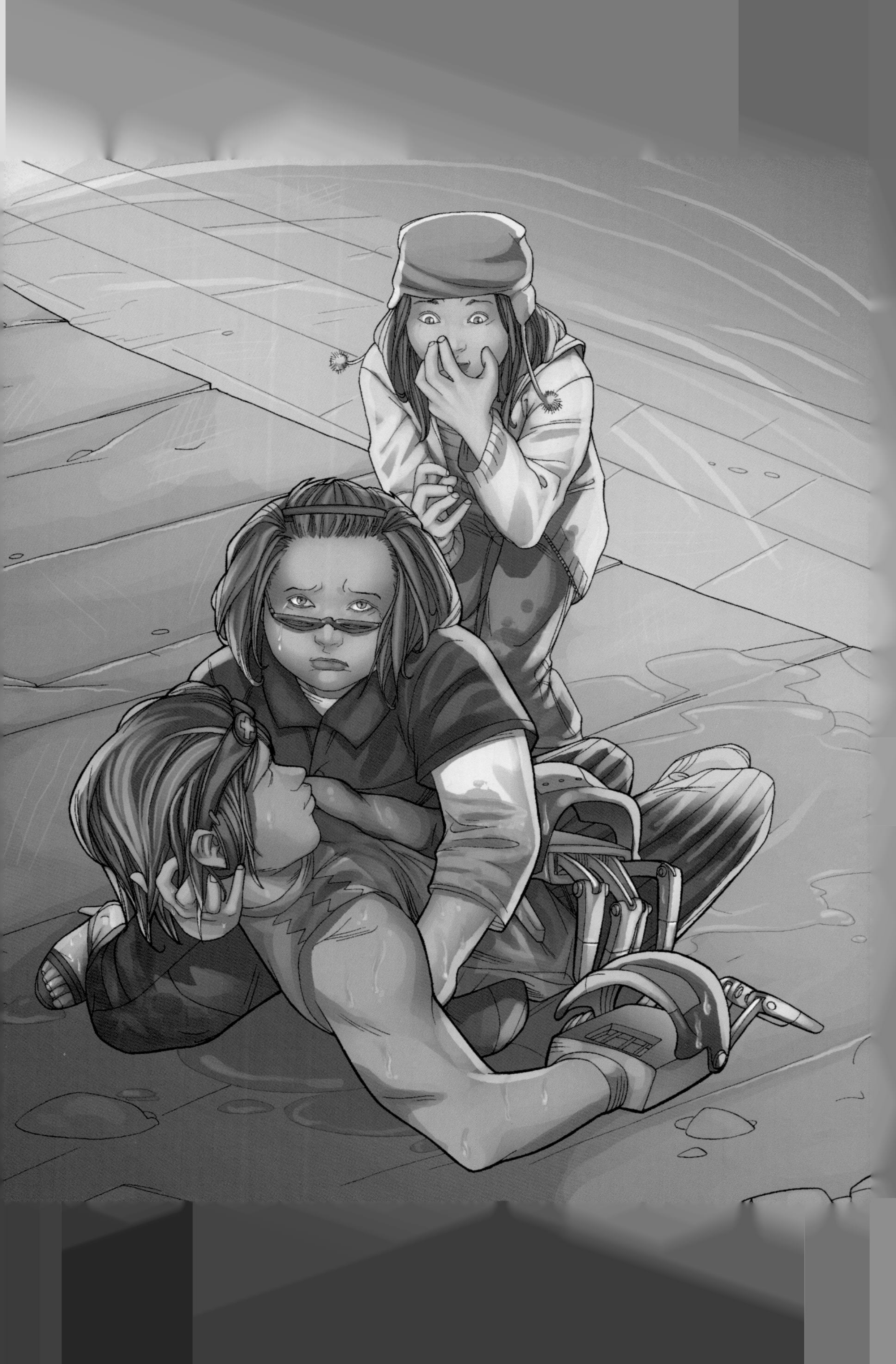

BIOGRAPHIES

BRIAN K. VAUGHAN

Born in Cleveland in 1976, Brian K. Vaughan got his big break thanks to Marvel's **Stan-hattan Project**, a workshop for aspiring comic book writers. Since then, he has written for a plethora of Marvel titles (**Cable, Captain America, Ka-Zar, Spider-Man, Mystique, Ultimate X-Men, Wolverine**) and DC characters (**Batman, Green Lantern, JLA, Superman, Wonder Woman, Swamp Thing, Young Justice**). In 2005, thanks to his work on **Y: The Last Man** (DC/Vertigo), **Ex-Machina** (Wildstorm) and **Runaways**, he was granted the **Eisner Award** as best writer. Among his most recent works, are **The Escapist** (Dark Horse), inspired by Michael Chabon's Pulitzer Prize-winning novel **The Amazing Adventures of Kavalier & Clay**, and **Pride of Baghdad** (his first original graphic novel) illustrated by Niko Henrichon, and a **Doctor Strange** miniseries drawn by Marcos Martin. He currently lives in Los Angeles.

ADRIAN ALPHONA

Young Canadian artist Adrian Alphona studied graphic art at George Brown College in Toronto. Afterwards, he joined the small, creative studio Bright Anvil Studios before moving on and co-creating **Runaways** with writer Brian K. Vaughan. This was Alphona's first professional work as a comicbook artist, and allowed him to contribute to the plot and character development. His delicate and modern style added to the series' originality and success.

TO BE CONTINUED...

MAKE MINE MARVEL!

RUNAWAYS

There comes a time in every young person's life when they
believe that their parents are evil... but what if they really are?

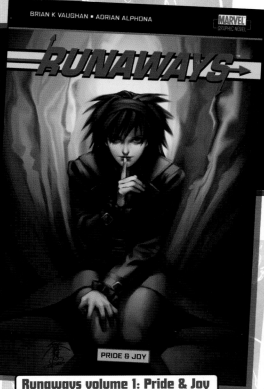

BRIAN K VAUGHAN • ADRIAN ALPHONA

RUNAWAYS

MARVEL GRAPHIC NOVEL

PRIDE & JOY

Runaways volume 1: Pride & Joy
ISBN: 978-1-84653-010-4 £8.99

BRIAN K VAUGHAN • ADRIAN ALPHONA • TAKESHI MIYAZAWA

RUNAWAYS

MARVEL GRAPHIC NOVEL

TEENAGE WASTELAND

Runaways volume 2: Teenage Wasteland
ISBN: 978-1-905239-76-4 £8.99

**WRITTEN BY HOT COMIC SCRIBE BRIAN K VAUGHAN
AND WITH AWESOME ART BY ADRIAN ALPHONA**